MORE THAN I
COULD EVER ASK

The Story of a Woman, Broken and Defeated,
Who Found That Dreams
Really Do Come True

LORI GRAHAM BAKKER

with
Connie Reece

NELSON
BOOKS

An Imprint of Thomas Nelson

Published in Nashville, Tennessee, by Nelson Books, an imprint of Thomas Nelson. Nelson Books and Thomas Nelson are registered trademarks of HarperCollins Christian Publishing, Inc.

Unless otherwise noted, Scripture quotations are from THE NEW KING JAMES VERSION. Copyright © 1979, 1980, 1982, Thomas Nelson, Inc.

Scripture quotations noted NIV are from the HOLY BIBLE: NEW INTERNATIONAL VERSION®. Copyright © 1973, 1978, 1984 by International Bible Society. Used by permission of Zondervan Publishing House. All rights reserved.

To protect their privacy, the names of certain individuals in this book are pseudonyms.

ISBN 978-1-4041-1192-9 (custom)

Library of Congress Control Number: 00-136407

ISBN 0-7852-6797-2
ISBN 978-0-7852-6812-3

Printed in the United States of America

19 20 21 22 23 24 LSC 6 5 4 3 2 1

He played such a heartrending tune that the Devil could not help himself; he bowed his head and wept.

When it was finished the Gypsy put his lips to one of the openings in the fiddle and drew in a deep breath. He kissed the fiddle and gave it and the bow to the Devil, who took them and vanished in a cloud of smoke.

The Gypsy took a handful of gold and went to the town to buy food and some better clothes, for he was in rags. Then he went back to the waterfall and filled all his pockets with gold. Now he was rich and he ought to have been happy, but he was sad. He missed his fiddle so badly. For three days he sat watching the water and thinking.

Suddenly the Devil appeared. He was very angry. "I've made a bad bargain," he growled. "You have the gold, but the fiddle's useless. When I play it people do not follow me, they run away. It's useless." He threw the fiddle and the bow at the Gypsy, who picked them up with a joyful heart.

"But why is it," said the Devil, "that I can't make music like yours?"

"It is natural," answered the Gypsy. "I promised to sell you the fiddle, but not to sell you my soul. I had breathed my soul into it. I took my soul back before I gave you the fiddle. Listen."

He put his lips to an opening and breathed into it. He tucked the fiddle under his chin and played a tune so merry that even the Devil had to dance madly till it was over. Then, with a scream of fury, he vanished.

So the Gypsy, with his fiddle under his arm and his pockets full of gold, went happily on his way.

That is how a Gypsy outwitted the Devil. And ever since then it is Gypsy fiddlers who have played the wildest, sweetest music.

AUTHOR'S NOTE

The stories in this book are based on folk tales which have been printed in the following: *Gypsy Folk-tales*, edited by Francis Hindes Groome (London, 1899); *The Journal of the Gypsy Lore Society*; and *XXI Welsh Gypsy Folk-tales* by John Sampson, edited by Dora E. Yates (Montgomeryshire, 1933).

I am greatly indebted to the Hon. Secretary of the Gypsy Lore Society, Miss Dora E. Yates, Litt. D., for permission to make use of transcripts in the Society's *Journal* and in John Sampson's collection; and to Mr. Bernard Gilliat-Smith for permission to use the story "Batim the Horse" which he took down in Romani from a Muslim Gypsy in Sofia.

I am much indebted also to Mrs. Margaret Weston, Mrs. Diane Crook, and Mrs. Glenys Carr for valuable help and advice, and to Mrs. Pamela Royds for much illuminating and sympathetic criticism.

The stories have been written down in many countries by students of Gypsy lore and most of them have been translated from tales told in Romani by illiterate Gypsies. The tales vary much from country to country both in style and content, and I have tried to reflect these variations. A few of my stories follow the transcripts almost word for word; most of them, however, have been considerably abridged and adapted to bring them within the scope of the young readers for whom this book is intended. But I have done my best to keep the spirit and flavor of the originals.

Many books have been written about Gypsy life and lore. One of the most fascinating is by Jan Yoors, who wrote the introduction to this book. It is *The Gypsies*, published by Simon and Schuster, 1967, and is an account of his own life among the Gypsies. Professor Walter Starkie, C.M.G., Litt. D., President of the international Gypsy Lore Society, is another writer who has lived with the Gypsies. He is the author of *Raggle-taggle* (London, 1933), *Spanish Raggle-taggle* (London, 1934, 1961), and *In Sara's Tents* (London, 1954).

John W. Hornby's *Gypsies* (New York, 1967) is intended for young readers and gives a comprehensive picture of Gypsy life. Other books of interest are *The Wind on the Heath*, a Gypsy anthology compiled by John Sampson (London, 1930); *Gypsies of Britain*, an introduction to their history, by Brian Vesey-Fitzgerald (London, 1944); *My Gypsy Days: Recollections of a Romani Rawnie*, by Dora E. Yates (London, 1953); and *The Gypsies* by Jean-Paul Clébert, translated from the French by Charles Duff (London, 1963). For specialists *The Journal of the Gypsy Lore Society*, which is published in Edinburgh, is invaluable.

The standard collections of folk tales in English are Francis Hindes Groome's and John Sampson's, noted above, and *A Book of Gypsy Folk-tales* selected by Dora E. Yates (London, 1948). The tales in this last, and in Groome's collection, are drawn from many European countries.

J. H.

1969

in loving memory of my father, Robert C. "Daddy Bob" Graham

in honor of my mother, the rock of my life, Charlene Graham

*to the most precious gift God has given me: my husband, Jim Bakker,
whose love continues to heal me*

to my brothers, Mark and Scott, who stood by me through it all

*to the children who are the joy of my life:
my nieces, Amber and Katherine, and my nephew, Thomas*

*to my beautiful grandmother, Lucille Thomas,
who has been my godly example*

*with special love for Tammy Sue, Doug, James, Jonathan, Jamie, and
Amanda, who accepted me and welcomed me into their family*

*and with gratitude to Lloyd and Chris Zeigler,
who modeled Christ and prepared me for ministry*

Contents

1

THE TABLOIDS STOLE MY TRIBUTE

The drone of the helicopter was my first indication that our storybook wedding would not have the requisite "happily ever after" ending. The noisy invasion signaled a reality check: this was not a fairy tale come true, though it had seemed like one as we stood under the gazebo outside the palatial home in the hills of Burbank, California, and exchanged our wedding vows. I had even received a pair of glass slippers, just like the heroine of my favorite childhood story. And now this.

Tommy Barnett, my pastor and Jim's good friend, had just made the announcement: "It is with great honor that I present to you Mr. and Mrs. Jim Bakker." The audience, some 250 family members and friends from all walks of life, erupted in cheers.

Jim told the guests, "We have requested a special song as we leave to take pictures. I'm so honored that Andrae Crouch, who wrote this song and who has been my friend for at least a hundred years, is here with us today." Jim smiled broadly and gave my hand a squeeze as he concluded, "This is *our* tribute to our God for what he has done."

For the recessional music we had chosen my favorite song, "My Tribute," which is more commonly known by the first words of its chorus: "To God be the glory for the things he has done." I had been absolutely floored when Jim called Andrae to ask if he would be available to sing it at our wedding. I was vaguely aware, of course, that Jim knew a lot of famous people from his television days, yet it hadn't dawned on me that he knew them well enough to just pick up the phone and ask them for a personal favor.

As Andrae stepped to the microphone to sing, the unmistakable whirr of chopper blades could be heard approaching the hillside.

Jim turned to me. "It's the press," he said softly, a note of quiet dismay in his voice. "They've got us now."

Distracted by the noise, Andrae paused for a moment before introducing the singer who would join him in a duet. There was a smattering of confused applause from the audience. No one was quite sure what to do. The music started and the helicopter flew closer.

"Can't you *do* something?" I implored Jim, feeling that my new husband had the power to make this intrusion go away.

Jim did something. He gently took me by the arm and nudged me closer to the steps of the gazebo.

Incredulous, I turned to my mom, who was my matron of honor. "It's the press."

"One step farther," Jim said, guiding me out into the open. "Now they can get a good picture," he said almost sarcastically.

I felt violated. A precious, private moment had been ruined.

2

NOT EVEN AN INKLING

Thursday, July 16, 1998

Kelli was late. *How typical,* I grumbled as I deposited a quarter in the coin slot of the pay phone. *I'm gonna kill her.* After retrieving my things from the baggage-claim area outside—the disadvantage of flying into the Burbank airport; the advantage is that it's closer to downtown Los Angeles—I had found a shady spot and waited in the blistering summer heat. *She'll come breezing up any minute and start rambling about some catastrophe. I don't care if she is like a daughter to me, this time I'm gonna kill her.* My plane had landed an hour ago, and Kelli, who was supposed to meet me, still hadn't shown up.

I dialed the one phone number I had for her: the inner-city office of Revolution, the ministry for which Kelli was a full-time volunteer. *Don't be unfair. Maybe there's a perfectly good reason she's so late.* The phone kept ringing until a machine finally picked it up. I recognized the voice on the recorded message. It belonged to Jay Bakker, who had started the Los Angeles branch of Revolution. I had known Jay for about four years, ever since he had first come to my church in Phoenix to get a fresh start on his life.

Beeeeeep. "Hi, Jay. This is Lori Graham. I'm trying to get in touch with Kelli. She was supposed to pick me up at the Burbank airport an hour ago. She doesn't have a cell phone, and no phone in her room, so I . . . well, anyway, if you can get a message to her, please tell her I'm still out here waiting." The irritation in my voice was evident.

What do I do now? I wondered. It was miserably hot. I was tired and cranky. I didn't know anyone else in L.A. I thought about splurging on a taxi, but I didn't even know the address of the place where I would be spending the night and then speaking the next day.

Many months earlier, Marja Barnett had invited me to speak to the women at the Los Angeles International Church—the Dream Center, as this dynamic inner-city outreach is rightly called. Marja's son Matthew and her husband, Tommy—who also pastors Phoenix First Assembly of God, my home church—had started LAIC as a mission in the ghettos of L.A., and the impact on people's lives there had been phenomenal. Marja oversaw the monthly women's outreach ministry for the Dream Center, along with Nancy Hinkle, another friend from Phoenix First.

My schedule had been so booked that it took quite a while to work out a time when I could come to L.A. Then, once I had locked in a date, I had to come up with the funds to accept this honor. Special speakers at the Dream Center come as volunteer missionaries: they receive no honorarium and they pay all their own expenses. Marja and Nancy had offered to send someone to pick me up at the airport, but I had assured them that wouldn't be necessary. Well, that's what I had thought at the time.

Come on, Kelli girl. Where are you? I tucked a strand of damp hair behind my ear. In spite of my aggravation, I couldn't wait to see her. I had been looking forward to this weekend for a long time. Not only would I get to speak at the Dream Center, we would get to have a mini-reunion of "Lori's Girls"—some of the young women I had mentored for several years. Kelli Miller, the one I was idly threatening to kill, was living and working at the Dream Center now. Jen Nicks and Jennifer Morgan were driving over from San Diego. It would be the first time in quite a while that we had all been together. These young women were an important part of my life, and I had missed them terribly.

Finally, after an hour and a half of waiting, I remembered the name of someone who worked in Pastor Matthew's office at the Dream Center. I got her on the phone and explained the situation. "I'll send somebody to get you right away," she graciously offered. While we were still on the phone, however, a black Jeep pulled up to the curb and out bounced Kelli, followed by Jay.

"Lori!" she squealed. "Wow! It's so good to see you. I'm so sorry! My car broke down on the freeway and I had to find a telephone and then Jay had to come get me and then the traffic . . ." Kelli always left her audience breathless.

We laughed and exchanged greetings as Jay loaded my bags into the car. "Thanks, Jay," I said to the handsome young man sporting tattoos and earrings. "You can ignore that frustrated phone message from me when you get back to the office."

Jay grinned. "Hey, no problem."

The three of us piled into the Jeep and headed for the heart of L.A. Jay looked a lot better than the last time I'd seen him. A few months earlier Jay and Kelli had been in Phoenix to meet with the national coordinators for Revolution. I had told the kids they could stay at my place; Kelli could share my bedroom and Jay could have the sofa. When I came home from a Bible study I was conducting, I found Jay asleep on the sofa. He was sick and running a fever. I had gotten him some medicine and tried to take care of him. It seemed the natural thing to do: my apartment was always full of ministry students, who affectionately called me Mama Lori.

"You are absolutely going to love Amanda," Kelli said. "She is just the best roommate and . . ." Kelli launched into a description of her good friend, who was also Jay's girlfriend. Amanda, originally from the Atlanta area, also worked with Revolution. Their ministry reached out to the counterculture kids: the Goths, with their black hair and ghostly pale faces; those into heavy metal, whether in music or body piercings; those for whom skateboarding was not a mode of transportation but a way of life.

It was late afternoon by the time we got into the downtown area. We stopped at a sandwich shop that was one of their favorite places to eat. After ordering, we settled into a booth. When Jay went to the counter to pick up our food, Kelli turned to me and casually asked, "Would you be interested in a man in his fifties?"

That came out of nowhere, I thought. "Stop right now." I held up both hands like a traffic cop. "I know exactly what you're implying."

"Jay once told me that if his dad ever met you, he'd fall for you big-time."

"Don't even go there." I chuckled in embarrassment. "I'm not interested, Kelli. I don't like being set up."

"Okay, okay. Chill." She rolled her eyes dramatically.

"Hush! Jay's coming back." *I can't believe she is trying to play matchmaker for me,* I thought. *And with Jim Bakker, of all people!*

I didn't know much about Jim Bakker except that he was Jay's dad. I was aware that he had been involved in some big scandal in the past and that he had been in prison, but I was not a Christian when all that had happened, and I hadn't paid much attention to it. All I really remembered from those days was the label the media had tagged on him: "fallen televangelist Jim Bakker."

I had seen the Dream Center complex on video many times before, but it was still an amazing sight the first time I saw it in person. In 1995, just a year after the Los Angeles International Church had been started, thousands of people across America sent contributions to help purchase the former Queen of Angels Hospital, located between downtown Los Angeles and Hollywood. At one time, some 70 percent of Los Angeles residents were born in this old hospital; now they came there to be born again.

As a teenager, Matthew Barnett had envisioned a church that would be open twenty-four hours a day, 365 days a year, and he saw that church as a place where people from the inner city could not only receive spiritual instruction but also have their physical needs met. Matthew's dream had become a reality, and now he was helping to revive the dreams of people who had completely lost their hope.

Situated on a hill overlooking the Hollywood Freeway, the Dream Center occupied nine buildings totaling some 400,000 square feet on 8.8 acres. The fourteen-story hospital was being renovated floor by floor, and the rooms were occupied by hundreds of people, from ministry leaders to ex–gang members. Several ethnic churches and more than a hundred outreaches to the community operated out of the Dream Center—not just gospel preaching and discipleship training, but feeding and clothing the poor, providing educational assistance and job training, even neighborhood cleanup and restoration.

Kelli and Amanda lived in one of the converted hospital rooms, in rather spartan living conditions. The room was tiny and incredibly hot—no air-conditioning; not even a fan to circulate the steamy air drifting up from the sizzling asphalt jungle below. These quarters were obviously a makeshift arrangement, with a twin bed against each side wall and a small hospital cabinet for their clothes. The bathroom held an antique toilet and sink; the communal shower was down the hall. Not the kind of place you'd expect to find two vivacious, up-and-coming young women. But Kelli and Amanda were not typical young women: they were deeply committed to sharing their faith and willing to pay the price for it.

The two Jennifers, Nicks and Morgan, arrived, and we had just enough time to freshen up before walking over to the gymnasium for church. The Thursday night evangelistic service at the Dream Center was *the* place to be. You needed to get there a half hour early to even get a seat. By the time we arrived, the music was pumping and the atmosphere was full of electricity. The five of us—Kelli, Amanda, Nicks, Morgan, and I— searched for seats in the back of the auditorium.

Kelli tapped me on the arm just before we sat down. "There he is. Jay's dad." She pointed toward the front. "The one in the ball cap."

He was sitting in one of the front rows, dressed in Levi's and a T-shirt and, as Kelli noted, a baseball cap. *How unpretentious,* I thought. He blended right in with the inner-city crowd. *Very humble, and not churchy at all.* I liked that. But I put it right out of my mind as I concentrated on the worship.

Pastor Tommy always came over from Phoenix for the Thursday night service at the Dream Center. And the list of guest speakers read like a who's who of preachers in America—people like T. D. Jakes and Joyce Meyer. That night Pastor Barnett asked his wife, Marja, to talk briefly about the women's meeting scheduled for the next day. She announced that I would be giving my testimony, and then Pastor Barnett asked me to stand up. Because I'm short—just over five feet tall—he told me to wave so people could see where I was standing way in the back.

There was so much excitement—so much *life*—in that place. It's unlike any church service I've ever attended. The tenor of the service may run from enthusiastic praise and worship—boisterous singing and clapping and dancing—to quiet reflection or noisy tears of repentance. The preaching is punctuated with more than the typical amens and hallelujahs. When a person who has known nothing but despair and destitution all his or her life finds hope and joy in Jesus Christ—well, it's hard to stay quiet. And this crowd did not even try to restrain its vocal expression. "Preach it, brother." "C'mon now." "I know that's right." "Yes, Lord!"

After the service, we exited through a door at the back into an area similar to an alley. First you walk down a very long ramp that descends behind the gymnasium into a loading zone. The hospital was built on a hillside, and what is ground level at one entrance is four or five stories higher than ground level at the other end. So from the loading docks in the alley, you have to walk up a very long, narrow flight of concrete stairs to get to the main parking lot of the Dream Center. It was dark, about 9:30 P.M., but dim lights illuminated the graffiti on the walls of the old hospital building.

And there, on the ramp, we ran into Jay and his dad.

"Lori, I'd like you to meet my dad, Jim Bakker," Jay said. I suppressed a grin when he introduced us formally—as if I wouldn't know who his dad was. "Dad, this is Lori Graham."

"Hi. Nice to meet you." We shook hands and exchanged pleasantries. My flock was with me and a small group of people surrounded Jim. I met Connie Elling, one of the volunteers in Jim's ministry. She prepared food for everyone who attended Jim's noon Bible studies. Armando Saavedra, a former gang member whose life had been radically changed at the Dream Center, was also there. I later found out that when Jim first arrived in L.A., Armando served as his unofficial tour guide and instructor in the ways of the ghetto and gang life. Over the months, Armando had become like a foster son to Jim, attending every Bible study Jim conducted and spending time with him in the off-hours as well.

We all chatted as we walked across the alley toward the row of Jeeps. I thought it was funny that Jay had one and so did his dad. And Pastor Barnett and Pastor Matthew also had Jeeps. It was like the Jeep had become the official vehicle of the Dream Center.

One of the girls said, "We're all going out to eat, and Jim wants to know if you'd like to go with us."

"Thanks, but I don't think so," I said. "I've got a major meeting in the morning, and I just want to go back to the room and rest and prepare for tomorrow." I wasn't avoiding Jim in particular, just crowds in general. I needed to stay focused on the reason

I was in Los Angeles, and that was to speak to a group of women, many of whom would be hurting. I knew firsthand just how deep their hurts could be, and I wanted to offer them something that could transform their lives.

I went back to Kelli and Amanda's crowded little room, and in the sultry heat I studied and prayed until late that night. I had absolutely no indication, not even an inkling of an idea, that I had just met Mr. Right. Jim would later say that he heard bells ring and violins play the minute he laid eyes on me. For him, it was love at first sight. For me, it was different. I thought I had simply met the father of a young friend, not the man who would be my life's companion. It would be another twenty-four hours before I even considered that possibility, and it would have to be pointed out to me by someone else, who saw it through spiritual eyes.

But that's the way it needed to be, because up to that point, my track record for choosing men was horrific—and that was putting the best possible spin on it.

3

IN THE SNARE OF THE FOX

I was a senior in high school when I met the man I thought was my knight in shining armor. Actually, my best friend and I discovered him at the same time.

"You have got to *see* this guy!" Dust cloth in hand, Bobbi stood glued to the window in my mother's bedroom.

I plugged the vacuum cleaner into the wall outlet. "C'mon, Bobbi. Let's finish cleaning, and then let's figure out how to get high." Mom wouldn't be home from work for hours, but I wanted to get the chores done quickly so I could see about replenishing my stash. I'd been smoking pot almost every day for a couple of years now, and I didn't like not having any around the house.

"But he's gorgeous!"

"A good-looking guy in our neighborhood? Since when?"

"Since today. I've never seen him before."

My curiosity piqued, I left the vacuum cleaner and moved to the window beside my friend. Bobbi had been like a sister ever since our family had moved into the neighborhood when I was eleven and she was nine—some six years ago.

"Oh, man, you weren't kidding!" I stared avidly at the guy washing the truck in the driveway of the house catty-corner from ours. He was about six feet tall with a beautiful head of shoulder-length, straight, dark blond hair. Very clean cut and well built. He definitely had *the look*. And he definitely was not a teenager. Must be in his mid-twenties, I guessed.

"Who do you suppose he is?" Bobbi asked.

"I don't know, but he's a *fox*." We both giggled.

"Remember, I saw him first!"

"Yeah, but I'm older. So he's mine."

"It's not fair, Lori! You get all the guys. You've got the looks, and you've got a better figure—it's just not fair!"

We argued good-naturedly as we staked our claim on the handsome stranger.

"Let's go outside and see if we can get his attention, okay?"

"I thought you wanted to finish cleaning the house first." Bobbi grinned at my change of tune.

"That was before I saw him," I quipped.

We checked our hair and put on lipstick before we went outside. Neither one of us was really a cigarette smoker (we only smoked pot), but we thought it looked cool. So we leaned against the tan Dodge Dart parked under the carport—my first car—and lit a couple of cigarettes. When the fox looked our way, I boldly waved. He waved back and started walking across the street toward us.

I flipped my long, straight hair over one shoulder as he said hello. "Hey, man, you got a joint?" I asked him.

"No, I was hoping you guys had some weed," he replied.

That's all I remember of my first conversation with Jesse, the man who became the focus of my life for more than a decade. I remember the date I met him: January 10, 1975. The fact that we talked about marijuana was a foretaste of things to come: much of our relationship would center on drugs.

Jesse and I clicked instantly and started hanging out together. Within a few weeks we were sleeping together. In fact, he spent almost every night at my house, and my mother never knew it.

My curfew was 11:00 P.M. We would say our good-byes and Jesse would go back across the street to his brother's house, where he lived. I would say good night to Mom and then go to bed. My bedroom was next to the family room downstairs, and my mother's bedroom was on the top level of our tri-level house. It was so far above mine that she never heard Jesse take the screen off and climb in my window. Early the next morning I would get dressed for school, and Jesse would sneak out and go home.

Mom was not aware of my drug use either. I was an expert at hiding it from her. I kept the house clean, was always home by my curfew, and never gave her any reason to suspect I was smoking pot daily and dropping acid on the weekends. She worked long hours in retail sales so we could afford to live in the same house on Citrus Way that we had grown up in. She wanted me and my two younger brothers, Mark and Scott, to have that kind of stability. But it also meant I had a lot of unsupervised time, and I took full advantage of it.

My father was not a part of our lives at the time. After years of emotional turmoil, Mom had divorced him two years previously.

Dad was remarried and wrapped up in his own little world. I can remember thinking that if my dad had been around, he would have sent Jesse packing before we ever had a relationship. At the time, I would have hated him for it. But, oh, the heartache it would have spared me.

Jesse quickly became a fixture in my life. He would take me to school in the mornings, dropping me off and then using my car during the day. He didn't have a car, and he didn't have a job, but that didn't concern me. All I cared about was that he was good-looking and charming. And he was twenty-six—nine years older than me. Jesse was a fox and he was cool—my chief criteria for a boyfriend—and I was very taken with him. I was also very deceived by him.

I was so naive, I didn't question where Jesse was or what he was doing all day. I learned things gradually: that he had been in jail on drug-related charges, that he had moved from Chicago to Phoenix to get away from a girlfriend. Each new revelation did not seem to matter; I was already too much in love with Jesse to ever see him objectively.

One day in April he came over. We sat in the family room of our house, where we had spent so many afternoons. "There's something I need to tell you," Jesse said. He looked as if he'd been crying. "I have to leave."

"Wh—what do you mean? Why?" I was shocked by the look on his face and the tone in his voice. It sounded so final.

"I'm no good for you, Lori. I—"

"But you are! I love you, and you—"

"Baby, I've lived a whole life, and you're just starting yours. I'm no good for you, and I know it. That's why I have to leave."

I begged and pleaded and cried, but I couldn't change his

mind. He said he wanted a lock of my hair to take with him so he could always remember me. Brokenhearted, I picked up the scissors and snipped off a piece of my hair. Then he kissed me good-bye and started to leave.

"Where are you going? Will I ever hear from you again?" I asked.

Jesse turned and looked at me for a long moment. "You don't need to know where I'm going, baby," he said softly. And then he was gone.

I was so devastated by Jesse's leaving me that I called my former boyfriend, a classmate of mine I had known since the first grade. We had dated off and on throughout high school and were very close. Up until the time I met Jesse, I had always figured I would marry Rick. We used to talk about getting married and having a lot of kids, but we never had a sexual relationship. I had dropped him instantly when I met Jesse; then when Jesse left, I immediately turned to Rick for comfort. He seemed so happy to be back together with me. But I was just using him, and I broke his heart.

My first separation from Jesse lasted ten days, and it started a pattern for our lives. He would walk out on me, and I would turn to another man. Then he would come back, and I would forgive him.

Jesse's brother and sister-in-law, who lived across the street from us, had two children, a boy and a girl. The little girl was about eight. One day she came over to see me. "Guess who's coming to dinner tonight?" she said.

"Who?" I replied.

"Uncle Jesse."

"You're kidding!"

"No, he came back to live with us. But you're not supposed to know. It's a surprise."

I was so excited, yet afraid to believe it. What if she had gotten things confused? I had butterflies in my stomach, waiting to hear if it was true.

It was. Jesse came over that night after dinner.

"I just couldn't stay away," he told me. "I can't live without you in my life. I've never felt this way before. I love you, Lori."

I was ecstatic to be back in his arms. I was Jesse's girl again, and the world was a wonderful place.

"I need to be truthful with you," he said earnestly. "I, uh, I've done things with women that weren't right. I've used them."

"Were you with another woman when you left town?" I wasn't sure I wanted to hear the answer.

"Yeah, my old girlfriend from Chicago came and picked me up in her Corvette."

"Where did you go?"

"Down to Mexico. We partied for a few days."

I couldn't help the tears, thinking about Jesse with another woman. He pulled me close. "Don't cry, baby. It's over. I couldn't stand being with her anymore." He stroked my hair. "You're the one I love, and I want to spend the rest of my life with you."

Jesse asked me to marry him that night, and I accepted. I didn't know that I was already pregnant.

4

WOUNDED HEALERS

Friday, July 17, 1998

I awoke to the sound of dreams being rebuilt: hammers pounding, saws grinding, music blaring, and people laughing. Volunteer workers were breathing new life into the decrepit old hospital, and even the paint fumes carried the scent of hope. How exciting to be right in the middle of it.

Exciting . . . and crowded. Five of us had spent the night in Kelli and Amanda's tiny room. Kelli had offered to let me have her twin bed, but I opted to sleep on the floor because she had hurt her back in an auto accident and was still in pain.

Getting up before the others, I spent a few minutes alone, praying, in the girls' private bathroom before getting dressed. As I prepared to minister that day, I sensed in my spirit that the upcoming service would be powerful. The meeting would include all the women at the Dream Center—those living or attending discipleship classes there, as well as the women volunteers and staff members.

Nancy and Marja had specifically asked me to preach my testimony. Many of the women in the audience would be hurting, and many of them would have been through the same types of painful experiences I had.

I opened my Bible to 2 Corinthians 1:3–4, which I had often prayed over in my ministry: "Blessed be the God and Father of our Lord Jesus Christ, the Father of mercies and God of all comfort, who comforts us in all our tribulation, that we may be able to comfort those who are in any trouble, with the comfort with which we ourselves are comforted by God."

"Heavenly Father," I prayed, "please help me to show my wounds today, so that you may use them as a source of healing."

It is never pleasant to relive the past when I share my testimony. But I do it because God uses it to comfort others. A hurting woman knows I understand her pain and suffering when she hears that I have been down the same road. And when she receives healing from God, she will extend that same comfort to yet others so that the circle of wounded healers widens.

I'll never forget the first time I shared a short testimony before a group of women at Phoenix First in the fall of 1990. I had panicked at the thought of standing before the pastors' wives and the matriarchs of the church and telling them even the briefest highlights of my sordid past. I had been a Christian for only about eighteen months, and I still carried a dump-truck-size load of shame about my past sins, even though I knew God had forgiven me and completely changed my life—in fact, he had called me into full-time ministry.

They're going to shun me, I thought. *They'll talk about me, and I'll never be able to hold my head high. I'll have to leave the church. They think I'm the perfect little Christian, but when they find out . . .*

On and on the accusing voice assaulted my mind. My stomach

was so tied in knots, I didn't think I could go through with it. I nearly backed out at the last minute, but I managed to battle my fear and honor my commitment to give a five-minute testimony.

I was petrified as I stepped behind the pulpit—the spot usually occupied by Tommy Barnett, one of the most respected pastors in America. What an incredible honor. Some one thousand women were in the audience, about six or seven hundred from the inner city and three or four hundred ladies from Phoenix First. The lights were dimmed, so I couldn't see their faces. But I definitely heard them respond when I took the microphone and said, "From the time I was seventeen to the time I was twenty-one, I had five abortions." The loud gasps throughout the audience paralyzed me for a moment, but I finished my story and then sat down to listen to the other testimonies. *Well, now they know,* I thought. I wondered if anybody would even speak to me, or if they would just avoid me.

One of the first people I saw afterward was Marja Barnett, my pastor's wife. Phoenix First Assembly is a huge church, and as I recall, she had never spoken to me before, except perhaps to say hello. This beautiful, gracious woman came over to me, kissed me on the cheek, and then clasped my hands. "Oh, Lori, you poor thing," she said in her lilting Swedish accent. "I never know you have such a horrible life—I can't believe what you go through. I'm so happy you are in our church. I love you so much!"

I don't remember exactly what she said after that. All I know is that Marja's love and acceptance flowed over my soul that day like a healing balm. Now, eight years later, she had invited me to the Dream Center, and my heart's desire was to extend the same encouragement to those who needed it.

About eighty women attended the meeting that Friday afternoon.

It was a treat to have my "girls" there—not only Kelli, Morgan, and Nicks, but Nina Atuatasi, my Samoan "daughter," who showed up just before the meeting. Nina, a gifted musician, had arrived in the Los Angeles area a few hours earlier and surprised me by driving over for the meeting. Before I preached, she sang two songs and ushered in the presence of the Holy Spirit.

"I don't trust people who haven't been through something," I told the ladies. "And I have a feeling that most of you have been through adversity. You've known some deep pain and heartache." Many women responded vocally. As I began recounting my personal story, I also preached about making choices—how bad choices get us into trouble, but "God choices" get us out.

In the back of my mind, I could hear my father—who sounded just like Archie Bunker on the old *All in the Family* TV show—saying, "You're a bad picker, Little Girl." Dad was so right about that. My teenage years were full of bad choices, with disastrous and far-reaching consequences.

I told the women at the Dream Center how Jesse and I had decided we would get married in the summer, after I graduated. My last year in high school, I was in the DECA (Distributive Education Clubs of America) program, so I only went to class for half a day, and then I went to my job. One afternoon in late April, Jesse picked me up after work, and he had an engagement ring for me. Standing there in front of Diamond's department store, he put a diamond on my finger.

My mother was devastated when I told her I was going to marry Jesse. "Lori, please wait," she begged me. "You're too young."

"I'm older than you were," I snapped.

"That's true—and it's why I know firsthand how hard it is." She looked pained. Mom had been just sixteen when Dad, who was eighteen, pressured her to get married.

"Besides, you can't stop me. I'll be eighteen at the end of August, and then I won't need your permission." I was stubborn and determined. "So either you sign the papers for me to get married, or we'll go to another state and elope."

Mom kept trying to talk sense into me, but I wouldn't listen. She knew that Jesse hated his mother, and that was a huge warning sign for her. "He doesn't have a good family relationship," she said, "and he won't be good to you." I turned a deaf ear to every reason why the marriage wouldn't work.

I told my dad the same thing. "Either you give your permission and give me a church wedding like you've always wanted, or I'm leaving." My heart was so hard.

When they both exhausted all the arguments, they finally gave in. We scheduled the wedding for July 26, 1975, at the First Church of the Nazarene, the church I had grown up in. The last service I had attended with my mom was Easter Sunday that year and Jesse had come with us. I never went back, and my wedding was the last time I would be inside a church for many years.

I was barely making it through school. My grades had suffered because my life had been focused on drugs and boyfriends. Now, I would sit in class and look at my diamond ring, and instead of taking notes I would practice writing out my married name. I was totally disinterested in graduation, or senior prom, or anything else. *This is kid stuff,* I thought. *I'm about to get married.*

That afternoon at the Dream Center, I looked out at the women and saw brown faces, black faces, and white faces. The color of their skin varied, but the pain in their eyes was the same. Hard living had aged many of them beyond their years: a girl grows up way too fast in the ghetto. They were listening intently, and I knew they understood my sorrow when I admitted that my bad choices far from ended with my decision to marry Jesse.

In May of that year I knew I had made another fateful error, I told them, when I missed my period. Jesse and I hadn't been using birth control. Pregnancy was a possibility I hadn't wanted to think about at the time, so I had just pretended it didn't even exist. I had always wanted children—had never wanted to be anything but a wife and mommy, in fact—but pregnancy was for the future. I was in love, I was getting married, and a baby was supposed to come along later. Yet the pregnancy was a reality now.

When I told Jesse, he was upset. He really didn't want to have a kid, he said. "Maybe someday, but not right now." And neither one of us wanted people to think we got married just because I was pregnant. We were in love and we *wanted* to get married. A baby would just complicate things, I rationalized. Anyway, there would be plenty of time for children later on—I was only seventeen.

It struck me as being odd that Jesse didn't want kids, since he was excellent with children. He coached my youngest brother Scott's Little League team, and both of my brothers loved Jesse and looked up to him. I could easily picture him as a father, but I pushed that tender dream aside. I was too afraid of losing Jesse, and he had made it clear that I had a choice: him or this baby.

I made the wrong choice.

I went to Planned Parenthood, where a friendly counselor told me about abortion. Some of my friends had gone to Mexico or California before abortion became legal in Arizona, and everywhere else, following the 1973 *Roe v. Wade* decision, so I knew the procedure existed. Yet I was completely ignorant about what an abortion really was. And I didn't get the straight facts at Planned Parenthood.

"It's just a little bit of tissue that needs to be cleaned up, and then you can go on with the rest of your life," the counselor told me. That was good news: a solution to my situation. I could get rid of the problem, then I could go ahead and marry Jesse and live happily ever after.

"The five-minute procedure is safer than a full-term pregnancy and delivery," she said. I remember that so vividly: *Only five minutes. Safer than having a baby.*

I felt I had no other option, so I scheduled an appointment for the abortion.

Jesse didn't go with me, of course. A girlfriend dropped me off at the clinic. I checked in and took the Valium a nurse gave me. "This will help you relax," she said. I nearly laughed. I had taken so many drugs that a ten-milligram Valium wouldn't even faze me. I got undressed and climbed onto the gurney. An orderly rolled me into a large room where about twenty others girls were lying on gurneys, all dressed in hospital gowns and socks, just like me. One by one they wheeled us away to the abortion room.

I recall noticing the girls on each side of me and thinking that they must have had some horrible tragedy in their lives to be going through this. I was feeling sorry for them, without even thinking about myself or what I was about to do.

Soon it was my turn to be wheeled off. I lay down on the table, put my feet in the stirrups, and had the life sucked out of me. Deep denial started setting in, and I have blotted out most of the details of that abortion, but my little "problem" was gone in five minutes. Someone gave me a glass of Tang and a cookie and made me wait a few more minutes to make sure I was okay. Then I got dressed and called my girlfriend to come pick me up.

"I'm fine," I told her. "Just fine." *I have to buck up, walk out of here, and act like nothing happened,* I told myself.

Jesse came over later to check on me, but he didn't stay with me that night. "It's no biggy," I told him. I had done what I had to do to keep him, so I put a big smile on my face and reassured him that everything was okay.

Over the past few months, I had learned a few things about Jesse that should have disturbed me but didn't. In the last few weeks before the wedding, I learned even more. The next thing I found out was that Jesse was using hard drugs. We smoked marijuana all the time and occasionally did acid together, but the one thing I thought was as low as you could go was shooting drugs into your arms. Only trash, the scum of the earth, shot heroin.

Jesse started staying out all night and not coming "home." After a number of times when he didn't sneak into my bedroom to spend the night, I finally got up the courage to confront him. I had not questioned Jesse earlier because I was afraid of losing him. He had already left me once, and I couldn't bear the thought of it happening again.

When Jesse admitted he had been mainlining drugs, I was shocked. I didn't even know where you could find stuff like that. He took me to the inner city of Phoenix, to a major drug house. People were slumped against the walls, injecting drugs into their veins. Someone offered me heroin, and I refused. "I would never go that far," I told Jesse. I was devastated that he was doing heroin, but I forgave him for it. He promised he wouldn't do it again, so I put it out of my mind.

I also found out Jesse had been frequenting topless bars. Several times he came home very late at night, and I could tell he'd been drinking. I asked him where he'd been and got vague answers. But once, when enough alcohol had loosened his tongue, he admitted that he had been at a bar watching the dancers. "Baby, those girls are just trash," he said.

"You're the most beautiful girl in the world. You're the kind of girl I want to marry."

That drunken confession didn't stop me from marrying him. Nothing derailed my decision to marry Jesse, not even the violent side of his personality, which I first saw just hours before we were married.

The day before the wedding, I had a get-together with my wedding party at the home of one of my bridesmaids. Bobbi, who was only sixteen, had to go home early. She wasn't allowed to hang out with me anymore, since her parents had caught her with some marijuana she'd gotten from me. They had agreed, however, to let her be the maid of honor for my wedding. The other two bridesmaids and I were just hanging out, drinking a little wine, and having fun.

Late that afternoon, Jesse called. I could tell from the loud music in the background and from his slurred speech that he was at a dance bar, and he was wasted. I was furious. "You need to get home," I told him. "We're getting married tomorrow!"

He started yelling and accusing me of being with another man. "That's ridiculous," I said. "You know I'm over at my girlfriend's house."

We must have argued for a few minutes. The next thing I remember is driving down Forty-seventh Avenue on my way home and seeing Jesse behind me in a car. We were just about a mile from my house. I sped up, and he ran a traffic light to catch me. At the next light, he got out of his car, yanked open my car door and pulled me out, then started shaking me and shoving me around. I was terrified. He was screaming incoherently that I had been with some other guy.

A man got out of another car and ran over to us. He flashed a badge. "I'm an undercover police officer!" he yelled as he pulled Jesse off me. Jesse turned around and pounded him to the ground.

Hysterical, I jumped back in my car and drove away. My eleven-year-old brother, Scott, was mowing the lawn when I pulled in our driveway. I knew Jesse wasn't far behind me.

"Go inside the house!" I yelled at Scott as I got out of the car.

"But why?" he said.

"Just do it!" I didn't want Scott to see Jesse like that, and I didn't know what Jesse was capable of doing when he was drunk and out of control.

Jesse came peeling into the driveway behind me. He got out and grabbed me and pushed me against the car. I don't remember how the fight ended; I just know that at some point I managed to get inside and Jesse went home.

Later, after Jesse calmed down, he came over to my house and apologized. He asked me to forgive him, and I did. We went back to his brother's house and were sitting in lawn chairs out in the backyard when the police came looking for him. They asked me if I wanted to press charges, and I said, "No. We're getting married tomorrow."

This big, tall cop looked at me and asked, "Young lady, you're marrying this man tomorrow?"

"Yes, sir."

"Don't do it."

"But I love him."

Jesse, who was standing beside me, put his arm around me. "It's cool, man. We've worked everything out," he said. "It won't happen again."

The police officer never took his eyes off me. "Young lady, if you marry this man, you will have to deal with a lot more than you've gone through tonight."

His words didn't register with me.

"I don't know what got into me. I was drunk," Jesse said. "I love her, and I'm going to take good care of her. Just leave us alone, okay?"

I had bruises on my arms where Jesse had grabbed me. I had never seen that side of him before. He was always so mellow and easygoing. Very soft-spoken. I had never once seen him angry, but that night he raged. Still, I didn't press charges. And I have no idea why they didn't arrest him for beating up an undercover cop.

After the police left, my mother arrived. Scott had sensed something was terribly wrong and called her at work, so she came home early. She was so upset. "Lori, do you understand that this will only get worse? If he's treating you like this now, think of what it's going to be like later."

"No, Mom. It'll be fine. He really loves me."

"I don't want to see you hurt. This is like a red light to stop you. Please come home with me," she said.

"I'll come home for a little while, but I'm getting married tomorrow." I started walking across the street with my mother, and Jesse came after me. We were standing in the middle of the street; Mom had hold of one arm, and Jesse had the other.

"Please, Lori, don't do this," my mother pleaded.

"Baby, I love you. I can't live without you, and you know you can't live without me," Jesse pleaded on the other side.

I made another bad choice. I didn't go home that night; I stayed with Jesse at his brother's house. We got up early the next morning, and Jesse coached Scott's Little League team in a championship play-off. And that night we got married.

Just before my father walked me down the aisle, he also tried to talk me out of it. "It's not too late," Dad said. Mom had told him about the altercation with Jesse. "You can back out of this, Lori Beth. So what if all these people are here? It doesn't matter. Please, don't do this."

"No, Dad. I'm marrying him. I love him." Then I walked down the aisle—straight into ten years of hell and heartache.

As I shared even more of my life story with the women at the Dream Center, I could tell that many of them related to the deep personal pain that stemmed from my bad choices. Some of them were sobbing openly; many had tears in their eyes. The joy is that I was able to share not just the pain and brokenness but the fact that God had loved me back to wholeness.

"God can only heal what you are willing to reveal," I told the audience. When I gave an invitation to come forward for prayer, the response was overwhelming. Most of these women had already committed their lives to Christ, but there were still so many deep hurts that needed healing. One woman who wanted prayer shared with me that she had had five abortions. She was praying and sobbing to the point of having dry heaves. Some of the other ladies were afraid she was going to throw up and wanted to help her, but I asked them to leave her alone. It doesn't happen that often, but sometimes a woman's grief can be so intense that she gets physically sick. In that case, it's actually best to let her get that out.

As I had sensed in my spirit, God did something powerful that day for these women. I was honored that he would use me as his chosen vessel.

5

CHOSEN VESSELS

After our prayer time at the altar that day, I made a special presentation to three women: Marja Barnett, Nancy Hinkle, and Willette Brown. I called them to the front and gave each of the ladies a beautiful vase, as I explained the concept behind a women's ministry I had started called Chosen Vessels.

I shared with the audience how Marja had poured herself into my life, helping to shape me and mold me as a Christian woman. "God loves his daughters," I said, "not for what we are, common sinners, but for who we are, women saved by his grace and personally chosen by him. Jesus told his followers, 'You did not choose me, but I chose you and appointed you to go and bear fruit—fruit that will last.'[1] I am the fruit of Marja and all the women at Phoenix First, and I thank them for that with all my heart. Women like Marja and Nancy are God's chosen vessels to help restore and rebuild women."

Willette surprised me when I made the presentation to her. "I'm very proud of Willette," I told the ladies. "She was a broken vessel who has become a vessel of divine hope, peace, joy, and love—'a vessel for honor, sanctified and useful for the Master, prepared for every good work,' just as the Bible says."[2] Willette had come a long way since the time I first met her in the housing projects of south Phoenix. Now she and her husband, James, and her sons, B. J. and Christopher, were living and working at the Dream Center, serving God faithfully.

The women applauded for Willette, and then she took the microphone. She began to share about our association and what her life was like before she accepted Christ as her Savior. "Lori just continued to love me through my sin," she said. Willette also told how she referred to me as B. J.'s godmother. She had brought Christopher to the meeting, and he came up to the front with her. With tears in her eyes, Willette told the ladies how I had once bought tennis shoes for Christopher because he had no shoes.

I had completely forgotten about that. As she told the story, it reminded me that when you do something for someone, you never know just how much it means to them. It also reminded me of the first inner-city kid I ever bought shoes for, a four-year-old named Roy.

My initial foray into ministry at Phoenix First had been with the bus ministry. On Saturdays, volunteers would take the church's fleet of rickety old buses into the inner city. We picked up kids and took them to a local Christian high school, where we held Sunday school–type classes for them. I worked as an assistant to Peggy Quan, who taught a class for the kids who were two to four years old. Peggy would bring her own children with her on the bus to the inner city, and once there, she lavished love on several dozen ragamuffins from the ghetto. Week after week her love for those runny-nosed, lice-infested kids overwhelmed me.

Somehow she imparted that love to me, and I got hooked on the inner city that summer.

One day a little boy named Roy came to our class. He was a tiny thing, small for his four years, with deep brown skin and dark eyes. His shy smile tugged at my heart as I pulled him up on my lap. I wished for a comb to tackle the cowlick in his stick-straight black hair, but I didn't have one with me. He was wearing shorts and a T-shirt, and he was barefooted.

"Where are your shoes?" I asked Roy.

"Don't got none." He spoke in a quiet voice, with his head hanging down.

It was summertime, and the temperature was well over a hundred degrees. *How could he be playing outside without shoes on the scorching pavement in this desert heat?* I wondered.

I asked his sister Jessica, who was five, "Why doesn't Roy have any shoes on?"

"He ain't got any," she said matter-of-factly.

But surely he had shoes of some kind—why, you could buy a pair of flip-flops at the drugstore for forty-nine cents. It was foreign to me that a mother could let a child go without shoes when you could get them for next to nothing. I was new to inner-city work, and I had never been exposed to the lifestyle.

Before we took the kids home that day, I made Roy stand on a sheet of paper so I could trace an outline of his foot to take with me to a shoe store. The next Saturday I returned with some high-top tennis shoes in his size. That pair of Nikes won him over; Roy was my buddy for the rest of the summer.

In the fall, I joined Master's Commission, an intensive discipleship and ministry training program. Divided into four groups, each with a specific bus route, we went into the inner city three times a week. The first time I worked my new bus route, we pulled into the parking lot of the housing project known as Sidney P. There was Roy, playing in the dirt field at Eighteenth Street and Van Buren, adjacent to the spot where we had parked the bus. I couldn't believe it. Out of all the projects in south Phoenix, I had been assigned to his area.

Our reunion was like the commercials where a couple runs in slow motion toward each other through a field of wildflowers. Only it was Lori and Roy, and we were racing across cement. I grabbed him and swung him in the air. "This is my bus route," I said. "You can come to church with me every week for a whole year!"

Roy was thrilled, and he wanted me to meet his mother. He took me by the hand and led me inside the housing project. It was like entering another world. I'd been coming to the inner city for several months, but all my work had been outdoors or in the school classroom. I was unprepared for the experience.

Like most public housing projects, Sidney P. consisted of a jumbled series of two-story buildings crowded together, seemingly laid out in a maze. The stuccoed walls must have been white originally, but they were dingy gray now. Trash littered the ground—bottles, cans, needles, dirty diapers. Bugs scurried everywhere.

Inside the stairwell that led to Roy's apartment, children were playing. Several toddlers were crawling up the concrete steps; no adults were around. As we walked up the stairs, I thought how easily they could have rolled down and cracked their heads. One of Roy's tiny hands clutched mine; with the other, he reached up and knocked on the door. Nobody answered. He knocked again, and this time the door creaked open; evidently it hadn't been shut all the way.

The assault on my senses was sudden and overwhelming. I

had never seen such filth as I saw inside the apartment. Trash piled on trash. Dirt piled on dirt. Walls smeared with human excrement—had the youngest kids tried to change their own diapers? There were tiny handprints in the filth.

A group of adults were lounging around on the few pieces of furniture in the apartment. This part of the scene, I recognized: they were partying—inhaling crack cocaine through a bong, a type of water pipe used for smoking various drugs.

Roy led me over to a woman who appeared to be about six months pregnant. "Mom, this is Lori." His little voice was raised in excitement.

"So you're the one I've been hearing so much about," the Hispanic woman said. Her black eyes flashed a look filled with hatred. "The kids come home singing their little Jesus songs, and it's Lori this and Lori that."

"I just wanted to tell you that I love your children," I said somewhat tentatively. "Thank you for letting them come to church."

"You get out of my house!" She started cursing and yelling as she raised herself up to her full five feet. "Don't you ever bring that church lady around here again, Roy."

I turned and walked to the door, but before I left, boldness struck me. "We have a special ladies' event coming up next month called Fashion Share. I'd like to invite you as my guest. You can come have dinner and then pick out some free clothes."

Her look softened. "Free clothes—for me?"

"Yes," I said. "It's not for the kids, it's for the moms. Think about it, okay?"

I found out later that she beat Roy for bringing me there. But Roy was persistent. He wanted his mom to know Jesus. I learned a valuable lesson: no matter how bad a mom is, the kids are loyal to her. Roy and his brothers and sisters covered for their mom so many times—when she was drunk, when she would beat them, when she had men in and out. They loved her through it all.

I went back week after week, and before long I had more or less adopted the entire family. Margie, Roy's mother, was only twenty-six years old. She had seven children and an eighth on the way. Veronica, the oldest, was eleven. Christina was ten; Priscilla, nine. The three oldest girls all had different fathers. Priscilla's father played a part in her life off and on, but not the others. Then there were Jessica and Roy. The middle two had the same dad, as did the three youngest: Sergio, who was three; Maricela, who was two; and the unborn baby. Eight kids by five fathers: a way of life in the ghetto.

On Thursdays our Master's Commission group conducted a big outreach service in the inner city. We would go to a different location within our area each week and set up a big stage and sound equipment. We would crank up the music—Christian rap—and some of the kids would start dancing. Several of the guys in our group performed "power" feats—breaking a stack of bricks with their hands or blowing up hot water bottles. We also did what we called "human videos," acting out a pantomime to a recorded song. Youth groups across the country perform human videos all the time now, but they started more than ten years ago with Pastor Lloyd Zeigler, director of Master's Commission.

My favorite assignment was canvassing the neighborhood to recruit people to attend the services. I loved talking one-on-one with the people. But I also participated in the dramas. Everybody pitched in—you realize quickly that you do whatever it takes. I learned to work with a team in those days.

The Thursday outreaches targeted teenagers and adults, but Saturdays were geared toward younger children. Our ministry teams met at 8:00 A.M. to board the old white buses—the *hot* old white buses with no air-conditioning. We parked at our first designated "fishing hole"—again, a different location each week. Two people would set up the stage and sound equipment while the others went knocking on doors to round up the kids. After you've cultivated a neighborhood for a while, the kids get to know you, and they're very excited that you're there. When we had gathered the children, we would do a whole program for them: songs, puppets, games, and Bible stories. Then we took the kids back home and went to the next location.

That's where I first learned how to speak using a microphone, by teaching Bible lessons to thirty or forty inner-city kids—*three times* every Saturday. When we finished at one location, we repeated the entire process at the next one: park the bus, set up the stage, round up the kids, conduct the program, take the kids back home. The most exhausting work I had ever done in my life, but I loved it.

On Sundays we brought the inner-city "flock" to the evening service at Phoenix First. The buses would leave the church at 4:00 P.M., and we would drive our route through the inner city. Our goal was to get moms and dads involved, so the rule was that the only way kids could come to church on Sunday night was to bring their parents with them. We broke the rule often—how can you say no to kids who are begging to come to church?—but we did manage to get some of the parents there.

Every Sunday afternoon I knocked on Margie's door and invited her to church. She wouldn't come, but after about six weeks she agreed to come to the Fashion Share event, another community outreach program birthed at Phoenix First. It reaches out to the bus kids' mothers and brings them into the church, where they are treated as a queen for the day. We put on a fashion show, have an elegant luncheon prepared, and then they get to shop for free clothes and accessories that have been donated by the women in the church and local merchants.

On the designated Saturday I drove to the inner city to pick up Margie. We left the projects in the south end of town and drove north to the church. As we got close to our destination Margie asked me, "Are we still in Phoenix?" That floored me. I learned that she had never once been out of the inner city. Her mother had been raised in the projects, Margie was born and raised in the projects, and now she was raising her kids in the projects. When we drove onto the church grounds, Margie thought it was one of the most beautiful sights she had ever seen. I couldn't help being excited for her, and I loved introducing her to my friends and some of the pastoral staff at church. She told me later that she had never felt so much love in her life.

That was the day I gave my first five-minute testimony, the one I had been so petrified over that I nearly backed out of it. I had practiced my speech a bit on Margie on the way to the church, but she was still very moved to hear me give it in front of a thousand women. When the keynote speaker gave the invitation at the end of the service, Margie went forward to invite Jesus into her heart, and I went with her. But she didn't change overnight.

She did, however, let me into her life. That was the beginning of our relationship. For the next eight years her family became mine. I celebrated holidays with them, bringing Thanksgiving and Christmas dinners every year, and Christmas presents and Easter baskets. I threw birthday parties for Margie and each one of the kids and also scraped together money to buy birthday gifts. Clothing and furniture were obtained for the family. They moved every four to six months, often leaving everything they owned behind. My family and friends helped me furnish several complete apartments for Margie over the years.

Every Sunday I continued to invite Margie to church. She rarely came. Many times I would knock on the door and she would make some excuse. "I'll come next week," she would say.

I'd go back the next week, all excited, just knowing she would come because I'd prayed so hard for her. Then she wouldn't answer the door. "Margie, I know you're in there," I'd say. "Come on, you promised me." Often she would be drunk or would have a man over, so she just locked me out.

Occasionally she would come to the big Easter or Christmas productions at church. But there was no consistency. I became the only consistency in her and her family's lives, and that took a tremendous amount of determination. It was a 24/7 commitment.

One time, after I had known Margie about a year, I was really heartsick because of all the broken promises. I had driven my car to Margie's on a Sunday night to pick her up for church. She had been using the excuse that she didn't want to ride the bus with all the screaming brats, so I said I would drive over and pick her up personally. When I got there, she stood me up.

Driving back up Highway 51, I started sobbing. If I hadn't been so devastated, I would have laughed. Men were all I'd ever cried over in my life, and here I was crying over an inner-city woman. When I got home, I went into my little walk-in closet and undressed. I was still crying as I put on my pajamas. "God," I said, "this woman has ripped out my heart, thrown it on the ground, and stomped all over it. She is just using me." All of a sudden I felt a stillness and a warmth in my chest—the sensation that often comes when God speaks something into my spirit.

That's exactly what you did to me for years, God whispered to my heart, *but I never gave up on you.*

I got the message loud and clear: God didn't give up on me, so I couldn't give up on Margie. I was not only doing it for her, I was doing it for the kids, and I had to keep that in mind.

As Willette Brown finished the story of how I had bought tennis shoes for her son and then thanked me for the presentation of her vessel, I said a silent prayer for Margie. She and her children had truly become my family, and I would never give up on them.

By the time the women's meeting was over that afternoon, it was almost five, and I was emotionally drained. But the most exciting part of my day was just starting. I had thought the highlight of my trip to L.A. would be that day's ministry to the women at the Dream Center. Instead, I was destined to be the featured player in a divine drama—a romantic comedy God himself had been scripting for years—and one of my most cherished dreams was on the brink of coming true.

6

"Pay Attention!"

In hindsight, Kelli's breakdown on the freeway the previous day had been divine intervention: it meant I was stranded in L.A. until her car was repaired. I had intended to leave right after the women's meeting that Friday and have Kelli drive me to Newport Beach—about an hour away—where my brother Mark lived. An exhausting year at breakneck pace had taken its toll on me, and uppermost in my mind was the opportunity to spend the weekend relaxing and lying in the sun. Because Mark would be out of town for a couple of days, he had arranged for me to have a key to his condo. But now Kelli couldn't take me, and I was disappointed that I had no way to get there.

After the meeting, the girls were buzzing around me, full of plans.

"Don't worry," Kelli told me. "We'll put the car in the shop tomorrow. Then we can go to Newport Beach as soon as it's fixed." In the meantime, she said, a group of people were headed to the laser show at the planetarium. "Since you have to stay here tonight anyway, why don't you go with us?"

"Sure, that sounds like fun," I said.

"Okay, we'd better hurry. We don't want to be late. Amanda has it all planned out."

The girls whisked me away to Jennifer Morgan's car. She drove and I sat in the front seat; Kelli and Jennifer Nicks were in the back. I noticed we were following a white Jeep, and all of a sudden I realized that the other three people in the car had exchanged one too many conspiratorial looks.

"Who's in the Jeep?" I asked. *Must be the others from the Dream Center who are going to the planetarium,* I thought. *Has to be from the Dream Center—it's a Jeep. But it's not Jay's. His is black, and this one is white.*

"Oh, that's Amanda and Jay," one of the girls said.

"And who else?" I asked, instantly suspicious. "Looks like there are four people inside."

"Uh, Connie's with them . . ." Kelli paused and then added deliberately, "And Jim."

Nicks lost it and started giggling, and the others joined in.

"You guys! Now stop it!" I was aggravated. I'd had this conversation with Kelli yesterday. "I told you, I don't want to be set up."

"Hey, it's no big deal," Kelli said.

"Yeah, it's not like a date or anything," Morgan said. "It's simply a group of us going to the show together."

"Besides, I think Jim's a very nice guy," Nicks said. "Last night at the restaurant was the first time I'd ever been around him, and I liked him a lot."

I leaned back against the headrest and looked out the window as I listened to the girls chattering about Jim Bakker while insisting they weren't trying to pair us up. We drove past the open-air Greek Theater, a concert venue for the nation's top performing artists, and headed up a winding road through the vast public park toward the observatory. It wasn't the beach, but I was beginning to relax nevertheless.

Griffith Observatory, a Los Angeles landmark since the 1930s, sits on the southern slope of Mount Hollywood. The art deco building with its three copper domes is immediately recognizable to millions of moviegoers: it has been a popular background location for many films, including the James Dean classic, *Rebel Without a Cause*. In addition to a science museum and public telescope, the planetarium is also home to the popular laser show that was our destination. Laserium, the grandfather of light displays, was celebrating twenty-five years as the longest-running theatrical attraction in Los Angeles.

Amanda, who is Miss Organization, and the others were waiting for us at the entrance, and we breezed in moments before the show began. I realized someone must have already bought the tickets because we were finding seats and putting on our 3-D glasses before I knew it. The eight of us sat together on one row; I was at one end, and Jim was completely at the other. *Not very effective matchmaking,* I thought, *if that's what they're trying to do.*

I leaned over to the girls and asked, "Who paid for our tickets?"

"I think Jim did," one of them said.

As the sound system began to blast out a U2 song and the fiber-optic technology beamed millions of colors into the darkness above us, I dug in my purse for my wallet. I took out enough money to cover the admission for my group of four. "Pass this down to Jim for our tickets," I said.

In a minute the money came back to me. "Jim said he wanted to treat everyone," Kelli said.

"When the show is over," I told her, "I want each one of you to go up and thank him for doing this, and I will too." Our four tickets totaled thirty dollars, and I thought that was very generous of Jim.

I found myself wondering what he thought of the music. I

doubted he was familiar with the wildly popular Irish rock group with Christian roots. *I'm in an observatory, watching a laser show and listening to U2 music with the famous Jim Bakker. How weird is that.*

The 3-D laser show was enjoyable, and the unusual, colorful lighting effects—"visual music," the promoters called it—were an awful lot cheaper and infinitely less hazardous, I reflected, than my youthful experiences with hallucinogenic-inspired light shows. When Bobbi and I took LSD as teenagers, we would sit outside and watch the lights. An ordinary streetlight or traffic light would look like fireworks, with the light seeming to explode and then melt and trickle down.

After the show, we went into the observatory's Hall of Science and strolled through the free museum. One by one the girls went over and thanked Jim, and then it was my turn. He was standing in front of a large exhibit labeled FALLS AND FLIGHTS. Pieces of meteorites occupied the glass shelves inside the lighted display cases. I thanked him for our tickets, and we struck up a conversation on meteors. He began to explain what they were, where the meteorite samples came from, and what the Bible said about them. Now, meteorites were not a topic I would ever have thought to discuss with a new acquaintance, let alone Jim Bakker, but he was so interesting to talk to that I found myself asking questions and learning from him.

He is so into this, I thought, mildly amused. *And not at all like a typical preacher. Not rigid or superspiritual. Very down-to-earth and extremely intelligent.*

Jim's boyish face was animated as he spoke. "I'm sorry to ramble on," he said, "but I'm like a kid in a candy store." He was in the process of writing a book on Bible prophecy and the end times, *Prosperity and the Coming Apocalypse,* he told me, and his book included a chapter on asteroids and meteors. "So this subject is dear to my heart," he said sheepishly.

"It's okay—I'm intrigued by it. I just never thought about meteorites in a Christian context before."

"I know," he said. "For centuries, Bible scholars have said that some of the key Scripture passages—the stars of heaven falling to Earth, for example—were simply symbolic language, referring to powerful world leaders. And for the last few decades, preachers have said that the catastrophes predicted in Bible prophecies dealing with the end times—like the sky receding as a scroll and the mountains and islands being moved out of place—describe a nuclear explosion. But as I started studying Scripture and researching the topic, I began to doubt that theory. Now I believe the Bible could be describing the impact of a massive meteor collision with our planet."

As we walked from exhibit to exhibit, Jim fascinated me with both his depth of knowledge and his spiritual insight. Two very large meteorites, weighing several hundred pounds each, sat on the museum floor. "These are the oldest objects you will ever see," Jim said. "They are 'leftovers' from the formation of our solar system. These two huge rocks are actually tiny chunks of asteroids that were hurtling through space—some of them can be hundreds of miles in diameter. The ones that cross Earth's orbit make collisions possible, and when an asteroid enters Earth's atmosphere, it's called a meteor."

He told me that what we call "shooting stars" or "falling stars" are often meteors that can be seen with the naked eye. We talked about the movie *Deep Impact* and its biblical overtones, and how Jim believed that even the great Chicago Fire of 1871 could have been caused by a meteor impact, not Mrs. O'Leary's cow kicking over a lantern, as the popular explanation goes.[1]

I had been so engrossed in my conversation with Jim, I hadn't noticed that the others had gotten restless and wandered off in different directions. Jen Nicks came over and pulled me to the side. "You two have been talking for a solid hour," she said.

I checked my watch; she was right. It had seemed like only minutes. "I want to go to the car and put some lipstick on," I said. Jen seemed to jump at the opportunity to get me alone for a minute. *Something must be on her mind,* I thought.

Jen and I walked out to the parking lot and checked our makeup in the car mirror. As we started to go back inside, she blurted out, "Lori, there is something I have to tell you." There was a soft urgency to her voice as the words began to spill out. "You're not living the dream God gave you. I know you're living part of the dream, with the women's ministry and all your speaking and traveling, but you've always told me that your ultimate dream was to be married to the right man. That you believed God had called you to be a wife and to have a family." She pointed her finger at me as she emphasized each word: "That's your dream, and you're not living it."

"I think I need to sit down for this," I said, somewhat taken aback, but with the sudden impression that she did indeed have something important to say to me. This was a different Jen talking. Her angular face, usually wreathed in a wide smile, was somber. Frosted bangs fell over her eyes, which shone with tears.

"Look, I don't even know why I'm saying this," she started again. "You're always the one who is teaching *me* about life. But right now something inside me is screaming, 'Pay attention, Lori! Open your eyes!'

"You've always told us that everything happens for a purpose when you are committed to following God's will for your life. I

47

believe that, and I don't think it's mere coincidence that this particular group of people happens to be together on this particular night. God has crisscrossed our lives and brought us all together for some reason we don't know, and I think you need to pay attention to what is happening and what God may be doing.

"I'm not saying 'thus saith the Lord' or anything like that, and I don't know if Jim Bakker is the one for you," she went on. "But I do know that something special is going on. And I feel that he is the kind of person you need to be with."

"If he's interested in me," I said, "I sure couldn't tell it. I mean, all we talked about was meteors and the Bible."

"Oh, he's interested all right. You can see it every time he looks at you, and even in the way he talks to you and treats you. He's not only attracted to you physically, he thinks you're someone special."

Ordinarily, I might have bristled at this complete role reversal, but I began to feel the presence of God as Jen talked, almost as if we were surrounded by an invisible force field. People were milling around on the observatory lawn, but we seemed to be completely shielded from any intrusion.

"I can tell that Jim is a very gentle man," she said. "A godly man. A mature man—and that's exactly my point. You're forty years old now, Lori, but because of your work with Master's Commission, you're surrounded by all these young twenty-something guys. That's who you're used to seeing, but that's not who you need in your life. You need someone mature who knows how to love you and care for you, someone you can be in ministry with, someone . . ."

Once Jen had gotten wound up, she just couldn't seem to stop. " So I don't know if Jim Bakker is *the* man for you, Lori, but he's the *type* of man for you. God is showing you, through this man, the standard for your husband. This is the kind of man he wants to put in your life. And you need to open your eyes and take a good look at Jim. That's all I'm trying to say: pay attention to what God is doing here!"

Both of us were very emotional at that point, sniffling and wiping our eyes. As we went to rejoin the group, I knew that the Holy Spirit had just spoken to me through one of my girls. The mentor had needed mentoring, and at a critical moment in my life, she had been willing to play the role I had so often played in hers.

Days later Jen Nicks told me that as she and Jennifer Morgan had driven to L.A. from San Diego, they had prayed for the women's meeting at the Dream Center. Nicks had also been going through some of her own struggles and had been short with me recently, so she had asked God to forgive her and to use her in my life in a special way. She never imagined that God would use her to point out the husband he had chosen for me. I know now that our conversation that night was the beginning of an incredible adventure in fulfillment of one of my favorite verses of Scripture, Ephesians 3:20, which says that God is able to do far more than we would ever dare to ask or even dream of.

Back at the observatory, we walked up the outer stairway and through the stone archway to the roof area, where a crowd had lined up to look through the large twelve-inch Zeiss telescope. It was a clear, starlit night, and we enjoyed the spectacular view of Los Angeles from the balconies as we waited.

What Nicks had said was true, I realized. It was as if I had been wearing blinders and had not really seen Jim Bakker at all. For the first time I looked at him in a different light—and I liked what I saw. I liked the way he looked, the way he smiled, the way his eyes lit up when it was his turn to step up to the telescope and gaze into the heavens.

I opened my eyes and started to pay attention.

7

Pop Quiz

As we left Griffith Observatory, Jim suggested we all go out to eat—a popular suggestion, it turned out. Connie knew of a family-type restaurant that was on the way back to the Dream Center, so the girls and I again followed Jim's white Jeep through the streets of L.A.

The hostess at the House of Pies pushed a couple of tables together for us, and Jim orchestrated the seating so that I was next to him. *Is he starting to make his move?* I wondered.

Everyone was already in high spirits, and the mood around the table kept lifting as we laughed and cut up. Jay and Jim were the only two men in the group, and the Bakker boys did a masterful job of keeping six women entertained. I had seen Jim's intense side and his innate intelligence during our conversation at the observatory; now I had the opportunity to see his lighthearted side and his keen sense of humor. I could also tell that he was trying to get my attention now, and he began to flirt with me a little.

After we placed our order, Jim had the idea of giving us all a quiz that would reveal something about our personalities. "I don't even know why this popped into my mind," he said, "because I haven't done this since college, but it's a lot of fun." He told us the quiz was something that Fern Olson, his former pastor's wife and a great evangelist, had used with the church kids back in the early '60s while Jim was in Bible college in Minnesota. I'm a people person, and I love discovering personality traits, so the quiz sounded like fun to me.

"Okay, everybody get a pen so you can write down the answers to these questions." Jim gave us a minute to dig around in our purses for pens, and then we used the paper place mats and napkins to jot down our answers as he administered the quiz. (You might also want to try this—the quiz is a fun personal assessment.)

"Now, close your eyes or just let your mind wander. Imagine you are walking down a quiet country lane, and you come to a crossroads. You take the fork to the left, and as you travel down the road you see a house. What kind of house is it?"

We all scribbled on our makeshift writing pads.

"Are there any trees around the house?" Jim asked. "How many trees, and what kind are they?" More scribbling.

"You walk inside the house, and there is an entry hall table to your right. What kind of table do you see?" He paused to let us answer. "Now you go back outside, and you see a huge bear in the front yard. What is your reaction?"

A few giggles from the girls broke the silent atmosphere of a school exam. I couldn't wait to hear their answers.

"You go back inside and wander through the house, and eventually you walk out into the backyard. You see water. Describe what kind of water you see. Next you notice a cup lying on the ground. What do you do with it?"

We kept jotting notes on our napkins.

"Finally, you leave the house and walk down the country lane again. You come to the end of the road. What do you see?"

Jim paused to let us finish writing. "Okay, that's the end of the test," he announced.

"Now you have to tell us what it means," somebody said. "Yeah, let's find out how crazy we are," another person chimed in.

I was sitting next to Jim, so he turned to me and asked, "Lori, will you go first?"

"Sure." I smiled, wondering what aspects of my personality I was about to reveal to a man I had just met. A man who, I was now pretty sure, was as interested in me as Nicks had said he was. "The house I saw was a Southern-style mansion," I began. "A big two-story white house with pillars across the front. It was open and airy and very spacious."

"And the table?" he asked.

"It was beautiful cherrywood with fine lines, like the kind you would find in a typical foyer—a narrow table placed right against the wall." I looked up from my notes. "Okay, what does it mean?"

"The house," Jim said, "shows the image you present—how you see yourself; and the table represents the real you—what you are really like."

"That's you, all right," Kelli said. "Stately and gracious like a mansion."

"The two images match," Morgan noted. "The table, which is the real you, is exactly what you would expect to find inside the mansion, which is your image of yourself."

Nicks spoke up. "The table was in the foyer. You're always out front mixing and mingling with people. And it was solid cherrywood. You're solid all the way through, Lori."

"Beautiful, with fine lines." Jim quoted my description of the table with an admiring glance in my direction. *Yep, the guy was interested.*

"Wait a minute," I said, eager to move to the next question. "You skipped the part about the trees."

"Sorry," he said. "What kind of trees did you see around the house?"

"It wasn't very wooded," I replied. "The lawn was like a grassy knoll, with a few large, beautiful oak trees."

"What you see around the house reflects the number and kind of friends you have."

Bingo, I thought. I'm always surrounded by people, but I have very few close friends. Those I do allow to get close to me loom large and significant, like the few tall oaks I had seen. "Let's hear the answers from the rest of you guys," I said.

We went around the table one by one and listened to everyone else's responses to the first few questions. As I listened to Kelli and Nicks and Morgan give their answers, I was amazed at how accurate some of the answers were at showing personalities. I also learned more about Connie and Amanda, whom I had just met, and Jay, whom I did not know very well even though I'd been acquainted with him for several years.

The discussion came back to me. "All right, Lori. Tell us about the bear," Nicks said. "This I gotta hear."

"For a minute I was frozen in shock," I replied. "Then I just turned around and ran back inside the house and locked the door. But I didn't scream—because I sure didn't want to startle that mean ol' bear."

Everyone got a good laugh over that. "What did I just tell about myself?" I asked Jim.

"The bear represents your problems and how you react to

them. Many people climb a tree," Jim explained, "meaning they go to their friends in times of trouble. The fact that you ran back inside the house means that you probably turn inward, go within yourself, when you're dealing with a problem."

"That nailed you, Lori," one of my girls said. "You're always helping us with our problems, but you never want to let anyone know when you're struggling with something."

"I guess that's why I didn't scream at the bear," I admitted. "So no one would know I had a problem." I shrugged and groaned exaggeratedly. "Okay, what's next? Give me the bad news so I can run back inside the house."

Jim grinned from ear to ear. "The water represents your love life, or your capacity for romance."

"All riiiiiiiight!" The girls giggled and high-fived. "Tell the truth, Lori. What did you write down?"

"I don't know what it means, but my house was on a lake. That's the water I saw behind the house."

"A lake—that's good," Jim said with a delighted smile. *"Really good."*

We all went around the table and discussed our answers. Someone had seen a rushing river; someone saw a gently flowing brook; another person saw a swimming pool. Everyone had something funny to say about the interpretation. Jim said that one person in his college had seen a garden hose with a tiny trickle of water coming out. "We figured he wasn't going to have much of a chance for romance in his life," he said. By this time we were all laughing so hard we were wiping tears from our eyes.

"I'm almost afraid to ask about the cup," I said.

"What did you do when you saw it?" Jim asked.

"I picked it up and threw it away. What does that mean?"

"The cup shows how you handle your romances."

Another boisterous round of laughter erupted. "I can't believe you threw it away!" Kelli said.

"Lori collects beautiful teacups," Morgan told the others. "She loves them."

"Yes, but the cup I saw by the lake was a paper cup," I said in my defense. "That's why I threw it away."

As the others told what they had done with the cup, I reflected on my answer. So many times over the years—I had been divorced for thirteen years, celibate for the last nine—I had almost despaired of ever having true romance in my life; it seemed as if I had indeed thrown the possibility away. Jen Nicks had just spoken strongly to me about not living my dream. The dream of being married—to the husband God picked for me. The evening had certainly taken a strange twist.

Jim was winding up the quiz, I realized. "The final question—'What do you see at the end of the road?'—is your interpretation of eternity. What did you see, Lori?"

"A beautiful scene," I said. "It was a bright, sunny day, and I saw a huge expanse of blue sky over a big open meadow."

Everyone at the table had seen an open space of some sort. "Christians always see beyond the end of the road," Jim said. "Fern once told us that every time she would test unbelievers, they would see a wall or something that blocked the view. They could never see beyond."

A very pleasant hour or more had passed while we ate our food and laughed over our answers to the personality quiz. "I haven't laughed this much in years," Jim confessed. "It feels great."

He had obviously been having so much fun—we all had—I hadn't stopped to think that for a long time Jim Bakker hadn't had anything to laugh about. An ordinary evening spent talking and enjoying ourselves around a dinner table could be an extraordinary joy for this man who had gone through scandal, prison, and divorce—all before a watching world.

Once or twice during the evening I caught Jay looking from his dad to me and then glancing away quickly. He could see the sparks flying between us, and I sensed Jay was having trouble with that. Did he resent his dad's interest in me? I thought I knew what the problem was, and it wasn't necessarily with me. Jay felt as if he had just gotten his father back, and he didn't want to lose him again—to anyone.

8

A Puppy Dog in a Sunday Suit

A few years earlier I had had a brief glimpse of Jim and Jay's struggle to have a close father-son relationship.

Jay came to Phoenix in the fall of 1994, not long after his father was released from prison. The two of them had been living in a small farmhouse in the mountains of North Carolina, and while it was a dream come true to be living under the same roof with his father again, Jay also felt isolated and bored. He started going back to Charlotte and hanging out with the wrong people, toying again with the drugs and alcohol that had tempted him during his early teen years.

Through a former ministry associate, Jim learned about Master's Commission at Phoenix First and, knowing Tommy Barnett personally, Jim picked up the phone and called him for assistance. Jim was up front about Jay's battle with drugs. Pastor Barnett offered to help Jay any way he could, and even said that

Jay could live with his family if he wanted to enroll in Master's Commission. Lloyd Zeigler, the director of Master's Commission, also agreed that Jay would be welcome and that he could come anonymously. Unless he wanted to tell them, no one would have to know that Jay Bakker was actually the Jamie Charles Bakker who had grown up in front of the cameras on his daddy's television program. Jamie had gone by the name Jay for several years now, and he looked completely different from the little boy everybody had seen on television and in news photographs. Because of my longtime association with Master's Commission—I had just left my full-time volunteer staff position with Master's to start Truth, a new ministry working with postabortive women, but I was still involved with the students on a regular, if informal, basis—I was one of the handful of people at Phoenix First who knew Jay's true identity.

Although Jay loved God and wanted to get his life straightened out, he was not sold on the idea of an intense discipleship training program like Master's Commission. But he promised his father he would visit Phoenix to consider it. While there to check it out, Jay met Mike and Heather Wall, who had also just left the Master's Commission staff to start a ministry called Revolution. Kelli Miller, another Master's graduate—and one of my "girls"—was helping Mike and Heather birth this new ministry to kids on the fringe of society, those who would never set foot inside a church. Jay immediately clicked with Mike Wall and Revolution. In fact, he moved in with the Walls, and he grew under Mike and Heather's discipleship.

Revolution was definitely "not your father's ministry," to paraphrase General Motors' television commercials with the slogan, "This is not your father's Oldsmobile." The group's leaders didn't look or dress like typical pastors—they looked more like rock musicians—and they held church services in a building where the walls were painted black and a live band pumped out music. They read poetry as well as the Bible, and they had a heart for kids who just didn't seem to fit in anywhere else. I used to attend Revolution's Sunday night services to show my support for the youth.

In spite of his struggles with drugs and alcohol, Jay had always had a heart for ministry and longed to reach out to the hurting. With Revolution, he found a vehicle for doing just that. Before long Jay had cut his black hair and dyed it blond, grown a goatee, and acquired earrings and a tattoo. He became more and more "alternative" in his appearance, yet more and more effective in his impact on kids who were tired of being judged by the way they looked.

I don't remember the first time I met Jay, but I periodically came into contact with him at Phoenix First. One night after church we were at a restaurant with a group of people, and Jay sat next to me. Kelli had already told him, "Lori has done everything there is to do, so if you need someone to talk to, she'll understand." That night Jay began to tell me about his problems with drugs. He said that occasionally he still had flashbacks from tripping on acid.

"I totally understand," I told him. "Been there, done that." We talked for a long time that night, and Kelli brought Jay with her a few times after that when she dropped by to visit. I was like the mother hen of Master's Commission, and even after I left Master's, students continued to hang out at my house or come over just to talk. Jay became a part of that extended circle of kids I tried to nurture while they were away from home and learning to work in a ministry.

Jay stayed at Phoenix First for only a few months, so I did not get the opportunity to know him back then as well as I would have liked. I had thought he would be someone whose path crossed mine occasionally through our common connection with Kelli. But looking at him across the table now at the House of Pies, I wondered if he might be destined to become a more significant part of my life.

I looked at Jim and then across the table at Jay, who was grinning at something Amanda had said. The physical resemblance between father and son was striking—the same soulful eyes, the same cherubic smile. Seeing them together now reminded me of another time I had seen them together—a moment that was not as carefree and casual as this, a moment I would never forget. It was the highlight of Jay's time in Phoenix; in fact, some people have said that it may have been a highlight in church history. And it was the only time I had ever seen Jim Bakker in person until Jay introduced us at the Dream Center just twenty-four hours earlier.

During the first week of February, Phoenix First hosts an annual event called Pastor's School. Each year approximately ten thousand pastors come from all over the world to go through three days of training in the ministries of Phoenix First. For the 1995 event, Truth Ministries had been tapped to appear onstage as one of three ministries spotlighted at the Monday night Parade of Ministries. Revolution would be one of the other new ministries featured, and Jay Bakker was scheduled to give his testimony at this spectacular event, where almost two hundred members of lay ministries, some wearing costumes or uniforms, parade through the sanctuary with banners and signs and balloons. It takes more than an hour for the hundreds of people involved just to march past the audience.

With so many vital, active ministries in the church, it is a great honor when Tommy Barnett chooses your group to be presented onstage for this annual event. That Monday night I sat on the front row with my camera, so I could take pictures of the other ministries and Mom could take pictures of me. The first ministry, an outreach to bikers, made a dramatic entrance riding their motorcycles across the platform. A few tough-looking guys in black leather showed just how tender their hearts were as they shared a short testimony.

Next, Pastor Barnett called the leaders of Truth Ministries to come forward, and I had a knot in my stomach. It was one thing to share my testimony with inner-city women or the women of my church, but now I would be standing before ten thousand church leaders from around the world, telling them that I had had five abortions. The three of us who started Truth Ministries each spoke briefly, giving a bit of our backgrounds and telling how we ministered to other women whose lives had been deeply scarred by abortion. It was pretty traumatic for me, standing next to Tommy Barnett and talking so openly about my past to this vast audience, but my pastor is so loving and gracious that his mere presence beside me infused me with strength.

After I sat back down in the audience, he introduced Revolution by showing a wild music video, and then Mike and Heather Wall and their group of youth rushed enthusiastically onto the stage. Mike told about his vision for Revolution and the impact it could have on an entire generation. Then Pastor Barnett called Jay Bakker forward and introduced him. He had saved Jay's testimony till the very end because of a surprise he had planned and kept very secret.

Jay began to tell why Revolution was so important to him. "My dad got out of prison a few months ago," he said. Tommy Barnett leaned over and said something to Jay, evidently encouraging him to identify his father. "Jim Bakker is my dad," Jay said—somewhat hesitantly at first and then more strongly—"Jim and Tammy Faye Bakker are my parents." Then he looked startled as the crowd began to stand and clap.

I could hear people yelling "We love you, Jamie" over the applause. Jay broke down and wept. He could barely speak when the applause died down. "You don't know how much that means to me," he managed to choke out through his tears. With an arm around Jay's shoulders, Pastor Barnett encouraged him to continue. Jay told the thousands of pastors and church leaders assembled what it had meant for him to find a group like Revolution to help him, how hurt he had been by the way people—church people—had treated his family in the past, and how he had rediscovered his faith in Jesus Christ. When he finished, the crowd erupted in another standing ovation.

It took a while for Tommy Barnett to get the audience to settle down. When they finally did, he told Jay that if anybody had the right to hear a young man's testimony, it was his father. Jay's face lit up with hope as Pastor Barnett said he had invited Jim Bakker to come and hear his son speak. But then he said that Jim had refused the invitation because he "didn't want to be an embarrassment" to his son, and I will never forget Jay's crestfallen look when he heard that his father thought he would embarrass Jay by being there. It was obvious to me that he wanted his father to be there more than anything in the world.

Not wanting to prolong Jay's agony, Tommy Barnett immediately announced his surprise: "But Jim's here tonight!" The entire evening had been emotionally charged, and now the crowd roared happily as Pastor Barnett said to Jim, who was sitting in the audience, "Come on down here and give your boy a hug!"

Jim started walking from the very back of the auditorium as the audience continued to applaud and yell encouragement. He kept his head down and never looked up as he proceeded down the long center aisle to the front. When he walked right past my front-row seat on his way to the stage, I got a very good look at the notorious Jim Bakker, and I was shocked. Jim is not a large person to begin with, but that night I thought he was the smallest man I'd ever seen—and it had much more to do with his demeanor than his physical stature. He looked like a pitiful little puppy dog wearing a Sunday suit.

When Jim climbed the steps and reached Jay, they fell into each other's arms and sobbed. The audience continued to clap and shout, "We love you, Jim!" Many people in the congregation wiped tears from their eyes. I was crying, too, but I managed to take a lot of photographs from my front-row vantage point; I gave Jay a set of prints later.

After a minute or two with Jay, Jim went over to Mike Wall and Tommy Barnett. He hugged them and said brokenly, "Thank you for loving my son." The audience kept applauding, and Jim kept on weeping and hanging on to his son. It was the longest ovation I've ever experienced. I've watched the videotape of this service many times, and the ovation lasts around four minutes on the edited version. But I was there in person, and I remember hearing the noise for close to ten minutes before Tommy Barnett could bring order to the service and continue.

During the long ovation, Jim had kept his back to the audience. Now Pastor Barnett handed him the microphone and urged him, "Say a few words." Jim looked up and blinked under the glare of the bright lights. He appeared frail, as if he might crumple, and I wondered if he would be able to speak at all. Finally, he said those few words the pastor had requested, and they were straight from a father's heart: "I'm proud of my boy." The crowd cheered.

I didn't know much about Jim Bakker. I hadn't paid attention to the scandal or the trial or his incarceration and didn't know why he was such a pariah or what had brought him to this point. But I knew one thing from the scene I had just witnessed: Jim Bakker was an anguished, broken man who loved his son deeply. And I respected him for that.

"This is my first public appearance in six years," Jim said slowly, obviously groping for words. Then he turned around and looked at some of the bikers who were still onstage. "Boy, am I glad you're up here," he said. "I feel right at home. This is my group!" The place went wild again. One of the bone-crushing bikers broke ranks and gave Jim a big hug. I wasn't exactly sure what was happening, but I knew that a lot of healing was taking place—both on the stage and in the audience.

I suppose the old Jim Bakker must have surfaced a bit, because he gained enough composure to speak to the crowd. He referred to a few of his accomplishments and the great people he had been privileged to know. "But I want to tell you pastors something," he said. "I had to go to prison for this boy to spend the first day with me in his lifetime." He told how Jay had driven to prison by himself on his sixteenth birthday because it was the first time he was old enough to visit without a guardian. "After we had spent the day together," Jim said, "my son told me it was 'the best day of my whole life. I've spent my whole life trying to get your attention. I wanted just to spend one day with you and have you to myself.'"

The pain on Jim's face spoke volumes to the pastors in the audience. But lest they miss his point, he drove it home. "Preachers, don't go win the world and lose your own kids." He confessed that he had been too busy building Heritage USA to give his young son the attention he needed, yet "all he wanted was his dad." The moment Jim finished speaking, Pastor Barnett asked for those who would like to pray to come down to the front. Hundreds of people filled the aisles and streamed forward. Pastors fell on their knees and began to repent for neglecting their children for the sake of their ministries.

The Parade of Ministries had turned into a major prayer meeting. I stayed until almost midnight, and people were still praying at the altars of the church. Several pastors came up to Tommy Barnett and said they weren't staying for the rest of the conference; they were going home to spend time with their families. What had motivated their return was witnessing this momentous reunion of a father and the son he had almost lost.

Now, three years later, I was watching Jim Bakker and his son interact again—not observing from a distance this time but sitting intimately around a dinner table with them. And they weren't weeping on this occasion; they were laughing and having a good time. Were Jim and Jay destined to be a part of my future? I didn't know. But as we left the restaurant that Friday night, I knew that if I was going to have any kind of a relationship with Jim, I needed to proceed with caution for Jay's sake. The last thing I wanted to do was to come between this father and his son.

9

FULL DISCLOSURE

Saturday, July 18, 1998

When sunlight began streaming into the window just after 5:00 A.M., the girls' room at the Dream Center was already hotter than hades. We had stayed up half the night talking, and it was far too early to think about getting up. I shut my eyes against the increasingly bright light and slept fitfully until a knock on the door woke us around nine o'clock.

"Who is it?" Kelli asked, her voice hoarse with sleep.

"It's Jim."

Kelli sat up in bed. "Jim has *never* come to our room before—it's because of you!" she said. Amanda raised her head and exchanged a puzzled look with Kelli.

"What do you want?" I raised my voice so it would carry beyond the closed door.

"Last night you said the girls didn't have a fan in their room, and I thought we could go to the drugstore and get one. And whatever else they need—the things you mentioned."

Kelli's eyes widened in surprise. "You told him we needed stuff?" she whispered.

"Well, yes. Revolution is operating under the umbrella of Jim's ministry, and he should know that you two don't even have the basic necessities." I stretched and yawned. "I figured *you* wouldn't tell him you were doing without things, so I went to bat for you girls."

"But we were going to get my car fixed this morning so I could take you to your brother's house," Kelli said.

Jim spoke again from the hall. "So, Lori, do you and the girls want to go shopping with me?"

"We'll worry about the car later," I told her. "Let's get some supplies first." Not waiting for Kelli and Amanda to agree, I got up from my bed on the floor and walked over to the door. "We'd love to go shopping," I called out. "We just woke up, so can you give us about thirty minutes to get ready?"

"Okay, I'll be back," Jim said. I listened to the squeak of rubber-soled shoes on linoleum as he walked down the hall.

The three of us—Nicks and Morgan had returned to San Diego after our evening at the observatory and the House of Pies—flew around the tiny room getting dressed, throwing things to one side and grabbing clothes and crowding around the mirror to put on our makeup. Miraculously, we were ready to go when Jim returned a half hour later.

"I'll walk you ladies downstairs," he said when I opened the door. "Jamie's down in the Jeep with the air conditioner running."

Jim looked absolutely adorable, standing there grinning broadly, a tan baseball cap perched on his head. He had on a tan shirt and tan shorts—freshly pressed and creased—and he was wearing some kind of hiking boots with socks. Everything matched perfectly. He looked so crisp and clean, and he smelled good too. *Just too cute for words,* I thought as we left the room. I found out later that he had roused Jay, who likes to sleep late, out of bed at eight o'clock in order to get ready to take us shopping. Jim had been thrilled that I had given him such a perfect excuse for seeing me again.

Jay had double-parked the Jeep outside the old hospital building. Amanda climbed in the front seat as Jim held the back door open for me. Instead of going around to the other side, Kelli immediately scooted in behind me and motioned me to the far side, which left Jim no option but to follow the two of us. Now sandwiched between Jim and me, Kelli kept looking straight ahead, avoiding my pointed glance in her direction. Jim had maneuvered the seating at the restaurant the night before so he could sit by me; I felt sure he had intended to sit next to me this morning, but Kelli had outmaneuvered him. *Is my would-be matchmaker now having second thoughts?* I wondered. *What's going on?*

Jim had picked up a stack of books and papers as he got into the Jeep. Now he handed the top item to me, reaching across Kelli. "I was wondering if you had read my book *I Was Wrong?*"

"No," I said, "but I saw the copy you gave Pastor Lloyd. He loved it." I stared at the heavy hardcover book. *How wrong was he?* I remember thinking. *Wrong enough to write six hundred-plus pages, I guess.* "Is this for me?" I asked him, speaking around Kelli, who was sitting there as stolid as Mount Rushmore.

"Yes, I'd like you to have it," he said.

I opened my mouth to thank him, and he immediately handed me another hardcover book; this one was older, with no dust jacket. "This is a book on Heritage USA and our lives there," Jim said.

"I never knew much about Heritage," I said, thumbing through the book, which was full of pictures. "In fact, I'm not even sure I knew about it at all until I met your son."

"This will tell you all about it," he said, "if you want to know more."

"Well, sure. Thanks," I said, not really knowing what to make of this gesture.

"And here is some information on meteorites." His offering this time was a sheaf of papers. He passed them in front of Ms. Stone Statue, who suddenly seemed incapable of even blinking. *He's giving me scientific articles to read?* I wondered in amazement as I reached across Kelli for the material.

"All of this is for me to keep?" I asked, a bit overwhelmed.

"Yes—if you'd like to have it, that is . . ."

"Of course. Thank you very much." I put the meteorite materials behind the books and started flipping through the volume on Heritage and the Bakker family. There were pictures of Jim and celebrities—presidents and preachers and musicians—pictures of Jamie Charles and Tammy Sue when they were kids, pictures of the Grand Hotel and the Heritage water park and the television studio, and a lot of pictures of Tammy Faye. My curiosity was piqued. What kind of marriage had Jim and Tammy had? What kind of relationship did they have now?

"Are you still in love with your ex-wife?" I asked rather bluntly.

"No," he said softly, "I'm not in love with her." He adjusted his ball cap a fraction of an inch. "I guess you could say I still have a love for her because she is the mother of my children. But I'm not in love with her."

"I, uh, was just wondering what your relationship was," I said, a bit embarrassed that I might have offended him by blurting out the question. But I didn't know what to think. Here was a man who was obviously interested in me, yet he had just given me a book chock full of photos of his ex-wife. What was he trying to tell me?

Though I wasn't sure what to make of the book, I appreciated his honest answer. And I very much respected the fact that he did not speak disparagingly about his ex-wife. He had every right to, based on what I'd pieced together from talking to Jay and Kelli over the last few years—I knew Tammy Faye had divorced Jim while he was in prison in order to marry the man he had considered his best friend. Jim's careful choice of words and the lack of rancor in his voice sent his personal stock soaring on my inner ticker tape. If he had bad-mouthed his ex-wife in front of me, it would have indicated that he might say the same kind of things about me if *we* had a relationship and he ever got mad at me.

I now knew two important things about Jim Bakker: he loved his children deeply, and he was not bitter toward his ex-wife. Okay, make that three things: he was also a very attractive man.

We stopped at a Rite-Aid drugstore, which was being remodeled. While the five of us picked our way around the scaffolding and selected the items the girls needed—some toiletries and cleaning supplies—Jim and Jay got into a disagreement about a new tattoo. Jay's tattoos were tasteful, as far as tattoos go, and they all had spiritual significance for him—one referred to God's grace, for example. Jim objected to the fact that he kept getting additional tattoos, and that they had now crept below the sleeve of his T-shirt, making them visible all the time.

I started to back Jim up because I had the same reservations about Jay's so-called body art, but Kelli quickly pulled me to one side. "Don't go there," she said. "You're going to get in the middle of something, and you don't want to." She knew the tattoos had been a sore spot between Jim and Jay, and she also had the good sense to know I shouldn't meddle in a potential father-son conflict at this point.

"I don't understand. It's like you're defacing your body," Jim said to Jay.

"You just don't approve of me," Jay accused.

"Son, I approve of you—you know that. It's the tattoos I disapprove of."

"Same thing."

"No, it's not." Jim shook his head sadly and left it at that.

The one item we did not find on the shelves at Rite-Aid was a fan; they were completely sold out—no surprise in this heat wave. So we went to another drugstore and bought a fan, and by the time we got through shopping, it was noon.

"Why don't we go get some lunch?" Jim suggested.

"Great!" the girls said.

"We really need to get Kelli's car fixed," I said, "because I need to get going. I'm supposed to go visit my brother in Newport Beach."

"Well, you have to eat lunch anyway. We can do that first."

I capitulated with minimal persuasion. I was hungry and everyone wanted to go and, I'll admit, I was enjoying Jim's company.

As we climbed back in the Jeep, I again picked up the stack of books and papers Jim had given me. My curiosity was drawn to the Heritage USA book. I stole a quick glance at the pages inside; the spot I turned to featured a full-page photo of Jim and Tammy Faye. I wondered again how much he had loved her, and if it had been a great struggle to forgive her for what she had done.

The difficulty of forgiving an ex-spouse was something I had had to deal with in my own life.

By the spring of 1989, I was getting my life together. The ten-year nightmare of my ill-advised marriage was over. I'd been divorced from Jesse for four years, yet he continued to drift in and out of my life. I didn't do hard drugs anymore, although I still smoked marijuana every day—not to get high, because it no longer had that effect on me; pot was just something I did to make me feel normal. I had a good job managing a retail furniture showroom, and I was making good money for the first time in my life. I had long ago left the church of my childhood, but I loved to watch Christian television. And even through all the years of drug abuse and promiscuity, I had never stopped believing in God.

So I decided to go to church on Easter Sunday that year. *After all,* I told myself, *doesn't everybody go to church on Easter and Christmas?* I chose Phoenix First Assembly of God as my destination because I had visited the church before and seen their fabulous Christmas productions. I never do anything halfway, so when I made up my mind to go to church on Easter, I made plans to attend the sunrise service. I had not been to a sunrise service since I was a child; I was now thirty-one years old.

I got up very early that morning and smoked a joint while I got dressed for church. That's just part of your lifestyle when you smoke pot: you smoke from the time you get up until the time you go to bed. If you go out to dinner or a movie or a concert, you smoke a joint first. So I smoked a joint before I went to church.

Something very unusual happened that Easter Sunday in Phoenix, Arizona: it rained. It's a rare event when it rains, and it's usually a cause for celebration. But on this day it meant that the sunrise service could not be held at the amphitheater, which overlooked the hills across the street from the church. I'd been told the setting looked like Jerusalem, and I was eagerly anticipating the outdoor presentation, so I was disappointed to learn that it had to be moved inside. I was committed to attending a sunrise service, however, so I flowed into the sanctuary with the other worshipers that morning.

It's interesting to me how God uses certain people in your life, how some individuals seem to be woven into the fabric of your existence like threads running through a tapestry. God had prepared two threads for my spiritual loom that day: one of these godly men had entered my life years earlier, and the other was brand-new to me—but both of them would reappear at critical moments of my life. The old thread was an associate pastor of Phoenix First, Larry Kerychuk, who was preaching when I walked into the sanctuary that morning in 1989. Two years earlier he had prayed with me when I visited a class he taught. Of all the people who could have been conducting the sunrise service, it was Larry Kerychuk. I was immediately at ease because of his familiar face; I might not have stayed, otherwise.

After the sunrise service, I decided to stay for Sunday school. I was already inside the church, and I had my sixteen-year-old niece, Mark's stepdaughter, Krysten, with me. It just seemed the logical thing to do, even though I hadn't attended a Sunday school class since I was thirteen years old.

Krysten and I walked up to the information counter. Phoenix First is a huge church that seats more than six thousand people.

A facility of that size can be intimidating, so it helps to have a central place to go for information and directions.

"Could you help me find a Sunday school class for my niece?" I asked the lady behind the counter. "She's sixteen."

The woman gave instructions for Krysten to find the room where the high school students met, then she turned back to me. "Now, how about a class for you?" she said. "Are you married or single?"

"Single," I replied.

"We have a great singles Sunday school class," she said.

"Oh, I don't think that's for me." I wanted to get her away from that suggestion quickly. I figured all the lonely hearts and losers would be in the singles class; there wouldn't be any good-looking guys there, just some nerdy types. I may have been in church, but I still had the mind-set of the world. I wasn't against finding spiritual nourishment; I just didn't want to find it with those I had unfairly characterized as social misfits. "That's okay," I said. "I'll just go to the youth group with my niece."

"No, you'll really enjoy this class," she insisted. I don't know why, but I relented and decided to attend the singles class, so I let her give me directions.

I sent Krysten on her way, then I walked out of the main building and headed toward the room where the lonely hearts club met. As my high heels clicked across the pavement of the parking lot, I silently told God, "If you're real, and if you're listening to me, I want you to know something. If I walk into that Sunday school class and some pencil-necked, skinny preacher is standing there in high-water pants—I'm out of there. I don't need this."

God has a great sense of humor. I walked into the classroom, and standing behind the podium was a very tall, very handsome man who looked more like an athlete than a preacher. In fact, Associate Pastor Jack Wallace—the second thread God wove into my life that day—had been a star football player in college.

I wonder if he's married, I thought as I took a seat on the inside aisle about four rows from the front. (He was, and is, to a beautiful woman named Gael; the two of them remain my dear friends to this day.)

The spirit of God began to soften my hard heart as I listened to Pastor Jack's words. Of all the things for him to teach on that Sunday morning, he chose to speak on forgiving others who had wronged you.

Just hours earlier—around midnight—I had received a collect phone call from my ex-husband.

"Listen," he said, "I'm in jail down here in Mexico, and I need you to help me make bail."

"What happened?" I asked.

"I don't know, babe. I got drunk and married some girl on a whim. And when I woke up and found out what I'd done, I guess I went a little crazy."

"What did you do? What'd they arrest you for?" I figured he'd tossed the girl around, but she evidently wasn't his target.

"I beat up some federales."

I let Jesse just keep on talking. I shouldn't have been surprised, and yet I was. We'd been divorced four years and yet here he was calling me up and asking me to bail him out of jail because he'd gotten drunk and married a girl in Mexico and then beaten up some cops.

"So I really need a thousand dollars. That'll get me out of here," he said. "How soon can you get the money to me, Lori?"

Something inside me clicked into place, as if a swinging gate had suddenly been shut and latched.

"No," I said.

"Maybe Mark could help you get the money."

"No," I repeated firmly. I had the money in the bank; that wasn't the problem. He still felt free to use me—that was the problem, and I had finally had enough. For the first time since I was seventeen years old, I said no to Jesse. "I'm not going to do it this time."

He proceeded to cuss me out and tell me what a horrible person I was. His language was vile, and his ranting opened up all the old wounds. All the hurt and the pain and the hell I had been through with that man was instantly real to me again, and I was devastated. I should have hung up the phone immediately, but I listened to him for a minute until I finally found the courage to say good-bye.

Sitting in Jack Wallace's Sunday school class several hours later, my wounds were still fresh and raw. Yet here he was teaching on forgiving those who had wounded you. "You must make a conscious choice to forgive that person so you can go on with your life," he said. "If you don't forgive, *you're* the one who will continue to hurt." Then he began to speak about God's forgiveness for sin, and how Jesus Christ paid the penalty for our sins. We could receive divine forgiveness, he said, by receiving Jesus into our hearts as Savior.

Tears streamed down my face as I silently made that conscious choice to forgive my ex-husband. I knew it would be one of the hardest things I ever had to do, but I also knew it was absolutely necessary for my own survival.

I prayed for salvation right there in my chair, asking Jesus to come into my heart, to cleanse me from my sin, and to give me a new life.

"Now, if you have made a commitment to Christ here in

Sunday school," Jack said, "then you need to go forward as a public profession of your faith when Pastor Barnett gives the invitation in the main service."

So that's what I did. Just before noon I walked down the long aisle of the main sanctuary and crossed over to the center to reach the altar. There I knelt and repeated the Sinner's Prayer. It was the longest walk of my life—not in terms of physical distance but spiritual distance, for I had crossed over from darkness into the light.

I closed the book Jim had given me about his life and glanced over at him—looking across Kelli, who had managed to slip in between us again. Jim was smiling at me from his side of the backseat. *There's at least one thing we have in common*, I thought. *We both know what it is to forgive an ex-spouse who wounded us deeply.*

As Jay started the Jeep and we left for the restaurant, I placed my new library on the floorboard of the car. Jim and I laugh a lot now about how nerdy he must have appeared—talking my arm off about meteorites the first time we were together, and then handing me a huge stack of books and papers the next time I saw him. But his policy in starting a relationship with me, as I was soon to discover, was one of full disclosure.

10

WE LOVE LUCY

Jim decided we should all go to the CityWalk, "the coolest street in America," for lunch. This popular tourist attraction—with dozens of restaurants, scores of shops, and an eighteen-screen multiplex cinema—sits on top of the hill at Universal City, California, just outside the gates of Universal Studios. Like all famous L.A. landmarks, the CityWalk was very crowded on a Saturday in the middle of summer, so we window-shopped and talked as we waited for a table. Then we laughed and enjoyed ourselves over a meal, as we had the evening before.

After lunch, Jim wanted to take us all to Universal Studios—"since we're already here," he said. "My treat. We'll have fun."

I wasn't sure if it had been a spontaneous idea or a premeditated plan on Jim's part, but everyone was having such a good time that I decided I could put my trip to Newport Beach on hold for another day. After all, I would be in the Los Angeles area for a few more days.

The five of us had a ball at Universal Studios, and we quickly gravitated toward an exhibit honoring Lucille Ball, the Queen of Comedy. As we waited outside the museum, a woman dressed as Lucy entertained the crowd. Her red hair pulled back and tied with a scarf, she was wearing a polka-dot dress and playing the saxophone. She played and danced, weaving her way through the people gathered around, and suddenly she pulled Jim out of the crowd to dance with her. Everyone laughed and clapped for Jim, who managed to look suitably embarrassed and yet boyishly excited at the same time.

"I can't believe I danced with Lucy!" he said breathlessly when the number was over.

"And you were wonderful," I said. "It's so strange that of all people, she picked you. Do you suppose she knew who you were?"

"I don't think so, but you never know. It was fun, though."

"I adore the old *I Love Lucy* show," I told him. "It's probably my favorite TV show of all time."

"My absolute favorite too," Jim said. "Lucy was always bigger than life. When I was a kid, back in the 1950s, we didn't have a television set. Every Monday night I went to the neighbors' house and had popcorn and Realtime lemonade while we watched Lucy."

Jim and I discovered that we both collected Lucy memorabilia, and that we much preferred the old *I Love Lucy* and *Andy Griffith* reruns to anything airing on television today.

"The programs today are so raunchy," Jim said, "but those old shows are simple and funny."

Inside Universal Studios' *Lucy: A Tribute,* we both got misty-eyed as we watched rare home movies of Lucy and Desi, looked at photographs and outtakes from the TV series, and saw her Emmy awards and hundreds of items from her personal life and her career.

"It's sad how their lives ended," I said. "Lucy brought joy to so many people, and yet she had so much unhappiness."

After the Lucy exhibit, we took the Backlot Tour, where we saw some of the most recognizable movie sets in Hollywood films: *King Kong, Psycho, Earthquake,* and *Jurassic Park.*

And this time, Jim beat Kelli in the race to sit beside me. He jumped onto the tram a fraction of a second before she did, and as I scooted to the end of the bench seat, he moved in next to me. In fact, he sat so close that his leg brushed against mine, and soon he had draped his arm along the back of the seat behind me.

I'm not sure about this, I thought. I had only known him a little over twenty-four hours. I liked Jim, but I didn't really have any romantic feelings for him at this point. It was a little strange yet also fun.

When we got off the tram and headed for the next attraction, Kelli got Jim off to one side and talked to him privately. *Perhaps they're debating who'll get to sit by me next,* I thought in amusement. *No, they're probably talking about something to do with Revolution. Or just talking in general. She's known him a lot longer than I have.*

We wore ourselves out traipsing through the amusement park under the sweltering sun. It seemed as if Jim had started to flirt with me, and then he backed off. I didn't know what to think, but a lot of emotions were starting to rise up in me. Before long, it was dinnertime and we were back at the CityWalk, choosing a different restaurant this time.

I cornered Jay and asked him a question. "I want to get your dad a thank-you gift for everything he's done today. What kind of souvenir would he like?"

Jay thought for a second and then shrugged. "I don't have any idea."

I strolled through one of the studio shops, looking for something that might catch my eye. It was obvious that Jim was a giver and truly enjoyed doing things for people. He'd taken us to lunch, paid our way into Universal Studios, and was now about to buy dinner. I wanted to give something back to him, although I didn't have much to spend. I finally paid seven dollars for a picture of Lucy as the Vitameatavegamin girl. We had laughed together at the clip we'd seen of that episode, where Lucy gets tipsy doing live TV commercials for a health tonic. The photo would be a memento of our day and a reminder of one of the things we had in common.

After dinner I was exhausted; I'd had only a few hours of sleep the night before and the heat had tired me out further. But Jim wasn't ready to let the day end. "Let's go see a movie," he said. "Look at all the choices we have right here. And we can just make a ten o'clock showing."

What is up with this guy? I thought. *We're all much younger than he is, but he's still going strong.* He had so much energy it was unbelievable.

So the five of us went to see a brand-new film, *The Mask of Zorro.* We slipped in right before the movie started, and it was so crowded that we had to sit on the front row with our necks craned at an uncomfortable angle. Jim managed to outmaneuver Kelli again, so he was on one end, I sat next to him, then Kelli, and then Amanda and Jay.

Even though I was sitting next to Jim, I didn't talk much to him during the movie. I was very tired, and Kelli and I got to giggling like schoolgirls because we thought Antonio Banderas was so handsome on the big screen.

By the time we got back to the Dream Center, it was almost 1:00 A.M. We all thanked Jim profusely, and I gave him the Lucy picture, which he loved. Then we said good night. I had been with Jim Bakker for the last fifteen hours, and while I couldn't exactly call it a date, I did think it had been a very special time. Kelli and Amanda and I stayed up very late talking. I discovered that Amanda had wisdom beyond her years and that she was very knowledgeable about the whole Bakker family because she had been around them quite a bit. I quizzed her about Jim, and I talked openly about my feelings—or lack of them.

"I'm numb inside," I told her. "I have no feelings for this man one way or another. I don't dislike him, but I don't like him. Romantically, I mean." I settled down on my bed on the floor as she turned out the lights. "If he's interested in me, he needs to come after me a little bit more. It's like he started to do that, then he backed away."

"Welllllll . . ." Kelli's voice floated above me in the darkness. "I talked to him about that," she said. I suddenly remembered her private conversation with Jim earlier that day.

"What did you say to him?"

"I said that maybe he should back off a little and not move too fast, because you've been wounded by a lot of men—"

"Kelli!"

"Well, you have, Lori."

"But I'm not some fragile little wallflower."

"I didn't mean that," Kelli said. "I just don't want to see you get hurt, that's all."

So that's why she kept trying to jump between Jim and me, I thought. *Yesterday she was playing matchmaker, and today she was playing protector.* As with Jen Nicks the previous night, a role reversal was taking place with Kelli.

I drifted off to sleep wondering what Jim Bakker thought of me and trying to decide how I felt about that. *I'm paying attention, Lord,* I prayed silently. *Are you trying to tell me something?*

11

CONFIRMATION

Sunday, July 19, 1998

You must see Jim Bakker today.

Is that God speaking to me, or is it just my own thoughts? I wondered. I had shut myself in the tiny bathroom of the girls' room at the Dream Center so I could spend some quiet time with God before starting my day. As I prayed, I continued to feel the same urgency: *You must see Jim Bakker today.*

What am I supposed to say? I asked silently. No answer. Just the knowledge that it was important to see Jim, and a sense that I could trust God to provide the words when I did.

I got dressed with excitement that morning because I had the opportunity to do something I love to do: minister to someone from the inner city. Some of the ladies at the Dream Center had just gotten a young woman off the streets, and they asked me to take her under my wing that Sunday morning. I gave her some clothes and helped her put on makeup and fix her hair, and then I took her to church with me.

When we walked into the gymnasium for the worship service, I immediately began to look around for Jim. We had arrived a few minutes early, so I used the extra time for a thorough search; but I didn't see him anywhere. When I realized he wasn't there, my heart sank. *Why wouldn't he be at church?* I wondered. *That has to be unusual. Is he sick? Off preaching somewhere?* I felt so let down. And then I realized that my disappointment at not finding Jim meant I *did* have feelings for him. I was beginning to care about this man very much.

The worship service at the Dream Center was wonderful, as expected, and the girl I had brought to church went to the altar to pray when the invitation was given. That thrilled me. We talked with people for a few minutes after the service, and then I prepared to find us something to eat—hopefully something better than cafeteria food.

As soon as we walked out of the gymnasium, Jim came walking across the parking lot. My heart skipped a beat. *You must see Jim Bakker today.* The thought came rushing into my mind again. I hadn't been able to find Jim on my own, now suddenly here he was. He was wearing a black ribbed T-shirt and jacket, and I thought he looked so sharp—casual yet dressed up in his solid black coat-but-no-tie outfit.

Jim's face lit up as he spotted me and said hello. "Well, I see everybody is dressed in black today," he said.

I surveyed the usual group of staff members and friends surrounding Jim—Armando, Connie, Aaron Jayne, Kendon Alexander, and Jennifer McDivitt. None of them had on black; Jim and I were the only two wearing black. I suppose in his eyes we were the only two who mattered, and I confess that I did think we looked very good together in our monochromatic clothing.

"I want to thank you again for a wonderful night Friday and

then all day yesterday—the shopping trip, Universal Studios, everything," I said. Earlier that morning I had thought I didn't have anything to say to Jim, but I began to find plenty of words. "You didn't have to do all that, but it was so sweet of you, and we all had such a terrific time."

"It was my pleasure," he said, still grinning broadly. "I had a great time, and I'm glad you enjoyed it."

"I really had a lot of fun." We chatted about absolutely nothing for a minute, and I knew Jim wanted to ask me out, but he was being very bashful about it. He looked like a shy, awkward teenager, his hands stuffed deep in his pants pockets as he glanced down and shifted his weight from one foot to the other. The others had moved back slightly to give us a little space, yet they were still standing nearby talking. I wondered if Jim would have the courage to say something in front of them.

"Anyway," I continued, "I'm going to be taking off for my brother's in Newport Beach soon, so I wanted to say thank you again and tell you good-bye." The word *good-bye* seemed to galvanize his resolve.

"I was wondering . . . ," he began hesitantly. *Come on, you can do it,* I mentally urged him. ". . . wondering if there was a possibility . . ." *Yes, that's it; I'm listening.* ". . . since you're going to be in the area this week . . ." I smiled reassuringly, but he ducked his head again and missed my signal. Nevertheless, he took a deep breath and finished his sentence. ". . . if maybe you and I could go out to dinner alone—without the kids." *Whew! He finally got it out.*

"I'd like that," I said.

"Really?" Jim's head shot up. "You would?"

"Yes, I really would."

"That's great." Relief relaxed the strain on his face. "What are you doing the rest of the day?"

"I'm taking my guest out to eat, and then Kelli's dad is coming over from Tustin to help us get her car fixed. Then they're going to drive me over to Newport Beach."

"Oh." His face fell. "I was going to ask you to go with us to San Diego. I'm speaking at Jerry Bernard's church there tonight."

"So that's why you weren't in church this morning."

"Yes, I was studying and preparing for the service tonight. It will be a long drive and we'll be late getting back, I imagine."

"Here, let me give you my brother's number." I wrote Mark's phone number on a scrap of paper I fished out of my purse. "Why don't you call me this week, and we can make plans to get together for dinner."

"That would be great, Lori." He studied the slip of paper with the phone number on it as if he couldn't quite believe he possessed so great a treasure. "I'll call you."

We were stuck at the Dream Center again. Kelli's dad had been unable to get her car running when he arrived after lunch; the vehicle would definitely have to go to a repair shop on Monday. To get out of the terrible heat, we spent the rest of that Sunday afternoon in Jim's office, where Kelli worked. The room that Jim's New Covenant ministry used as an office at the Dream Center had air-conditioning, and it was tolerably cool there.

About six that evening I placed a call to my mother. "I want to tell you what's been going on this weekend," I told her after we said hello. "It's so strange, really, but I've met somebody."

"Somebody . . . as in somebody special?" she asked.

"I think so. And you won't believe who it is—Jim Bakker." I

began to tell her the whole story of how we met and the time we had spent together and how he had asked me to have dinner with him—a real date, this time. "So, what do you think?" I asked her. "Doesn't that just blow your mind—me and Jim Bakker?"

"Actually, I'm not surprised." She paused a moment. "Lori, I need to tell you something."

"Okay." I didn't know what to think. She sounded kind of serious, but Mom has never been the type to lecture me or try to interfere in my life. She has been an incredible influence on me, always by example and through lots of positive encouragement and support.

"I met Jim Bakker before you did . . . and I saw you two together."

"You what?" I couldn't believe it. "What do you mean you saw us together? And why didn't you ever tell me?"

"It was only a month or so ago," she said. Earlier that year Mom had moved from Phoenix to the San Francisco area to work for Mario Murillo Ministries. Recently she had traveled to L.A. when Mario was invited to be a guest speaker at the Dream Center, she told me. "I ran into Kelli just before the Thursday night service, and she sat with me. Afterward we saw Jim and Jay out in the parking lot—"

"Just like we did!"

"Yes. And then we all went out to eat together."

"Yeah, that does seem to be the chief entertainment here at the Dream Center." We laughed at the priority we Christians seem to put on "breaking bread" together at every opportunity.

"Tommy Barnett asked Jim to go with us," she said, "because Mario had wanted to spend some time with Jim while he was in L.A. So there was a big group—ten of us, I think. Matthew

Barnett came, too, and Mario's wife, Rose, and their two boys, as well as me and Kelli and Jay. We had to go in separate cars, and Jim and I happened to be in the first group that left. It took a while for Pastor Barnett and Mario to get away from the crowd, so Jim and I had time to visit for a while before they arrived.

"Anyway, we sat at this huge corner booth with a table dragged up beside it, and we started talking. I had never met Jim before—"

"Isn't he cute, Mom?" I giggled, and then I remembered the serious tone she had started the conversation with. "Did you like him? I really want to know what you think of him."

She agreed that Jim was an attractive man and that she liked him. "He was friendly and not at all arrogant—actually, very shy in person. But he really opened up when I asked him what he was doing these days and what kind of vision for ministry he had. It was quite a conversation." Mom hesitated briefly, as if remembering the details and deciding how much to tell me. "Lori, as I listened to Jim talk that night, I couldn't help thinking I was listening to you. It's as if he had an identical heart for ministry. He talked about the inner city, about lifting up those who had fallen, about restoring the dreams of broken, hurting people. He spoke with such passion and such compassion—and it was word for word what I've heard you say. And that's when I saw the two of you together in my mind. I had a powerful premonition, if that's what you want to call it, that God might bring you and Jim together someday."

"Wow." I was dumbfounded. My mother had already met Jim Bakker and she had the impression that God meant for us to be together.

"It wasn't the first time I'd had that thought either," she added.

"Okay, now you've really got my attention. How long have you been thinking like this?"

"Do you remember the Pastor's School a few years ago when Jay gave his testimony and Jim came to see him?"

"Yes," I said, "that was the only time I'd ever seen Jim in person until this week."

"Well, I had the same thought that night."

"You're kidding me."

"No, it was just a fleeting thought—a flash. Jim walked right in front of us and I had a mental picture of the two of you side by side. But it wasn't that specifically. It was more that I could see you marrying that type of man, and I had an insight into the type of ministry you could have together. I forgot all about it until I met Jim in Los Angeles recently. Then it came back to me."

"Why didn't you ever tell me this?"

"Because I know you too well." She laughed. "You would have said 'no way' and dismissed it without ever considering it." Turning serious again, she said, "Besides, I knew that if it truly was God's will I was glimpsing, *he* would have to put the two of you together—not me."

"Do you think that's what God is doing now?"

"It could be, Lori. You have to consider that. I don't think this is all coincidence."

Later that night as I lay in bed, Mom's words replayed in my mind. Kelli and I had gone to sleep early, but I woke up about one in the morning. I threw the sheet off and let the fan blow over me. Jim's oscillating gift had helped, but it couldn't come close to cooling the room in this heat. I noticed that Amanda wasn't home yet, so that meant Jim and the rest of the team had not returned. I tend to be a worrier, so I began to wonder if something had happened.

Thinking of Jim brought my phone call to Mom back to mind. She had confirmed the direction God had been leading me since Friday night. First, Jen Nicks had opened my eyes and suggested God was doing something incredible in my life, that my being with Jim was not a coincidence. I had prayed about that in the intervening two days, and now my mother had confirmed it. What Mom had said weighed heavily on me because she is not the type to see visions or dream dreams and attach spiritual significance to them. She's a strong Christian and believes very much in supernatural guidance. But she's always been a businesswoman—very logical and practical and realistic. So for her to have such a strong inner impression about Jim and me was an important signpost.

Kelli heard me stirring and woke up. "Amanda's not home yet," I told her, "and it's after one. Do you think we should be worried?"

"I'm sure she's fine. Jim said it would probably be a late night."

"But church would have been over hours ago, and they've had plenty of time to make it back from San Diego by now."

We talked for a while as the fan droned in the background. Amanda finally made it home about two o'clock. She gasped as she flipped the lights on. "You scared me," she said. "I didn't expect you to be here—I thought you two were going to Newport Beach."

"Yeah, well, we did too," Kelli said. "But we couldn't get my car fixed, so we were stuck here."

"What happened?" I asked Amanda. "I was getting worried."

Amanda pulled her long, straight honey-colored hair off her neck as the fan blew a warm breeze in her direction. She chuckled and motioned toward me. "You happened," she said. "Jim was so fired up after seeing you that he preached for three hours."

"He preached *how* long?" My jaw dropped.

"He must have been really wound up," Kelli said.

"Three hours," Amanda reiterated. "And I've never seen him so wound up."

I lay back down as the girls giggled and joked about my effect on Jim's preaching. It occurred to me that I had never even heard Jim preach, yet I now thought God was putting us together as a couple, perhaps as a ministry team. Last night I had lain in this same bed and said that I was numb, that I had no feelings for Jim one way or the other. Tonight I *knew* I had feelings for him. I had started my day by believing God was telling me, "You must see Jim Bakker." I ended it by thinking that I would probably be seeing a lot of Jim Bakker in the days ahead, and that it might very well lead to a lasting relationship.

So much was happening so fast.

12

BROTHERLY LOVE

Monday, July 20, 1998

The ocean breeze made the heat bearable, and I reveled in lying lazily by the water and soaking up the peace and quiet as well as the sun. I had finally made it to Newport Beach, three days later than I'd intended. What a hectic but exciting three days they had been. I desperately needed the time and space to sort through everything that had happened and to let my body catch up on some much-needed rest, so I relished being by myself for the day.

Mark was still out of town and wouldn't arrive until late afternoon. He had promised to take me out to dinner, and I was looking forward to spending time with my brother. We always had a lot of catching up to do, but especially this time. I wondered what he would think of my dating Jim Bakker. I still wondered what *I* thought about dating Jim Bakker. It was all so new to me, and yet it felt so right.

I picked up the picture book of Jim's life and ministry at PTL.

I was glad he had given me the two books to read, because I suddenly wanted to know everything I could about this man God seemed to be bringing into my life. I leafed through the pages of this photographic chronicle, and I began to see the man Jim Bakker had been—a very different person from the man I was getting to know now, I thought. I smiled at the funny hair-dos and outdated clothes from the early days of his ministry, marveled at the famous people who had posed for photo ops with the head of PTL, oohed and aahed over the pictures of his two precious babies and then noted how quickly they had grown up—all in front of the cameras. And on page after page I saw the woman whose name was indelibly linked with his in the public's memory: Tammy Faye.

The only thing I knew about Jim's ex-wife was what all of America had seen on television: a heavily made-up woman with mascara running down her face because she seemed to always be crying. *Was she for real?* I wondered. She certainly seemed at home in front of the camera. I knew she was part of his past, and I would have to deal with that if I was going to date Jim. But I did not enjoy seeing his ex-wife so vividly displayed, especially all the pictures of the two of them together.

Weeks later I would learn that Jim had removed the oversized book's dust jacket prior to giving it to me because it featured a full-length photo of the two of them. He was sensitive to the fact that such photos might bother me, yet he felt it was extremely important for me to know everything about his former life. He needed a woman who could accept his past and move beyond it, someone who would not run when the inevitable ghosts appeared, but who could face the truth up front. He had gambled that I was that kind of woman when he gave me these chronicles of his personal history.

I put the picture book aside and started reading Jim's book *I Was Wrong,* an autobiographical account written after he had served almost five years in prison on charges of fraud stemming from a building program at Heritage USA. Here I began to get a glimpse of Jim's life behind the public facade and the incredible suffering he had endured in the years subsequent to PTL's demise and the failure of his marriage. "I have been branded for life by the events you will read about in this book," he wrote. "Strangely, perhaps, I would not have it any other way."[1]

As I read the first few chapters, I developed a deep admiration for Jim's honesty and integrity. He wrote forthrightly about the mistakes he had made in his ministry. With openness and yet dignity, he told of the long-standing problems in his marriage. Without wallowing in the details or glorifying his sin, he reported his brief sexual encounter with Jessica Hahn one fateful afternoon in a Florida hotel. "I knew I was wrong the moment I entered the hotel room," he wrote. "I should have run out of that place. Nobody forced me into the room or to stay once I was there. Yet I rationalized the situation: I was feeling rejected by my wife; I knew that Tammy Faye was seeing another man; I was wondering whether I was much of a man at all. Suddenly, I felt as though I were an adolescent boy who had to prove he was a man by having sex."[2] Afterward, he said, he was horrified that he had not stopped to consider the consequences of such an absurd attempt to make his wife jealous. Jim quickly confessed his sin to a trusted Christian counselor and then apologized to Jessica Hahn. After repenting and seeking forgiveness, he thought the situation was over and done with. But he was wrong, as the title of his book declared.

My heart hurt for Jim as I read his words. I had committed the same sin—and not just once; I had made a lifestyle of adultery for a period of time. But my sin had remained hidden from all but a handful of people, while his had been emblazoned on the front pages of newspapers and magazines from literally around the world. My bad choices had caused me untold heartache and misery; his bad choices—his original sin and his approval of his closest advisers' ill-conceived attempt to buy a woman's silence long after the fact—ultimately led to the downfall of his ministry and the final unraveling of his marriage. And because he was a well-known figure, the eventual publicity of his sin had wounded millions of people and brought shame to the body of Christ.

I removed my sunglasses and wiped my eyes. Reading Jim's story had made me cry, and I had to put the book aside for a while. I lay back and dozed off, wondering how he had lived with the burden of that shame. Add the stigma of prison and it's no wonder he had seemed so broken and fragile that one time I had seen him in Phoenix.

A few hours later I sat across the dinner table from my brother. Mark had chosen an elegant restaurant for our evening out. The servers wore white shirts with black ties and black pants, and the tables were attired in starched white linen cloths with sparkling crystal and gleaming silver. I was relaxed and refreshed and so excited to see my "big brother." Actually, Mark is three years younger than I am, but in many ways he has played the role of an older brother in my life. And he's physically a big man—tall and handsome, with dark hair and a set of dimples my girlfriends had all drooled over when we were younger.

Mark had been a protector and provider for me, and we had been through so much together, both good times and bad times. He was the only one in my family who had known exactly how wild a roller-coaster ride my life had been. As my buddy during our rebellious teenage years—my friends and I had turned him onto drugs when he was only twelve—he had stuck with me through the sex, drugs, and rock 'n' roll of the Jesse years. Then when I finally let God turn my life around and went into full-time Christian work, Mark applauded my commitment and even supported my ministry financially. And in the last few years Mark had turned his life around too. He had stopped using drugs, become successful in business, and had rededicated his life to Christ.

As we studied the menu, I could hardly wait to tell him about the direction my life had just taken and to get his brotherly advice about the new man in my life. I decided to wait until after we ordered to spring the news on him. Suddenly I remembered a conversation we'd had ten years earlier, a conversation about the man in my life then: my ex-husband, Jesse.

I was living in Flagstaff at the time, closing out one of the waterbed stores for the company my mother had a financial interest in. I spent the summer and fall of 1988 there, and Mark refers to those months as "the beginning of the end" for me—for my self-destructive lifestyle, that is. I had plenty of time to myself in Flagstaff—time to reflect on my life. Physically removed from the insanity of my partying pals, I knew I needed to get my act together. So it was a very introspective period for me, one that was accompanied by a great emotional and spiritual struggle.

It was also one of the last times I saw my ex-husband. I was living in a hotel until I could find a place to rent. Jesse called one day and said he wanted to see me. We had been divorced for three years by then, but it was not unusual for me to hear from him out of the blue like that. We continued to have our "interludes," as I referred to them. I could never call Jesse, even if I wanted to, because he would never tell me where he lived. "I'm no good for you, babe, and you need to go on with your life," he would always say. "I love you enough to stay away from you."

Yet he never stayed away for too long, and he always managed to find me through my family—usually Mark. So when Jesse found me this time, I said, "Sure. Come on up." That's the kind of bond Jesse and I had for so many years: we couldn't live together, but we couldn't stay apart for too long either.

As always, I had mixed emotions about another rendezvous with him. I was excited and hopeful and discouraged and sad, all at the same time. But I could never say no to him. He was like a drug I couldn't stay away from. And just like all the other drugs I ever took, the "Jesse high" never lasted. There would be a crash afterward, and I would come down hard. I knew that, could see it coming, and yet was powerless to resist it. I craved emotional and physical intimacy with this man, even after everything I'd been through with him.

Jesse spent the weekend with me. We slept together, smoked pot, and drank—the usual stuff. Then he left as suddenly as he had arrived, telling me he had to get back to his girlfriend. I felt so empty, so very sad and lonely, when Jesse left.

Trying to fill the void, I turned to my familiar rituals. I lit a joint and poured myself a glass of wine. And I turned on the TV.

Billy Graham was preaching a crusade. That night he talked about being single and how sexual relationships outside of marriage are wrong. *Is there an exception for having sex with your ex-husband?* I wondered wryly. No, I knew there wasn't. Maybe that's why I felt so empty. I was beginning to see that only God could fill this void.

Right there, as I sat at the little table in my hotel room, I felt God's presence. For almost three hours I sensed him speaking to my mind, and I wrote a lot of it down. God said it was time to get my life straightened out, and that he had a plan for my life that was more wonderful than anything I could imagine. Not only would I get my life together, he said, but through me my family members and my friends would also get their lives together. "Don't preach to them; just live it by example, and they will come around one by one."

A few years earlier I had tried to act like a Christian. When I was married to Jesse I became extreme for a time, trying to fix what was wrong in my life through my own efforts. I would watch only Christian television and listen to only Christian radio. I tried to go to church. I even threw out all of our drug paraphernalia and got rid of Jesse's rock 'n' roll collection. He was furious. "You're crazy," he yelled at me. "You've completely lost it." Then he stormed out. The bongs could be replaced, but I had tossed away his classic albums: Cream, the Allman Brothers, Eric Clapton, old Beatles records. You might say I had gone off the deep end in my attempt to be religious. But it didn't last, because it was all done in my strength, not God's.

After watching the Billy Graham crusade and hearing this awesome personal message from God, I called my brother Mark.

"Guess what I'm doing?"

"What?" he asked.

"Smoking my last joint. I'm giving it up. Quitting."

For a second there was silence on the other end of the line. "Really? Wow!"

"I have to get back to God, Mark. I really need to start doing the right thing."

"That's great. I support what you're doing—it *is* the right thing," he said slowly. "I wish I could say that about myself now."

Mark and I had always wanted to come back to God; we just didn't know how to do it. It sounds kind of crazy, but no matter how far we wandered from the faith of our childhood, we always talked about God and even witnessed about Jesus. We would sit around smoking dope with our friends and say things like, "I'm serious, dude. Jesus is the Savior." For a few minutes we would engage the group in a sublime spiritual discussion, until one of us would realize that a smoker was sitting there, engrossed in the conversation, with a lit cigarette dangling from the corner of his mouth. Then we'd complain, "Hey, quit bogarting that joint, man." (You bogart a joint when you take more than one hit before passing it around—a breach of etiquette in the drug culture.) How quickly we could move from the sublime to the ridiculous.

That night on the phone I also told Mark about Jesse's visit and how sad it had left me. We had a long conversation about why I still loved Jesse and why I couldn't get over him. Mark had been very close to Jesse, and had always looked to him as an older brother. As much as anyone could, he understood my conflicted emotions about my ex-husband. One minute I would tell Mark, "It's such a relief to be out from under that situation. How did I ever live that way?" And the next minute I would be crying and saying, "But I still love him, and I miss him so much."

Now, ten years later, I was about to tell Mark of the new man in my life, one whose name he would surely recognize, and I wondered what he would say.

After the waiter took our order, I couldn't stand it any longer. "Mark, I have something to tell you," I said. "I've met somebody, and I think he's the one I'm going to spend the rest of my life with."

A slow smile creased his dimples. "Who is he?"

"Well, this is the interesting part. I think you might have heard of him."

"Oh, really?"

"Yes. It's Jim Bakker."

"You mean . . . *the* Jim Bakker?" Mark's question, uttered in his deep, resonant voice, was one I would hear over and over again in the ensuing weeks.

"That's the one," I said. I began describing Jim and how I'd met him at the Dream Center. Mark is a thinker, so he just took it all in, listening attentively without saying much.

Mark knew who Jim was, of course, from the media. Like me, he had known virtually nothing about the man though.

"I knew a little about Jim from my association with Jay," I said. "Now I'm learning a lot more." I told Mark about the books Jim had given me. "Isn't it weird? I got saved and involved in the church world in 1989, and that's the year Jim went to prison."

"All I remember," Mark said, "is what I saw on TV."

"I remember the way Tommy Barnett handled it in church—both the scandal swirling around Jim and the thing with Jimmy Swaggart. Pastor always said, 'We should pray for these men.'"

Mark's cell phone rang, interrupting our conversation. Cupping his hand over the mouthpiece, he whispered. "It's Dad. Do you want to talk to him?"

Soon I was repeating my story of meeting Jim to my father.

"Jim Bakker . . . *the* Jim Bakker?" Dad asked. *Here we go,* I thought. He was taken aback by the news, and yet he sounded happy for me. Or perhaps he was just excited because Jim was still something of a celebrity. My father was the kind of man who valued people primarily for what they could do for you, not who they really were.

"It's not that big a deal," I told Dad. "I'm just going out on a date with him this week. That's all."

Mark teased me when I finished talking to Dad. "Maybe this will put you at the top of the List," he said.

He was referring to an imaginary list we had often joked that my father kept. Whichever of his three children was in his good graces at the moment was at the top of the List. We all rotated in and out of the number one position, depending on Dad's current opinion of us. And one of us was always *off* the List, period—alienated from Dad and not even a part of his life for that time. He was a very controlling person, and he played us against each other.

Mark was probably at the top of the List for the longest single stretch. When he first became successful in business, it really got Dad's attention. He had verbally and sometimes physically abused Mark as a child, always cursing him and telling him that he was stupid and would never amount to anything, and haranguing Mom for raising a wimp. Mark had dropped out of the eighth grade and had nearly wasted his life—as I had, for many years—but he eventually prospered in the business world. That finally won Dad's approval and made him proud of his son.

During Mark's reign at the top of the List, I was relegated to being simply Little Girl. Especially in the early days of my ministry, Dad would belittle me for my "excessive" faith and tell me I needed to quit leeching off my mother and go out and get a real job. There were long stretches of time where I was the alienated one.

Scott's nickname was Brat Baby or Prince Scott. I think my father was somewhat intimidated by his youngest son's scholastic achievements as well as his athletic ability. The "prince" name implied that Scott thought he was better than the rest of us because he went to an Ivy League school, which wasn't true at all. Scott was a very disciplined, hard worker, and even though he was dyslexic—like my dad—Scott graduated from Brown University. It was a very proud moment for our family, and that put Scott at the top of the List for a while. He became the revered one. But Scott got bumped from the number one position when Dad decided a college education had turned Scott away from the things of God. You just couldn't count on staying at the top of the List.

"I'm just kidding about Dad," Mark said. "I'm very happy for you, and I hope it works out. No one deserves 'happily ever after' more than you, Lori."

I appreciated the fact that, as always, Mark didn't try to talk me out of it, even if he did have any reservations about my involvement with Jim. He just listened and cared and supported me.

So did Scott when I later told him. Both of my brothers are very protective of me and very perceptive about me. Today they each love and respect Jim very much. But they quickly got over the original "*the* Jim Bakker?" response. To my brothers, Jim is not some Christian celebrity or even a respected man of the cloth; he's simply the guy who married their sister, and they don't hesitate to let Jim know he'd better treat me right. Of course, they also feel free to tell me when they think *I* step out of line. That's the great joy and blessing of having two wonderful brothers.

As Mark and I left the restaurant that night, I was so thankful we'd had the chance to talk. Mom had been the one who confirmed the direction God was leading me, but Mark was the first one to whom I had verbalized the thought that I had just met the man I was about to marry.

Jim and I hadn't even been on a real date yet, but I knew in my spirit that he was God's choice for me.

13

FALLING IN LOVE

Tuesday, July 21, 1998

Mark had to leave immediately on another business trip, so I had his condo to myself again the next day. I spent a quiet morning praying and reading more of *I Was Wrong*.

With every page I read, I got angrier. I cringed as I looked at some of the photos in the book, especially the still photo of the humiliating television footage broadcast around the world—the one clear image I retained in my mind from the news of those events. The photo showed Jim weeping profusely, his suit jacket draped over his handcuffed wrists, with two federal marshals literally holding him by each arm because he could barely stand. The caption read, "I debated long and hard before including this picture in my book. This is one of the lowest moments of my life—a time during my trial when I suffered a nervous breakdown and was put into what I call an 'insane asylum' inside the prison at Butner,

NC."[1] It was a gut-wrenching piece of photojournalism, and I admired Jim's courage in publishing it.

A beautiful photo of Tammy Sue holding her firstborn son, Jim's namesake, was followed by these words: "This picture is the only possession I was able to somehow take with me into almost every prison to which I was assigned. There were times when simply looking at this picture of my grandbaby gave me the will to hold on just a little longer."[2] The next page showed the federal marshals leading Jim away from the courthouse in chains, his wrists and ankles shackled.

Jim's original sentence of forty-five years had seemed excessive even to many people who believed he was guilty. Jim not only steadfastly maintained his innocence, a federal jury in the subsequent civil trial handed down a decision—two years after his release from prison—that PTL had *not* fraudulently sold securities by offering lifetime partnerships at Heritage USA, as the criminal case alleged. Because the judge in the criminal case had shown a prejudice against Christians, Jim's sentence was eventually reduced to eighteen years. Yet he was denied early release, in spite of his stellar behavior inside the prison system and the recommendation of all his counselors and many prominent civic and religious leaders.

My anger at the *in*justice against Jim of the criminal justice system, however, was far overshadowed by a deep grief at the vicious behavior of some Christians toward Jim and his family and his ministry. No wonder Jay had wept when he received a standing ovation at the Pastor's School several years earlier. I recalled his words from that night, how he said he had been hurt by what people—Christian people—had done to his family. *What an understatement,* I thought as I read Jim's account of how several prominent church leaders, fellow ministers of the gospel, had conspired to use their knowledge of his illicit liaison with Jessica Hahn to expose him publicly—not for the purpose of bringing correction and restoration to a fallen minister, but in order to mount a hostile takeover of his television network. Their skillful, behind-the-scenes manipulation of Jim's vulnerability led to the loss of the ministry he had worked so hard—too hard, admittedly—to build. And it very nearly destroyed his family in the process. His children suffered deeply from the trauma, and his marriage, already foundering, did not survive the long separation of prison.

Less than a hundred pages into the book, I had to put it down. The pain Jim went through had become personal to me, and it was more than I could take. I was becoming emotionally involved with this man, and I had a difficult time facing the enormity of the truth behind the fall of PTL and the scandal that had brought Jim and his ministry down.

I quit reading and started praying urgently. "Dear God, please shut the door if this relationship with Jim is not supposed to happen, because he does not need to be hurt anymore. The last thing I would want to do in this world is to hurt this dear man, who has already been through so much. And I don't want to be hurt again either. We shouldn't go *anywhere* from this moment on, if this is not from you, Lord. I'm starting to feel very attached to Jim, and the two of us don't need to be falling in love if we're only going to wind up wounded. Please, God, stop us in our tracks if this is not your will for us."

That afternoon I got a call from Kelli. "We were wondering if we could drive over to Newport Beach and take you out to dinner," she said.

"Who's 'we'?" I asked.

"Jay and Amanda and Jim and I."

"Sure, I'd love to go." *What's going on?* I wondered as I hung up the phone. I had thought Jim would be calling me for a date—"dinner alone, without the kids," he had said on Sunday. Perhaps he'd changed his mind about wanting to see me. But if that were so, why would he even want to tag along with the rest of the group? Was God about to close the door on our relationship? I thought about it but didn't fret over it as I got dressed to go out. I still felt strongly that Jim and I were supposed to be together, but I trusted God to change our direction suddenly if we had indeed headed down the wrong path.

The four of them were in a great mood when they arrived in Newport Beach. They were also starved, so we quickly selected Joe's Crab Shack for our meal. It was noisy and crowded, and we nearly drooled while we waited for one of the newspaper-lined tables and watched the bib-draped diners use mallets to tackle heaping plates of steaming stone crabs. When the hostess called our party, Jim scooted in next to me on one side of the booth; Kelli and Amanda and Jay took the other side. Jim sat as close to me as he possibly could and still remain respectable. *Okay, that's obvious. He hasn't changed his mind about wanting to get together with me,* I decided.

The fresh seafood was absolutely delicious and we had such a fun time. The five of us were becoming a close-knit group, and we enjoyed one another's company immensely. Jim and I stole meaningful glances at each other as we all joked and laughed. I figured the others couldn't help but notice that we were attracted to each other, even though we were trying not to act too much like a couple.

After dinner we decided to take a stroll down the Newport Pier. The gorgeous sunset had almost completely faded by the time we drove the short distance to the pier and parked the car.

A van full of hippies pulled up about the same time we did, and Kelli migrated over to say hello and talk to them about Jesus. The rest of us took a few flash photos in the deepening shadows. We looked in the direction of Catalina Island, usually visible from this vantage point, but we couldn't make it out in the gray-violet haze of early nightfall. We slowly cut across the sandy beach toward the pier, taking our time so Kelli wouldn't lose sight of us.

She rejoined us after a few minutes, and the kids walked slightly ahead of Jim and me as we started down the pier. With the sun down, the wind sweeping across the water had turned the night air chilly, and I tugged down the pushed-up sleeves of my lightweight cotton pullover. Neither Jim nor I said much. We simply walked leisurely and enjoyed being outdoors together. I was very calm on the outside, but inside my mind was swirling like the bubbling surf on the sand below us.

About halfway out, the others kept on going while Jim slowed down. "Lori, can we talk a minute?" he asked me.

"Okay," I said with a smile. My heart started to beat a little faster as he put a hand on my elbow and guided me toward one of the wooden benches spaced along the pier. Jim motioned for me to sit down, but he remained standing. In the second or two of quietness while he gathered his thoughts before beginning to speak, I listened to the roar of the ocean. *This conversation is going to be a significant milepost in my life,* I realized.

"Lori, I'm starting to fall in love with you." Jim's face was somber, his soft brown eyes earnest. "And I don't want this to go any farther if there's no hope of you feeling the same way. But even if you might possibly be interested in me, you need to know what it would be like for us to have a relationship. It wouldn't be like dating anyone else. Unfortunately, I bring a lot of baggage with me."

The breeze ruffled his thinning hair, and I resisted the urge to reach up and smooth it into place. I thought once again how attractive he was—not just physically handsome but personally appealing. I was discovering that Jim possessed many endearing qualities. His gentleness and his generosity, for example. Another trait I appreciated was his openness and vulnerability, which was exactly how he appeared to me now. Vulnerable. So afraid of being rejected that he seemed not to want to pause long enough to let me respond. He just kept plowing ahead with his disclaimer spiel, so I watched him and listened patiently; I wanted to hear what he had to say, although I already knew how I would answer him.

"That baggage is my past," he continued. "I remain a very public figure, even though PTL and Heritage are long gone. For some reason I haven't figured out, I'm still pursued by the news media. It seems utterly insane, but the whole world wants to know everything that goes on in my life. And that affects *everybody* in my life. So if we both were falling in love and dating, and especially if we were to get married, well, the media attention could be overwhelming. The press would be constantly following us, and you would find yourself in situations you've never been in before. A lot of people in life are starstruck by fame and imagine how wonderful it would be. But it's far from glamorous being in the limelight. In fact, most of the time it's a heavy burden because you're not able to have any kind of a private life."

He smiled tentatively. "But that's what my life is like. And on top of that, I'm older than you, I've got two grown children . . . and even a couple of grandkids, and . . . well, anyway, I don't know if you could even begin to handle all that, but would you be willing to try? Would you consider the possibility of dating me, or maybe even more? I mean, could you rule it in or out, perhaps?"

When Jim's vocal locomotive finally ran out of steam and he

paused, I stood up to give him my answer. He had almost made it sound as if I'd have to be crazy to want to date him. "Yes, Jim," I said, "I would be interested in pursuing a relationship with you."

His expression was positively jubilant. "That's wonderful," he said. We were standing very close, and his fingertips brushed mine. "Is it okay if I hold your hand?"

Just then I saw Jay and Amanda and Kelli returning. "No," I said as I quickly moved back. "Only because of Jay," I told Jim, who looked disappointed. "It's too much too soon for him, I think."

But that was too much to ask of a man who had just bared his soul to a woman he was falling deeply in love with—much more in love than he had even disclosed at that point. The next minute he slipped his arm around me, needing to feel close to me, and needing to stake his claim, I suppose. I didn't mind it at all; it felt very natural. And yet I wanted to try to protect Jay's feelings. I didn't know what he thought about my dating his dad. *Have they talked it over?* I wondered. Had father and son stayed up late at night talking about me the way Kelli and Amanda and I had talked about Jim?

Kelli looked very surprised when she saw Jim with his arm around me. Later she confessed that while they had walked to the end of the pier, she told Jay, "Get ready, because Lori is letting your dad down gently. She'll be nice about it, but that's what she's doing." When they got back and found out that the opposite had happened, she was shocked.

As we walked back to the Jeep, Jim and I made plans to go out on our first date alone the next night. Both of us knew that it was far more than a first date; we were already falling in love. And we knew that it was God bringing this love into our lives at the very time both of us had just about given up on ever finding love again.

14

NOT EXACTLY
THE GRAND HOTEL

Wednesday, July 22, 1998

Kelli picked me up in Newport Beach on Wednesday morning, and we fought our way through the L.A. traffic to get back to the Dream Center, so I could attend the Bible study Jim taught every weekday at noon. We walked down the steep stairs into the bowels of the old hospital building—we were literally underneath the parking lot—and entered a large concrete room with only a few tiny windows placed high on one wall.

"What is this place?" I asked Kelli.

"Used to be the laundry for the hospital. Jim fixed it up himself."

I could tell the room had recently been renovated with fresh paint and carpet. Drapes hung on the walls, even the walls without windows. The heavy fabric of the draperies would cut down on the echo from the concrete walls, I realized. At Master's Commission we had made similar modifications to old buildings.

The large room was crowded, and Kelli and I quickly gravitated to the several odd-sized rectangular tables covered with white cloths and spread with food. Jim's ministry, New Covenant, fed everyone who came to the noon Bible study. It wasn't nearly as spectacular a miracle as the Feeding of the Five Thousand, yet I was very impressed that a couple of volunteers, operating on a shoestring budget, could put together a smorgasbord for two hundred or more people, five days a week—with no kitchen facility. Connie Elling and another worker prepared the food in New Covenant's office space, using one hot plate and a microwave oven, and then carted everything across the alley and set it up in the old laundry room.

After we had filled our plates, Armando waved and motioned that he had saved a place for us. We threaded our way through the narrow path between the round dining tables, also covered with white tablecloths. The big concrete room was built more like a bunker than a hotel ballroom. There were no chandeliers, and we were eating off of paper plates rather than fine china, yet the atmosphere was that of a banquet hall.

Just as we sat down, Jim began to teach. Wearing his usual ball cap, T-shirt, and Bermuda shorts, he sat at a table on a raised platform, with a Bible laid out in front of him and a tabletop microphone stand within reach. When Jim saw me, he lit up like a Christmas tree. I smiled back at him, thinking he looked absolutely smitten, and I rather liked that.

Jim was teaching a series on the gospel of Matthew, and as he shared what he had learned in prison—while spending hours every single day studying the words of Jesus—I was amazed. Because my home church was one of the nation's leading megachurches, I had been privileged to sit under some of the finest Bible teachers from America and beyond. That day I discovered that Jim Bakker ranked with the best I'd ever heard. *This is deep, in-the-Word teaching,* I thought. *No wonder his Bible studies are standing room only.*

I stopped taking notes for a moment and looked around the audience. It was sweltering in the unair-conditioned room. Some people were mopping their foreheads from the heat, but they were all listening intently. Like every event I had attended at the Dream Center, the noon Bible study had attracted a cross section of people. The middle and high school students from the Dream Center Academy were easy to spot in their school uniforms. A fresh-faced, well-scrubbed gaggle of teenagers that looked straight out of the Midwest was probably a church youth group spending a week in L.A. as a summer ministry. Groups of all ages from churches across the country regularly came to the Dream Center to help with the remodeling and participate in evangelistic outreaches to the inner city. A few well-heeled individuals sat among former gang members with shaved heads and little old ladies in bright dresses—the kind of ghetto women who might be poor but dressed in their best and put flowers in their hair because they held on to their dreams and their dignity.

"I used to preach and even write books on how to get rich," Jim told the crowd. "But after months of studying the words of Jesus in prison—literally writing down every word Christ spoke as recorded in the Scriptures—I concluded that He did not have one good thing to say about money. When I came to the realization that I had actually been contradicting Christ, I was horrified—physically nauseated. Yes, God can take care of his people. He promises to supply all our needs—our *needs*, not our every wish or whim. He can and does bless us, but our main focus should never be on material blessings. Our focus must be on Jesus and our total love for him."

I was thrilled to hear Jim openly challenge those who promote a materialistic Christianity. From my work in the inner city and a life-changing mission trip to El Salvador, I knew firsthand what kind of damage such teaching could do to poor Christians who love the Lord and who walk by faith even while living in abject poverty.

Amazing, I thought, *that Jim Bakker had once come into the homes of millions of people.* Now he was feeding a small inner-city flock, and he appeared to be in his element.

About one o'clock, Jim said a prayer of dismissal over the diverse crowd of eager Bible students. Armando went to the front, where people had immediately gathered around Jim. Kelli and I sat at the table and talked to Amanda and Jennifer McDivitt. I wanted to see Jim, naturally, but I did not want to push my way through the crowd.

In a few minutes, Armando came back to the table. "Jim asked me to come get you," he said. "He's very generous with his time, so he has a hard time getting away from people sometimes. And he *really* wanted me to make sure you didn't leave before he could get back here to see you." Armando grinned, which wiped the tough-guy look right off his face. With his muscular build and tattooed arms, he looked like a street-hardened gang member, which is what he had been. But when he smiled, his face reflected what he had become—a tender young man transformed by the grace of God.

"Jim has changed since you've been around," Armando told me as we walked toward the front.

"How's that?" I asked.

"Oh, he's a lot happier. He was kinda depressed before that."

He looked anything but depressed to me now as he animatedly explained a passage of Bible prophecy to one of the Dream Center kids who was questioning him. When he noticed me standing there, Jim wound up his explanation, closed his Bible, and put an arm around the young man next to him. He started to introduce us. "Lori, I'd like you to meet someone. This is my—"

"B. J.!" I suddenly recognized the gangly boy.

"You two know each other?" Jim asked as I hugged my young friend.

"Good grief, you're taller than I am now!" I said to B. J. We laughed and stood back-to-back to compare heights. "Yes," I told Jim. "I've known Willette Brown, B. J.'s mother, for years. She calls me the godmother to her two boys. This handsome rascal is my godson!"

"I can't believe it." Jim looked shocked. "He's my godson too."

"You're kidding!" It was my turn to be amazed.

"No, Willette gave me the same honor recently. She asked me to be a godparent to B. J."

"Guess you're both stuck with me," B. J. said with a laugh, then he ambled off with one of his friends.

"What are the odds of that?" Jim wondered out loud. "*You* meet Willette Brown in the ghetto of Phoenix, and she asks you to be B. J.'s godmother. Then she moves to L.A. and gets involved at the Dream Center, and she makes *me* his godfather. That's, well . . ."

"It's weird," I said.

"More than a coincidence, I think." Jim looked intently at me.

"Maybe so." I returned his gaze. *How strange that we would have this unknown connection through a young black kid from the inner city.* "So, how's he doing?" I asked.

"B. J.'s doing great," Jim said. "He is so turned on to the

Bible. I've been teaching the words of Jesus, and because of the prophetic words of Christ in Matthew, I often tie them into the book of Revelation. That's what he was asking me about just now. These kids love to study prophecy. They're hungry for the Word of God."

We sat down at one of the round tables, and Jim continued telling me about B. J. "For his birthday, B. J. didn't want a Game Boy or a computer or any of the things you figure a kid would want. He let everybody know he wanted a Greek and Hebrew study Bible. So some of the people here went together and got him one for a birthday present."

For a leisurely half hour or so we sat and talked, stopping our conversation from time to time as Jim graciously posed for a photo for a visitor or greeted one of the regular attendees.

"I started this daily Bible study," Jim told me, "after I recalled a mistake I had made at Heritage USA. At its heyday, we had over three thousand staff members, plus a host of volunteers. In the early days we had taken time out of our workday to have prayer and Bible study. But as we grew larger, we got so busy working for God, we didn't take time to study the Word together as a staff. Besides, it was too expensive, the accountants said. Somebody estimated it cost us two hundred thousand dollars in lost work time whenever we held a staff Bible study. So we eventually dropped them altogether.

"When I got here, we had so many kids who were coming off the streets to be discipled, and they just couldn't get enough Bible teaching. I noticed the staff members wanted more Bible study as well. So when I thought about the tragic mistake we'd made at Heritage, I decided to include the Dream Center staff and volunteers as well as the students in my daily teaching ministry. Before I knew it, we had two hundred people attending.

Some days we have to turn people away because we just don't have the room."

Volunteers moved around us, picking up the paper plates and plastic utensils, clearing the room so they could start all over again the next day.

"Not exactly the Grand Hotel, is it?" Jim asked.

"No, but it has a certain style. I like what you've done with the place."

"I scrounged or bought everything you see," he said, obviously pleased with my comment. "Well, the 'buffet tables' were already here. They're old pool tables. We put long plywood planks over them and covered them to the floor with white cloths." We laughed at the thought of converting the pool tables to a nobler use. "Mainly, I tried to find hotel stuff, like the round tables. Paid a dollar a panel for the used drapes—and they're even fireproof, as the fire marshal required. A local business gave us the carpet out of their computer center. And I did the scraping and painting myself, with some volunteers. I actually enjoy remodeling work."

He looked supremely satisfied as he surveyed his handiwork. I recalled all the pictures of Jim in the books he'd given me. I'd seen the same look on his face when he had been wearing a hard hat on a construction site, overseeing multimillion-dollar building projects at Heritage. It wasn't the size or the scope of the project that mattered to Jim, I realized. He truly did enjoy building and renovating as a creative endeavor.

"You're happy here, aren't you?" I asked him.

"Happier than I've ever been in my life," he said quietly. "Especially now that you're here."

15

ALONE—AT LAST!

That night Jim took me to an Italian restaurant in the Burbank area. We dined alfresco in the courtyard, and we were both glad to be alone together—at last. In Jim's mind, we had been dating for almost a week—our previous outings were "group dates," as he calls them. But to me, that Wednesday night with just the two of us at a nice restaurant was our first real date— even though he had more or less proposed to me the night before, although without a ring. Standing on the pier, Jim had talked me through what life with him would be like, from dating all the way to marriage, so this evening was unlike any other first date I'd ever been on. It was certainly fraught with more significance.

And yet it was not awkward at all. I was already comfortable being around Jim. Now I was excited as well, because I was beginning to fall in love. He was head over heels, that was plain to see. He couldn't take his eyes off me, couldn't wipe the smile off his face, couldn't stop touching my hand or leaning close to me—and I didn't want him to stop. I enjoyed the attention, and now that I had decided it was okay to fall in love with Jim, I started letting go of the defenses I'd built around my heart.

Over a delicious dinner we talked about anything and everything. Jim is an insatiable learner and knowledgeable on a wide variety of subjects. He is also able to talk openly and transparently about any aspect of his life. I wasn't sure if he was that way by nature or if so much of his life had already been made public that he had simply gotten accustomed to being candid with new acquaintances as well as old friends. Of course, he'd already said he wanted me to know everything about him, and he was definitely still operating in the full disclosure mode.

We talked about our work in the inner city and how we had both become involved in it. I briefly told him about Roy and Margie and how they had become like family to me. He told me about first coming to the Dream Center and what a welcome reception he had received.

"I came here to minister to the people in the inner city," Jim said. "But they are the ones who ministered to me." He talked about Aaron Jayne, a former alcoholic and drug addict, now a youth pastor at the Dream Center. "Aaron took me on as his project those first few weeks, making sure I knew where to get food and supplies, seeing to it that my laundry got done, introducing me to everyone. And he constantly encouraged me, telling me I was one of the best preachers he'd ever heard—"

"You are," I interrupted. "I thought the same thing today."

"Thank you, Lori. That's kind, but …" He shook his head, as if to protest.

"It's true. I've heard some of the very best at Phoenix First, and I could have listened to you for hours. You really *fed* the people—a lot more than sandwiches, I mean."

"Well, I'm a far *different* preacher than I used to be. A different *person* than I used to be. Prison changed me. But when I first came to L.A., my self-confidence was still zero—I worried that people would never see beyond the stigma of prison and the public failure of my past—so I desperately needed the kind of approval Aaron and the others gave me. If anyone here had rejected me, I think I would have fled back to the hills of North Carolina and buried myself on the farm. But they didn't reject me. They respected me. They loved me. And they cared for me—in so many ways."

"I've found the same generosity of spirit in the inner city, from a lot of broken people who still have a great capacity to love."

"Of course, you've met Armando. He's another one who has really encouraged me, and I've been able to teach him and mentor him."

"He told on you earlier," I joked.

"What did he say?"

"That you had changed since I've been here . . . Armando said you'd been depressed before that."

"He's right about that." Jim paused a moment. "It *is* odd that I would meet you now," he said.

"Why is that?" I didn't quite catch his jump in the conversation at first.

"Because I'd finally given up. Stopped looking."

"Looking for . . ."

"A wife."

"Oh."

"And that's why I was depressed . . . because of the loneliness. It got to me."

"I know what that's like," I said.

We sat silently in our intimate corner of the courtyard, each daring to hope that God had brought us together to end the years of loneliness.

"In prison I was lonely, but there's so much going on," Jim said after a moment. "You're working all the time, and there are always people around. Then when I went to the farm, the loneliness gnawed at me. I would lie in bed at night and just ache from the hurting inside my chest. When I came to the Dream Center, I found so much love and acceptance, and I poured myself into ministry. I've been tremendously blessed in that ministry, and it's the most fulfilling work I've ever done, and yet . . ." His voice trailed off.

"Yet it doesn't meet the need for the love and companionship of a spouse."

"No, it doesn't." He paused to take a sip of water. "You understand that, don't you?"

"Yes, even though I wouldn't trade the last nine years for anything in the world. In my early years in the ministry, I fell in love with Jesus, and *he* became my husband. I've been very, very happy. But being single can be tough sometimes. I've had those nights where I ache from the loneliness too. Like at Valentine's—"

"Oh, Valentine's Day is the *pits*," Jim said.

"Especially those years when you don't even get a card or a phone call, let alone flowers. It's hard *not* to feel blue," I said.

"I hate to watch TV the first two weeks in February. You start to think you're the only person on the planet who doesn't have someone special. And don't even walk into a card shop. It'll make you want to cry." We both laughed at his exaggeration; but the thought was funny only because there was a kernel of truth in it.

"Then there are the weddings—everybody else's. I've been a bridesmaid so many times I've lost count. I'm not jealous of my girlfriends when they get married; I'm excited that God has brought someone into their lives, and I can genuinely rejoice with them. Yet there are times when you have to wonder, 'Will it ever be *my* turn?' A wedding just emphasizes the loneliness that's always lurking in the background."

Jim nodded. "You think you're dealing with it just fine, and then suddenly the loneliness reaches out and slaps you in the face. A couple of weeks ago that happened to me. That's what Armando was talking about when he said I'd been depressed. When I get depressed, I tend to withdraw. That weekend I didn't come out of my room; I just stayed in bed and slept all day Friday and Saturday. I took the phone off the hook so I wouldn't have to talk to anyone.

"Finally, on Sunday, Armando invaded my room. He lives next door to me, and I had given him a key. 'Jim, you've got to get out of bed,' he told me. I said no and told him to go away. He wasn't taking no for an answer, though. 'C'mon, you're gonna take a shower and go somewhere,' he said—and then he grabbed me by the arm and literally hauled me out of bed. I started to protest feebly, but he wouldn't have any part of it. He dragged me into the bathroom and turned the shower on. 'Now, don't make me get in there and wash you,' he said. I took one look at that burly ex–gang member and knew he meant what he said. So I got in the shower. After I got cleaned up, Armando took me over to Placita Olvera, the historic Mexican marketplace in downtown L.A. We walked around and shopped for a few things, and he finally got me out of my shell and got me talking.

"Later that night, I made a commitment to God. I had prayed for a wife for years. I wanted someone to work along-side me, someone to share my dreams and visions. As I traveled around the country, I would ask the pastors of the churches where I spoke to pray that God would send me a wife. 'Where do you find a godly woman?' I would ask them. I even enlisted the pastors' wives; they love to play matchmaker. I had a little formula I told them about. I always said that my number one requirement was a woman who loved God even more than she loved me. Then I wanted her to love me passionately and to be a helpmate. I also said it wouldn't hurt if she were good-looking.

"Occasionally one of the pastors would invite me to dinner and bring a woman he thought I should meet, but there was never a connection. You're the first woman who made my heart leap, Lori." The corners of his eyes crinkled in a silly smile as he melodramatically bounced a hand over his heart. "Anyway, that night I told the Lord that I would stop looking for a wife. That I was willing to be celibate if that's what he wanted—it wasn't what *I* wanted, but I was willing to accept his will, even if that meant I would be without a partner for the rest of my life. And then, two weeks after I gave up and committed it to God, *you* came into my life. Now I can't stop smiling."

We had finished our meal and the waiter had brought the check, but we were in no hurry to leave.

"Tell me, Lori. Have you been looking for someone too?"

"Oh, yes." I grinned. "And, just like you, I've had all my friends in the ministry praying up a husband for me."

"It's hard for me to believe that a godly woman as beautiful as you, and with so much personality and passion for people, is still unattached."

"Actually, I haven't even dated all that much. I was rather wild before I became a Christian, and I needed to go to the other extreme for a while, I guess. That's what I had to do to keep from falling back into that old lifestyle. So I put men out of my life along with the drugs. But I always wanted to be married again some day—and this time to the right man, the one *God* picked for me.

"After a while, though, I sort of gave up and quit looking too. You get so wrapped up in ministry, and God is blessing your work, so you just keep going and going. And somehow you put your deepest personal dreams on hold. Ever since I went into full-time ministry, I've had a dream of marrying a preacher or minister—someone to share my vision, someone who's not threatened that I have a ministry of my own but who wants me to partner with him in God's work. Over the years that dream has seemed pretty remote at times. Just a few months ago, I finally let God put that dream back in my heart, even though I knew it would take a miracle. I'm a woman with a very checkered past, and that past is part and parcel of my ministry. But marrying someone like me could ruin a minister's reputation . . ." I stopped, suddenly unsure and embarrassed that I had revealed so much of what lay deep inside my heart.

"Now, isn't it interesting," Jim said, "that I don't have a reputation left to ruin. Not a shred of respectability." We both burst out laughing.

"No, I guess you don't. And you made sure I knew that up front, giving me those books and practically trying to talk me out of even dating you."

"I knew it would have to be a gift from God if I ever found a woman who could accept my past." Jim had turned serious again. "I'm finding out now it's the same for you. I don't care what's in your past, Lori. But I want to know about it, simply because I'm falling in love with you and can't help wanting to know everything there is to know about you."

I'd felt the same way the last few days, reading everything Jim had given me, wanting to know all about him. It was natural for him to have the same curiosity about me, and I knew it was time for me to open up. If he truly were God's man for me—and I was pretty much convinced of that by now, even though this was our first real date—then I had no reason to withhold anything from him.

"What would you like to know?" I asked him. "Where do you want me to start?"

"Tell me more about your ministry. You've talked about your work in the inner city, and I know you also have a women's ministry. All I know is that it has something to do with abortion. That you've experienced abortion yourself and want to help other women find healing. Kelli told me that much. I've been asking questions," he admitted with a grin.

"That's something I've done the last four years, speak out about my abortions."

"Abortions—plural?"

"Yes, five. I've had five abortions." There was not a hint of condemnation on Jim's face, only compassion, so I continued. "Once I finally comprehended what I had done, I was devastated, and I didn't know where to turn for help in coming to terms with it spiritually."

"I can see where it would be hard to find help," he said thoughtfully. "Most people in our Christian circles wouldn't know how to deal with that—wouldn't *want* to deal with it. So many people sitting in church pews are hurting deep inside, with no one to talk to about their pain."

"Exactly. And if you can't talk about it, you can't find healing."

"You did find healing, though, and now you have a ministry to women in the same situation. How did it happen? How did you find the courage to tell someone, and how did God call you into that ministry?"

As I decided how to answer Jim, I thought back to the very first time I knew God had called me to speak to women about my own abortions . . .

16

A Little Boy's Voice

I fiddled with the knobs on the car radio as the kids chattered in the backseat. I had driven from Phoenix to Los Angeles to see Bobbi, and now the two of us were taking her daughter, Nikki, and her nephew Jason to the beach. It was a beautiful late summer day, blazing hot, near the end of August 1989.

Without being too obvious about it, I was looking for a Christian radio station. I figured Bobbi would want to listen to our usual rock music, so I reached for the dial first. Following my commitment to Christ five months earlier, I did not want to have anything to do with my former lifestyle, including the music.

A little girl's voice cut through the static on the radio. She was saying something about Jesus. *Great! A Christian children's program,* I thought smugly. *This is perfect.* I smiled and tapped my fingers against the steering wheel as the background music faded out and the dialogue started again.

As a new Christian I very much wanted to be a good influence on Bobbi and her family. After all, I had been responsible for leading her down the wrong path, introducing her to drugs and encouraging her toward promiscuity. And when Bobbi had wanted to straighten out her life and serve God two years earlier, *I* had been the one who kept drawing her back into the destructive party lifestyle. Now the tables were turned: I was on fire for God, and she was still trying to get me to snort crystal with her, tempting me with worn-out promises of a new and better high. For the first time in almost two decades, though, I wasn't buying it.

Bobbi was as close to me as any blood relative could be—and with all my heart I wanted to help her find the same joy I had found when I gave my life to Jesus. I breathed a silent prayer of gratitude to God for finding a Christian children's program. *What a great ministry tool,* I told myself. *Bobbi will have to listen to it for the kids' sake.* But as we cruised down the Pacific Coast Highway listening to the radio, I discovered the audio drama was not a children's program at all; instead it was directed squarely at me.

The broadcast that day by Focus on the Family was called "Tilly." The skillful blend of voices and music and sound effects captivated me, and I was quickly lost in the story. I identified with the character named Kathy, a depressed woman who has a dream populated with lots of children. She discovers something different about these children: they have no names and no parents, and they don't know where they came from. The ethereal background music clued the listener that these children were actually in heaven.

I gripped the steering wheel tightly as I tried to keep my emotions in check. *Children in heaven with no names and no parents. A woman who is depressed and doesn't know what is wrong. Dear God, I know what's wrong with her; I've been in her shoes.* I knew instantly that God was dealing with me about my abortions. I had not just stumbled across a Christian program for Bobbi's or Nikki's or Jason's sake. It may have been my hand that turned the knob, but it was God who tuned my car radio to the station *I* needed to hear.

I glanced in the rearview mirror at the kids in the backseat. Five-year-old Nikki was like my own daughter. I had been in the delivery room when she was born, and I had helped Bobbi raise her. Jason, who was nine, was like my own nephew. His mother, Bobbi's sister Kathy, was also a lifelong friend. Our relationship was so close that Nikki and Jason called me Auntie Lori. I loved these two children dearly, but they weren't my flesh and blood. I had destroyed my own flesh and blood, and now I would never have any children to call me Mommy.

Five children. I was supposed to have five children. The thought hammered into my heart relentlessly as I listened to the radio drama. *They were children—my children—and I killed them!* Oh, I hadn't done it by myself. Others helped me and encouraged me. Someone else actually did the killing, and it was all legal. But the bottom line was the same: my children were gone. And I was responsible. It was *my* choice to take their lives.

What tormenting thoughts. How could I stand them?

A glimmer of hope flickered across my mind. *They're in heaven. Like Tilly.*

Someone else had recently told me that, I remembered. One evening at a singles meeting at church, Craig Smith had shared his experience of being on drugs before he committed his life to Christ. Now he was a successful businessman with a beautiful wife and two daughters. *If he can come out of that lifestyle, so can I,* I thought. Yet I was a brand-new Christian, and I had just begun to struggle with the issues of my past, and I hadn't faced up to my abortions at all. As Craig spoke that night, it suddenly seemed to be too much for me to handle.

Not wanting anyone to see me cry, I had slipped outside. Melissa, Craig's wife, followed me.

"Do you want to talk about it?" she asked me.

"I don't know if I can." I had never told any of my new Christian friends about the abortions. Yet in spite of my hesitation at sharing something so personal and so shameful, all at once I started spilling it out to Melissa. I told her I had had five abortions. And she didn't judge me or condemn me. Instead, she accepted me and comforted me.

"Lori, your babies are in heaven," she said softly.

Babies? I had steeled myself not to think of them that way. Planned Parenthood had said they were blobs of tissue. I knew better, of course—at least on some level. But that's the only way I could live with myself, to think of them as "problem pregnancies," the flotsam and jetsam of an untimely conception, not as babies.

Heaven? Until that moment, I had vaguely thought of them as formless blobs out there in the universe somewhere. Were they really babies, really in heaven, as Melissa had just said?

"When my daughter was eighteen months old," Melissa continued, "she had a life-threatening experience. Actually, she died. Then they brought her back. Later, when she was old enough to talk, she told us about seeing Jesus during that time. She said she had seen Jesus with lots of children, and they were very happy."

I was spellbound.

"So that's how I know your children are in heaven with Jesus," she said. And then she hugged me as I grappled, for the first time, with the reality that I had aborted five children, not blobs. And they were in heaven, not floating around in space somewhere. They were real—real beings, real . . . real babies.

That conversation with Melissa Smith came back to me as I listened to "Tilly" and struggled to maintain my composure. On the radio, Kathy was crying and asking the daughter she had aborted to forgive her.

"Don't cry, Mommy. It's all right," a little girl's voice replied. The road blurred in front of me as I tried to blink away the tears. "I forgive you. I love you . . . Jesus forgave you a long time ago . . . I don't hurt anymore."[1] I bit my lip to stifle a sob and wondered if I would have to pull over and let Bobbi drive.

The broadcast ended and I managed to hold the car steady, but by the time we arrived at Huntington Beach, I was white-knuckled and shaken to the core.

I pulled into the parking lot and stationed the car under the swaying palm trees. Ordinarily I'm the fussbudget who gets everything unloaded and set up and arranged just so. But not that day; I could barely speak.

"I, uh, have to go for a walk," I stammered as Bobbi started to retrieve our beach gear from the car.

"Okay," she said, shooting me a surprised but sympathetic look. She busied herself with the kids as I stumbled toward the water. I thought I would take a stroll on the concrete pier, the longest on the California coast, but I never made it that far.

Sunglasses could not hide the tears streaming down my face, and I was glad the beach was not crowded that day. I walked toward the water, oblivious to the warm ocean breeze or the strident call of the seagulls. My shoulders slumped under the weight of the reality that now settled on me. *Dear God, what have I done?* My feet were leaden, my legs would no longer hold me. I sank to my knees in the hot sand, completely devastated. *I murdered my children.*

A man and a woman passed by me and discarded the remains

of their picnic lunch into one of the large trash bins dotting the beach. It occurred to me that I had thrown my children away, almost as unthinkingly as they tossed their soda cans in the garbage. I had killed my babies to keep my husband. A husband I wound up losing anyway. A husband who had betrayed me and abused me, again and again.

The years of denial had finally come to an end. The lies I had believed had finally been exposed. I was supposed to have five children with me right now. God had intended for me to be a mother. He had given me children, and I had wantonly destroyed them. I had asked Jesus to forgive my sins, but had he really forgiven me of even this? Could I ever forgive myself?

When I could bear my thoughts no longer, I felt the comforting presence of the Holy Spirit wrap around me like a soft cashmere shawl. I watched the waves racing each other to the shore, and suddenly I saw before me an ocean of women—millions of women, stretching all the way to the horizon—and I was speaking to them about abortion. The "still, small voice" of God's Spirit spoke to my mind in that moment: *One day I will place you on a platform where you will speak to these women.*

"But I murdered my children," I whispered. "I gave them up for a man who ruined my life." I choked back a wail.

Tell the women that. I will give you the platform.

I stared at the ocean. The multitudes of women were gone. I could no longer see their faces.

"Mommy, we love you." The lilting voice drifted over the waves. My heart skipped a beat.

"We're with Jesus. And you'll be with us one day, Mommy. But now you must go and do what the Master says."

I knew that voice was telling me that I had to fulfill my calling—whatever it was that God had put me on this earth to do. I also knew that the child's voice was not a figment of my imagination, even though I had listened to a little girl's voice saying something similar on the radio just moments before. This was a little boy's voice . . . and it was not the first time I had heard it.

That voice was familiar because I had heard it about a year earlier, before I had ever walked the aisle at church and committed my life to Christ. It was during that "beginning of the end" time when I was living in Flagstaff, not long after I had that final "interlude" with my ex-husband, Jesse.

I had rented a beautiful little cabin in the mountains and really enjoyed the solitude it afforded. One night I couldn't sleep. So I got up and turned on the television. I flipped through the channels until I found a Christian program. It was *The 700 Club*. Pat Robertson was talking about abortion. The topic made me a little uneasy, but I didn't change the station.

That night *The 700 Club* aired a video called *The Silent Scream*. This pro-life documentary was narrated by Dr. Bernard Nathanson, a former abortionist, and included live film footage of a suction abortion. For the first time I saw pictures of exactly what I had done. I was horrified, but I could not tear my eyes away from the screen.

"We are now looking at a sector scan of a real-time ultrasound imaging of a twelve-week, unborn child," Dr. Nathanson said in his professorial voice.[2] Then he pointed out the child's head and hand, the ribs and the spine. *Twelve weeks.* I had been a good sixteen weeks for one of my abortions, I remembered.

"The heart is beating at the rate of approximately 140 beats a minute. And we can see the child moving rather serenely in the uterus."[3] The black-and-white images were grainy, but there was no mistaking the perfectly shaped fetus. I began to feel sick to my stomach. Ultrasound was not available when I had my abortions. If I had seen pictures like this . . .

"You will note as the suction tip, which is now over here, moves towards the child, the child will rear away from it and undergo much more violent and much more agitated movements . . . The child has now moved back to the profile view and the suction tip is flashing across the screen. The child's mouth is now open . . . but this suction tip which you can see moving violently back and forth on the bottom of the screen is the lethal instrument which will ultimately tear apart and destroy the child."[4]

When I saw that baby, with its mouth open in a silent scream, pushing against the walls of its mother's womb, my world completely shattered. I fell out of my chair and onto the hardwood floor, crying hysterically. The full fury of my sin, which I had stuffed so deep inside of me, erupted in such searing pain that I didn't know if I could live through it—wasn't sure I wanted to live through it. I lay on the floor and sobbed until I heaved.

And that's when I heard the voice.

"Mommy, everything's okay. We love you."

That's all. Just a few words uttered in a little boy's voice. A voice so sweet and pure that it melted my heart.

Because I'd never had an ultrasound, I didn't know the gender of any of the children I aborted, so don't ask me how I knew this; I can't tell you. But somehow I knew in my heart that the voice I had just heard belonged to my son. He would have been my firstborn.

Now, on the beach, I understood why God had wanted me to hear the radio broadcast of "Tilly," and why he had spoken to me in the voice of my unborn child for the second time. He had already forgiven me, but he wanted to begin a healing process in me. I remember hearing a preacher say once that God does things in the heavenly realm that there are no earthly words to describe. I believe that with God, all things are possible. Whatever it takes for you to be healed, that's what he will do for you. That's what it took for me. I needed to hear that voice. Needed that reassurance.

God knew I could never have taken all the guilt and grief at once. So he restored me bit by bit, patched my broken spirit piece by piece. I did not get up from that experience energized and with a burning zeal to speak to women about abortion. In fact, over time, I almost forgot what God had shown me that day. Yet, I always remembered hearing that voice, and I remembered it as a healing time, a moment when God, in his infinite grace and mercy, put a Band-Aid on my bleeding soul.

After my hour alone on the beach, I was able to pull myself together. I got up, brushed myself off, and walked back to where Bobbi and the kids were soaking up the sun. I had lost the exuberance with which we had started the trip, but I was functional again.

Yet, it would be another five years before I would fully grieve for the loss of my children. And that would be the third and final time I heard my son's voice.

17

Our First Kiss

That night at the restaurant I started telling Jim how God had used my past to lead me into an unusual outreach to women. I did not tell him many details about my marriage or my abortions or even what I did in my postabortion ministry. I gave him a broad overview—the public version, much as I do when I give my personal testimony. It's not that I felt uncomfortable opening up to Jim or that I wanted to hide anything from him. But many of the details I didn't even remember; my mind had blotted them out as a defense mechanism. And I had been through so much healing of the painful aspects of my past that I never talked at length about what I did remember.

The main reason I did not reveal very much to Jim that night is that I didn't want him to carry that hurt inside him, and in one week I already knew him well enough to know that he would grieve deeply for my pain and for the loss of my children. To some extent, I was doing that myself. As I learned more about Jim, through reading his books and listening to him talk, it was as if I were reliving parts of his past, dealing with emotions and issues he had already struggled to move beyond. Over the next few weeks, however, Jim and I would talk for hour upon hour, sharing everything in our hearts and holding back nothing. In fact, we probably talked more in those seven weeks—from the time we met until we were married—than most couples do in seven years.

After our first dinner alone together, we went to a movie. We held hands as we walked down the aisle of the darkened theater. "At least we don't have all the kids with us this time," Jim said. "I thought I'd *never* get you all to myself."

"We've only known each other a week."

"Yes, a whole week! You make it sound short, but it seems like eternity to a man who is dying to be alone with a beautiful girl. All week long, everywhere we've gone, we've had chaperones."

I couldn't help laughing. "The younger generation does seem concerned about monitoring our behavior."

"Of course, it's been so long since I went out on a date, my son had to give me advice. He also told me to be sure I came home at a decent hour. Jamie's starting to sound more like a father than a son," he joked.

We saw *Dr. Dolittle* that night. I say that we "saw" it, but neither one of us can tell you a thing that happened on the big screen. We were so wrapped up in each other that we were completely oblivious to the shenanigans of Eddie Murphy and his talking animals.

As soon as we sat down, Jim put his arm around me and pulled me close. He held me all during the movie, whispering something to me now and then. I closed my eyes and leaned against him, savoring this tender, romantic moment.

Before the movie ended, we had shared our first kiss. It was a very sweet, tender kiss. I was forty years old, but I felt for all the world as if I were seventeen again. *This is exactly how you feel when you fall in love for the very first time,* I thought. It was so sweet and innocent and pure.

In my Master's Commission training I had memorized 451 Bible verses, and one of them came to mind now, 2 Corinthians 5:17: "Therefore, if anyone is in Christ, he is a new creation; old things have passed away; behold, all things have become new."

It was true. Old things had passed away. It was as if years had been erased from our lives. Nothing that had gone before mattered. God had wiped the slate clean and given us both a fresh start on finding love and romance. We had waited a long time for this, and it was wonderful indeed.

We certainly both felt like kids when Jim took me "home" after our date. There was no place we could go and be completely alone—not that we would have done anything except talk. But we had no place to talk in private. Jim lived in Casa Grande, the "big house" next door to the old hospital, and girls were not allowed in the guys' rooms on the second floor. With adjoining rooms connected by a bathroom, Casa Grande was a step above the dorm-type rooms of the remodeled hospital. Jay and Jim each had a private room and shared a connecting bathroom. That one room was the only "house" Jim had, and that's what all the residents called it—their room was their house. Before we were married, I could not visit Jim's home.

I was staying in L.A. that night, at the Dream Center with Kelli and Amanda. So after our date, Jim walked me to the door of the girls' room. He gave me a very quick good-night kiss— which was against the rules, but we risked it. We felt like teenagers, standing out in the hall and sneaking that kiss.

Old things had passed away. All things had become new.

18

TALKING HEART TO HEART

Thursday, July 23, 1998

I can't believe you shined shoes!" Jim's voice on the other end of
the phone line sounded sad.

"It's true. I was a shoeshine girl for a couple of years," I
replied. "That's how I supported my ministry financially." It was
late at night, and I was stretched across the bed in Mark's guest
room. He had completed his business trip, so I'd gone back to
Newport Beach to visit him. After Mark and I returned from
dinner that night, Jim called to chat.

"I wanted to cry when Kelli told me that today. I just couldn't
imagine my beautiful princess bowing down at people's feet!"

"I'm a preacher, not a princess." I chuckled at Jim for pro-
moting me to royal status.

"Well, you're a princess to me, and it hurts to think you had
to stoop to shining shoes."

"I *did* have to stoop—a lot. And it was fairly strenuous work.

But I only did it two or three days a week, and it was good, quick money. I needed that kind of flexibility in order to be in full-time ministry."

"But how did you ever get into something like shoe shining?"

"A lady in our church owned the shoeshine company at the Phoenix airport. She often hired church members, especially women. It was a smart business idea because it was unusual; I haven't seen that anywhere else. I worked as a team with another lady, also a blonde. We had side-by-side shoeshine chairs—those big old-timey ones that the customer has to step up on, and there's a drawer underneath for all your brushes and polishes and rags. We worked in the busiest terminal at the airport. A lot of travelers—mostly businessmen—passed right in front of our chairs, and many of them did a double take when they spotted us."

"I'll bet they suddenly decided their shoes needed some attention when they saw a gorgeous woman shining shoes." I couldn't see Jim's face, but I knew he was grinning and raising his eyebrows.

"We did do a steady business. And we had to be quick about it, because the customers were always catching a flight. So I would be exhausted after a four- to six-hour shift. My back and arms would be sore."

"That kind of menial work didn't bother you?"

"I never minded hard work. I was a waitress for years, and that's hard work too. But some days I would be embarrassed about shining shoes and would hope I wouldn't see anyone at the airport who I recognized. Other days it didn't bother me at all. One thing about it—I always had the opportunity to share my faith because the first question out of a customer's mouth would invariably be, 'What's a girl like you doing shining shoes?'"

"What did you tell them?"

"I would always say that it gave me the opportunity to earn some money so I could do the work of the ministry. Some of them didn't even know what I meant by that. So I'd tell them I had started an organization to help women, and they would usually ask me what kind of help. I didn't offer too much information up front; that way they would keep asking questions, and it didn't sound like I was preaching. Since the owner of the company was a Christian, we were free to talk about our faith; we just didn't go overboard because of working in a public place like the airport.

"When they asked me what kind of ministry I had, I would say that I worked with women who had been through abortion, to help them deal with the scars it had caused. Some customers wouldn't want to know one more thing; that would be it. Others would be curious and ask me to tell them more about what I did. I would tell them that I knew the pain of abortion firsthand, that I had been through an abusive marriage and a life of alcohol and drugs—I got all the basic facts out fast. I could give a complete testimony during a five-minute shine, polishing and buffing the whole time. They were usually quite shocked."

"I know I would be, if I met a good-looking shoeshine girl who was actually a minister. Were they ever rude to you?"

"A few. Every now and then some guy would try to hit on me, but mostly they were very polite, like one customer I'll never forget—an older gentleman, dressed sharply in a business suit, as most of the men were. He seemed very sweet and was interested in hearing my testimony, asking me questions and nodding his head. As he got money out of his wallet to pay me, he said, 'By the way, I'm a pastor.' He named a large church in San Jose, California; I recognized the name of the church. He looked at me as he handed me the money and said, 'Young lady, don't ever stop doing what you're doing for God.' He had such a kind voice, and I was touched by what he said.

"I refused to take his money. 'Listen,' I said. 'This shine's on me. Let me bless your ministry today.' I gave away at least one shine during every shift; it was my way of tithing. 'Okay, but I want to give you a tip,' he said, and pressed a bill into my hand. I thanked him and he walked off. As I went to put the money in my pocket, I unfolded it and saw that it was a hundred-dollar bill. God has often met my needs like that, surprising me with a financial blessing exactly when I needed it the most."

Jim and I continued to talk "shop" about ministry issues for a while longer, and then we turned to matters of the heart. We talked most of the night, sharing personal stories, learning all about each other as sweethearts do at the beginning of a relationship. He described the emotional devastation he had gone through in prison, and I started opening up about my past. He never pushed me to reveal anything I didn't want to, never even asked me that many questions. It was months later, for example, before Jim ever knew my ex-husband's first name. What Jim really wanted to get was a glimpse of my heart—to know the real me—and what a priceless gift that was.

One of the things I began to talk about was the crushing loss of my dream of motherhood. "Ever since I can remember," I told Jim, "all I wanted to be was a mommy. In my childhood photographs, I'm always carrying a baby doll—sometimes one under each arm."

"I can picture that," Jim said. "I've seen you with kids. You're so nurturing."

"I know, that nurturing was born into me. It was a gift of God, a gift he meant to be used for my children."

"You never had any children after your abortions?"

"No. I couldn't."

I acknowledged that my abortions had eventually robbed me of the opportunity to ever bear children, and I told Jim the story of my hysterectomy at the age of twenty-two . . .

19

Empty and Angry

I stared at the new-patient history form I was filling out in the surgeon's office. "Number of pregnancies," it said. I couldn't bring myself to fill in that blank.

Jesse was sitting next to me, thumbing through a magazine. I looked over at him. "It asks how many times I've been pregnant," I said.

"So what's the problem?"

"I'm embarrassed to say I've had five abortions."

"Why?"

You really don't get it, do you? I thought. "Never mind," I told him.

"It's not that big a deal, Lori. Just answer the questions so the doctor can find out what's wrong with you."

I finished filling out the form, and Jesse took the clipboard back to the receptionist. Just getting up and down from a chair hurt. I'd been in pain for almost a year—ever since my last abortion actually, although I had not made a connection between that event and my pain. My right side hurt all the time, and it kept getting worse. I have a high tolerance for pain, so I put off going to the doctor for a long time. When I finally couldn't stand it anymore, I sought help.

The doctor had sent me for an ultrasound—the technology was still fairly new in 1980—and then for a surgical consultation.

"From the ultrasound, it looks like you have a grapefruit-sized cyst on your right ovary," the surgeon said when I was finally ushered back to his office. "That's not uncommon. I'll go in and remove the cyst, and hopefully that's all we'll have to do."

"You mean you might have to do more surgery?"

"Possibly. But the most I'll have to do is take the one ovary. That way you'll still be able to have children—if you want to."

"Yes, I do. Very much."

"I see you've had several abortions." He was looking at the medical history I'd filled out, and I blushed as I confirmed it for him.

"But I would like to have children someday," I said.

"You're young and otherwise healthy. Even with one ovary you should be able to get pregnant, and we'll try to save both ovaries if we can."

I was so relieved by his answer. And so ready for an end to the pain.

A few days later, after surgery, I woke up briefly in the recovery room, and a nurse gave me a shot for the pain. When I awoke again, I was in my hospital room. Jesse was standing on one side of the bed and my mom on the other. Dad was pacing around the room.

The pain was excruciating, and no one had to tell me what had happened. I just knew. I felt empty.

I looked at Jesse and asked, "They took everything, didn't they?" My voice was groggy from the medication.

"Don't worry about anything right now, baby. Just get some rest," he said.

I didn't trust Jesse to tell me the truth, but I knew my mother wouldn't lie to me, so I asked her the same question. "They took everything, didn't they, Mom?"

"They had to, Lori." She looked as if she'd been crying. "They had to save your life."

"God, no . . ." I was still too sedated to even cry.

"You're going to be okay, honey. Just go to sleep and get some rest." Mom squeezed my hand as I gave up the struggle to stay awake.

I learned later that the surgeon had been astounded when he opened me up. It was not just a matter of a grapefruit-sized cyst on one ovary. My insides were mangled—all my female organs mutilated. The OR team called in specialists while I was on the operating table. "It's the kind of thing you see once in every thousand or so cases," the surgeon said. There was so much scar tissue, it was hard to tell what was what, and there were signs of a massive infection. The doctors felt that if they didn't do a complete hysterectomy, my life would be threatened.

The surgeon had gone out to the waiting room to tell my family, and to get formal permission to do radical surgery. He had begun to explain what was wrong. "We think that as a result of her last abor—" he said. Then he suddenly backpedaled as he remembered that I had specifically asked him not to mention anything to my parents about my previous abortions, but the damage had been done. That's how my mother learned she had lost several grandchildren, although we never talked about the specifics until many years later.

None of the doctors involved in my surgery had performed the abortions, so they were unable to compare my current condition to a prior medical exam. But they agreed that I had probably suffered complications from a botched abortion the previous year. More than likely the procedure had not been complete, and the abortionist had left a part of the baby inside me, which caused a severe infection.

A *five-minute procedure. Safer than carrying a pregnancy to term.* That's what I'd been told when I had my first abortion. Now one of those "safe" five-minute procedures had threatened my life and destroyed my ability to bear children.

Years later I learned the details of what happens in a suction abortion. The hands-on nurse presses on the woman's abdomen as the abortionist empties the womb. Afterward the nurse has to remove the contents of the canister attached to the suction apparatus and reassemble the body parts to make sure nothing was left inside the patient. She checks that there are two tiny feet, two legs, two arms, two hands, a head and spine. If any fetal tissue has not been removed, it can cause serious complications such as sterility or infection. That was the doctors' best guess as to what had happened to me. They couldn't prove it, but they didn't have another explanation.

After my hysterectomy, the anger and resentment I had stuffed down inside of me because of the abortions began to erupt, and I knew then my marriage would never survive my hatred for Jesse. "It's me or the baby," he'd said every time I'd gotten pregnant. Then he would lead me on. "Someday we'll have kids. There's plenty of time for that." He'd never meant it, and I finally realized that. And there *hadn't* been plenty of time. Now I was twenty-two years old and going through surgically induced menopause.

I was sick beyond sick, and I didn't think I would ever get over it. I couldn't watch a diaper commercial on TV without falling apart. More than anything in the world I had wanted to be a mother. Even as a little girl I would stuff a pillow under my baby-doll pajamas and walk around pretending I was pregnant.

God must have intended me to be a mother of many: I was a Fertile Myrtle, and I got pregnant every year from the ages of seventeen to twenty-one. Except for the first pregnancy, I was using birth control. But because of my drug use, I would forget and miss taking a pill here and there. I invariably got pregnant. Then I had an IUD for a while, but I took it out because it was painful. So I went back on the pill . . . and still managed to get pregnant.

But not anymore. The chance for that was gone forever. And as I began to realize that, I was incredibly angry with Jesse for taking away my dream. I was angry with myself, too, because abortion was ultimately my choice.

Before long I was numbing my emotional pain with drugs again—heavy drugs. I started shooting cocaine with Jesse, and when the high would begin to fade, we'd wash down a few quaaludes with alcohol—an incredibly dangerous combination. It's a miracle I never overdosed. When you abuse quaaludes—methaqualone, a powerful tranquilizer once prescribed as a muscle relaxant—you lose all your inhibitions. You'll do anything—*anything*—when you're on 'ludes, and I did. I figured I had nothing to lose.

Except Jesse. And as much as I hated him, I still loved him. At least, I thought this was love. I clung to him desperately, doing whatever he wanted me to do because I didn't want him to leave me. He had cheated on me from the time we were married, and it devastated me that he wanted other women. But instead of telling him to hit the road, I debased myself and became a partner in his depravity. I had to be stoned out of my mind to do it, but we became "swingers" with other couples.

Sin had become a permanent fixture in my life, and the only way I can even bear to think about such things is that I know my sins have been completely washed away. "Though your sins are like scarlet," Isaiah 1:18 says, "they shall be as white as snow." God's Word promises that when we turn to him and repent of our sins, he not only no longer holds them against us, but he even blots them out of his memory.[1] I have blotted them out of my memory, too, and the only reason I dredge them up now is in hope that even one reader who might think, *But what I've done is too horrible; God can't forgive me,* will understand the error of that thought.

My marriage to Jesse didn't survive, but my anger did. Only after I became a Christian in 1989 did I begin to deal with my deep-seated anger. During my years in Master's Commission, I received a tremendous amount of emotional healing from the wounds my ex-husband had inflicted on me and those I had inflicted on myself. But losing the dream of becoming a mother was by far the hardest.

One particular incident, about fifteen years after my hysterectomy, resurrected that pain and anger, and it became as raw and fresh as the day I first learned I would never bear children. It was Christmastime, and I was living with my mom in a two-bedroom condo. She provided a home for me while I was working in full-time ministry.

Mark's best friend, Tim, came to visit the day before Christmas Eve. I knew Tim had stayed in touch with Jesse over the years; he and Mark and Jesse had been close, almost like brothers. And I fully expected to hear from Jesse the next day because he always called then. He knew our whole family would be together exchanging gifts, so no matter where he was—and we never knew how to get in touch with him—Jesse would resurface on

Christmas Eve and either call or come by. He had done a lot of horrible things, yet there was a tender side of Jesse that everyone, not just me, had loved. And Jesse had been closer to my family than his own. So I expected to hear from him, even ten years after our divorce, and that's why Jesse was on my mind when I saw Tim that day.

As he got ready to leave, I walked outside with Tim. We were standing in the front yard, saying good-bye, and I asked him, "Have you seen Jesse lately? What's he doing these days?"

"His old lady is pregnant," Tim said. "About ready to pop that kid out any day."

"What?" I felt as if someone had just stabbed me in the heart.

"Yeah, it's a bad situation though. She's a real druggie . . ." Tim went on to tell me that Jesse's girlfriend was going to jail on drug charges as soon as she had the baby. I couldn't take it all in because I was reeling from the news that Jesse was about to become a father.

When Tim left, I went back in the house, still in shock. Then the anger started spilling out. I wanted to curse Jesse. *He robbed me of the number one thing I've wanted in my life,* I thought. *And now, if I ever fall in love and get married, I won't be able to have a baby. But* he *can go off and get a woman pregnant—and* he *can have a baby. It is so wrong. So horribly unfair.* I was screaming inside.

I ran to the phone and called Chris, one of the two friends with whom I had started Truth Ministries, an outreach to post-abortive women. Chris had been my mentor and helped me work through the pain of my own abortions. I was sobbing by the time she answered the phone, and I began to spill out what had just happened. "How do I deal with this?" I asked her. "I can't deal with it! I hate him all over again. I'm so furious."

"Lori, let it all out," she said. "You have to express the anger. Don't stuff it down inside this time. Don't take it out on anybody else, and don't express it in front of them. But get by yourself—in your closet if you have to—and scream and cry. These are very real emotions you're feeling, and you need to get them out."

Chris did most of the talking because I was crying. "God will help you through this," she said. "And then you have to do something, Lori."

"What?" I asked.

"You have to pray for that baby."

Pray for that baby. Jesse's baby.

I knew Chris was right. But I didn't know if I could do it. My heart was broken in a million pieces. How could I pray for someone else, even an innocent baby, when I was falling apart myself?

A few minutes after I talked to Chris, the phone rang. It was another friend, an intercessor who often prayed for my ministry.

"Lori, are you okay?" she asked.

"No, I'm very upset," I told her.

"I knew something was wrong. I've been up since four this morning praying for you, and I finally decided I had to call because I can't get you off my mind." It was late afternoon now; she had been praying for me for more than twelve hours. Even before I had gotten the news, God had urged her to pray. He had known what was coming, and that thought began to comfort me.

I told my friend what had just happened, and she prayed for me over the phone and said she would keep on praying.

For the next twenty-four hours, I wavered between profound sadness and extreme anger. I spent a lot of time on my knees, or curled up in a ball on the floor, crying and praying. I told God everything that was in my heart—all the sorrow and grief, all the fury and rage.

On Christmas Eve, as we gathered around the tree and opened our gifts, Jesse called. I got a knot in my stomach the minute I heard the phone ring. I took the phone outside because I didn't want the others to overhear the conversation.

"I hear your girlfriend is pregnant," I said evenly.

"That's right, she is." He sounded cocky, and I wanted to kill him for it.

I wanted to scream, "So why didn't you tell her to get an abortion? 'It's me or the baby,' isn't that your usual line?" But I didn't. Instead, I asked, "Do you know if it's a boy or a girl?"

"It's a boy," he said, and he told me the baby's first and middle names. *Oh, great. He even gets a namesake.* He sounded all three names out proudly, and each one was like a knife in my heart. *They've already named the baby. It's really happening.*

If I had not spent so much time in prayer over the last twenty-four hours, I would have lost my temper and let Jesse have it. I wanted to. Oh, how I wanted to tell him exactly what I was thinking and how badly I was hurting. But I didn't. With God's help I managed to remain calm while Jesse proceeded to tell me what an awful person his girlfriend was and how he didn't know what was going to happen to the baby once she went to jail.

"You have to be there for your child," I told him. "That baby will need his father. Be a good dad to him, Jesse."

Over the next year I let the anger out whenever it resurfaced. Chris was an invaluable sounding board; just being able to talk about it with her helped immensely. And God blessed my ministry—I had a deep empathy for women who had been in similar situations, and he directed many of them across my path.

The next Christmas Eve, Jesse called as usual. I asked him about his son, and he told me that for the first five or six months he had taken care of the baby by himself, while his girlfriend was in jail. *You got to take care of your own baby?* I thought. A pang of jealousy swept over me momentarily.

"Does he look like you?" I asked.

"He's beautiful. An incredible kid," Jesse said.

"So, are you still in his life?"

"No, I haven't seen him in a while . . . my girlfriend headed to California not long after she got out of jail, and she took him with her."

"Jesse, that's your son," I said. "You should be in contact with him. If you know where they are, you should call."

I was reliving the hurt all over again, but it was easier to do the right thing this time and encourage him to be a good father to his son. *His son.* Nothing—absolutely nothing—could have wounded me more than Jesse having a child of his own.

That was the last time I ever heard from Jesse. He never called again.

20

GOING STEADY

Friday, July 24, 1998

Kelli and I were stuck in traffic again. "Are the L.A. freeways *always* this bad?" I wondered out loud.

"Yeah, most of the time," Kelli replied.

She had picked me up in Newport Beach that morning, and we were headed back to the Dream Center. I planned on spending the night with Kelli and Amanda again, and then the next day, Saturday, I would return to the San Francisco area, where I was staying with my mom for the summer. To raise funds for my ministry, I would be doing some work for her at Mario Murillo Ministries.

"We're going nowhere fast," I said as the cars in our lane came to a complete stop again. "No way we can make it for Jim's noon Bible study, is there?"

"Doesn't look like it." She glanced over at me. "You're not getting carsick, are you?" She knew that riding in a car sometimes bothered me, and I was beginning to feel queasy.

"A little."

"Here—do something to take your mind off of it." She pointed to an envelope in the front seat. "Jim wanted me to bring this to you. He says it's very important to him."

I opened the manila envelope and pulled out a booklet that was actually a questionnaire, the kind of test you take by blacking out circles on a multiple-choice answer to each question.

"There's a number two pencil inside the envelope," Kelli said. "You have to use that because it's scored on a computer."

The booklet was titled "Temperament Analysis Profile." On the phone the night before, Jim had mentioned to me that he wanted me to take the test—"a snapshot of your soul," he called it. While in prison, Jim had studied to become a licensed temperament counselor through the National Christian Counselors Association, a professional organization that provides academic and clinical training to Christians of all denominations.

"The profile has an accuracy rate of over ninety percent in identifying a person's temperament," Jim had told me. "When a couple asks me to marry them, I won't do it unless they first agree to take the temperament profile. I know it will save them a lot of grief down the road—because you know how the other person will react in a given situation when you understand what makes them tick."

I'd never been trained as a counselor, but from my ministry experience, and from my own personal experience of a failed marriage, I knew that what Jim had said was right. I've always loved taking personality assessments like the temperament profile, so I enjoyed filling out the questionnaire and looked forward to getting the results.

Answering the fifty-plus questions took only ten minutes or so. Getting out of the bumper-to-bumper logjam took two and a half hours. We were too late to attend the Bible study, but Jim was still in the old laundry room talking to a handful of people when we finally arrived.

"Let's go for a walk," he suggested, "so we can be alone."

We walked a few blocks to Echo Park, an old public park that dated back to 1895. A large lagoon dominated one end of the beautiful park, and we crossed over the arched footbridge that spanned it.

"There's Angelus Temple." Jim pointed across the street to a large circular building. "The church Aimee Semple McPherson built." He entertained me with stories of the most popular radio preacher of the 1920s and 1930s, a flamboyant woman who had been through some public problems of her own but who had done a great work for God. "Sister Aimee had a penchant for high drama," he said, "and she once rode a motorcycle through the sanctuary during one of her famous illustrated sermons." We imagined this picturesque locale in its heyday, with crowds of churchgoers, decked out in their Sunday best, spilling out of the temple and sprawling across the park lawns for a picnic lunch.

Stopping in front of one of the large palm trees, Jim looked over his shoulder. "You don't suppose anyone from the Dream Center is around, do you?" He had a mischievous twinkle in his eyes.

I leaned back against the tree. "I don't think so. Why?"

He placed one hand beside my head and braced his arm against the tree. "Because I want to kiss you, Miss Lori Beth Graham," he said as he put his other hand on my waist.

I grinned and tilted my head up for his kiss. "I like that idea, Mr. Jim Bakker." *Falling in love. What a glorious feeling.*

"I feel like a schoolboy kissing my girl on the playground."

"We ought to carve our initials in the tree or something," I said.

"No, with my luck we'd get arrested for defacing public property—and I don't need that on my rap sheet," Jim joked.

We laughed over silly things and strolled hand in hand through the historic park. Over the next few weeks we would come here often, and we started calling it our Love Park. We had no place else to go for privacy. The Dream Center is like a little village, and all eyes were on us. The news had spread like wildfire—everybody knew that Jim Bakker and Lori Graham were an item. I was well known to many people there because of my association with Phoenix First, and Jim was well-known simply because he was Jim Bakker. Everybody knew who he was, and everybody watched him.

So when we wanted to be alone, or when we wanted to escape the bleakness of the ghetto, we would trek the few blocks to Echo Park. We were so in love, we could shut out the rest of the world and easily ignore the panhandlers, alcoholics, and street people occupying the park benches. To us, the park with its lagoon and palm trees was like being on a tropical island, our little corner of paradise. It was not until after we were married that someone pointed out to us just how dangerous the park was: people had been murdered there.

After that first walk in Echo Park, we met up with Jay and Amanda and Kelli, and we all went out to eat at a restaurant the kids liked. As had become our custom, we decided to go to a late movie afterward. There was plenty of time before the movie started, so Jim put Jay in charge of buying tickets while the two of us went off by ourselves for a while.

Jim and I talked as we looked in the windows of the few stores next to the movie theater.

"I wish you weren't leaving tomorrow," he said.

"Me too. I'm going to miss you."

"Not as much as I'm going to miss you."

"Wanna bet?" I laughed and squeezed his hand.

We had come to the end of the row of stores, but instead of turning around to walk back toward the theater, Jim stopped.

"Lori, I want to tell you something," he said. "In my own words." He looked very serious again. Very serious, and very much in love. I felt such tenderness for him already, I realized, as his eyes searched mine.

As we stood there next to the brick wall of the shopping center, Jim began to tell me some very personal things about his life. "It's one thing for you to read about my past in a book. It's another for you to hear it from me in person. And you deserve to be able to look me in the eyes when I say this." He told me all about his relationship with Tammy Faye—not the carefully worded version he had written for *I Was Wrong* but the gut-level version that never saw print. He even verbally took me inside the hotel room where he had the encounter with Jessica Hahn. Looking embarrassed and pained, he laid it all out—all the intimate details of that fateful meeting. "I've now told you more than I've ever told anyone else about what happened that day," he said when he finished.

I reached up and touched his cheek, wishing I could wipe away the shame of the past, wishing I could make it all go away so he wouldn't have to live with it anymore. "That doesn't bother me, Jim. It really doesn't. I understand it was strictly sexual and didn't mean anything. But I appreciate the fact that you wanted to tell me about it—"

"I don't want to ever have any secrets from you," he said.

"The emotional tie with your ex-wife, though, that means something. That's harder for me to deal with."

"The love I once had for her is long gone, Lori. I can't erase her out of my past, but I promise you, that part of my life is over and done with. Completely."

We started walking back to the theater to meet the kids, and Jim spotted a silver shop across the street. "Let's go there," he said. "I want to buy you something."

"No, Jim. You don't have to buy me anything." I knew he didn't have much money to spend. I'd found out that the only source of income for his ministry was from his speaking engagements; he drew a salary from New Covenant, then he turned around and spent most of his paycheck on the kids at the Dream Center.

"But I want to. Please let me." He looked like a lovestruck teenager, and there was no way I could refuse.

We went inside and looked at all the displays. You would have thought we were shopping at Tiffany's the way we pored over the silver bracelets. Finally, we picked out a very inexpensive one with rhinestone chips.

"Now it's official," Jim said as he fastened the bracelet on my wrist. "We're going steady."

21

RECOVERING WHAT
WAS LOST

Going steady. How corny, I thought later that night as I looked
at the silver bracelet dangling on my wrist. And how infinitely
sweet. A lump formed in my throat.

I thought of another Bible verse I had memorized: "I will
restore to you the years that the swarming locust has eaten."[1] God
was doing that in my life, giving back the years I had lost because
of my sin and rebellion. He had done it in several areas already.

Because I married at seventeen, barely graduating from high
school, I never had the opportunity to attend college. Yet when
I was thirty-two years old, I entered Master's Commission and
became a full-time "student of the Word" under Lloyd Zeigler's
tutelage. All the other students were straight out of high school
or in their college years, but somehow I fit in. And for the next
four years God allowed me to have many of the experiences I
would have had in college.

Having made the choice to have five abortions, I lost the opportunity to ever have children. Yet God had blessed me with many spiritual offspring—like "my girls," Kelli, Nicks, Morgan, Nina, and Michelle Murillo. He'd given me an inner-city family—Margie's family—complete with a namesake, Little Lori. Margie had been pregnant with her eighth child when Roy dragged me upstairs to meet her that first time. At the Fashion Share the next month, Margie had accepted Jesus as her Savior and the church had outfitted her with maternity clothes and accessories. Two months later I was in the delivery room when her baby was born.

My mind drifted back to that occasion, December 6, 1990.

The day before, Lloyd had interrupted one of my classes. "Margie's in labor," he said. "She called and asked for you."

I immediately left for the hospital, and I sat with Margie all that day and through the night; she was having a horrible time of it. The next morning, the doctors finally decided to do a C-section. Her previous children had all been delivered vaginally, and Margie had never had any kind of surgery before. She wanted me in the operating room with her.

"Do you think you can handle it?" the doctor asked me.

"I think so," I replied. "I've been through childbirth classes, and I've assisted with several deliveries. I want to do this." I had been present at the births of three children—Nicole (or Nikki Bee as we called her), Bobbi's daughter; my niece Amber, Mark's daughter; and the child of my close friends Christy and John—but I had never done anything like this. I wasn't worried, though, because I had discovered that a calming presence always came over me when a baby was being born, and it seemed quite natural to be in the delivery room helping. Previously I'd held the baby as it came out of the mother's womb. I had cut the umbilical cord. I knew I could do this, even though a C-section would be a lot different.

Margie was scared by this new—and traumatic—experience. Right before they put her out, she motioned to me, and I leaned over the gurney. "Jesus is here with me," Margie said. "He told me to just go ahead and go to sleep because he would stay with me."

"That's right," I told her. "And I'll be here too."

Scrubbed and gowned in hospital greens, I stood by Margie's side and watched the doctor cut open her abdomen. It was extraordinary, looking down and seeing a person inside of another person, and I was overwhelmed as the doctor reached in and brought out a baby girl in his hands. C-section babies are beautiful. Their heads are perfectly shaped because they haven't gone through the trauma of the birth canal. This tiny little girl with a full head of black hair yelped and gulped, filling her lungs for the first time outside her mother's womb. I was awestruck.

The anesthesiologist brought Margie around quickly, and the doctor presented her with a brand-new daughter.

"What do you want to name her?" he asked.

Margie didn't hesitate. "Lori."

"No! You can't do that," I said. We had never even discussed it.

"Yes," she said. "I want to name her Lori. I don't ever want to forget what you've done for me and my family."

Little Lori—or Little Luvins; I was Big Luvins—was seven now, and I'd been there for every milestone in her life—every birthday, every holiday. Maricela, Margie's next oldest girl, had tattled on Lori the last time I'd seen them. "Auntie Lori, Little Luvins says bad words." It was true, unfortunately; my name-sake could already cuss like a sailor.

The first child whose birth I had witnessed, Nikki Bee, was fourteen now. I'd been a second mother to Nikki since before she was born. In fact, she might not have *been* born if it hadn't been for me.

I recalled the day Bobbi told me she was pregnant. It was July 1983, and we were standing outside the house where Jesse and I lived across the street from the park. Talking outside seemed natural; Bobbi and I had done it since we were kids. I used to pull a green stool up to the wooden fence that separated our houses so I could see over into Bobbi's yard. We held many important conversations over that fence. No barrier separated us now, however.

"Are you sure you're pregnant?" I asked her.

"I took a test," she said. "It was positive."

"How far along are you?"

"About seven weeks. I . . . I called a clinic and made an appointment."

"No! Bobbi, please don't."

"Lori, I don't know what to do—"

"Who's the father?"

"One of the students at the technical institute where I work. Look, there's no chance of marrying him. He just graduated and moved away, and besides, he's five years younger than I am."

"Five . . ."

"Yes, he's only eighteen."

"Oh, Bobbi."

"I know, I know. It was a dumb thing to do." She sighed and shook her head, the dark curls falling around her face.

"Do you love him?" I asked gently.

"Not enough to marry him. He's a great guy, and I've known him for about a year. The employees aren't allowed to date the students, so I didn't have much outside contact with him until he graduated. He stayed here the week following graduation, and I went out with him, and—one time, Lori. I slept with him *one time,* and I got pregnant. I'm so embarrassed."

"Bobbi, you can't go through with it. You can't have an abortion." I felt so sorry for her, but I couldn't stand the thought of Bobbi going down the same path I'd been on. I had experienced so much hatred and bitterness toward Jesse, so much pain over the fact that I'd never have children of my own. What if something happened to her too? I couldn't bear it.

"What else can I do?" she said. "I can't raise a baby by myself . . ."

"I'll help you—whatever it takes, I'll do it. Just don't have an abortion. *Please,* Bobbi."

"You promise?" She looked at me questioningly, and I knew she didn't want to destroy this child; she just felt trapped and hopeless, like so many other women.

"Hey, I'm your best friend. Of course I promise." I hugged her tightly.

"Okay," she said over my shoulder. "I won't do it."

I made good on my word. The next week I helped Bobbi apply for financial assistance. Then I signed up to take Lamaze classes with her. It's not uncommon today to have your best friend as your childbirth coach, but in those days it was very unusual. We were the only nontraditional couple in the class. I'm sure the other members of the class thought we were pretty strange, but I didn't care. I was just thrilled that "we" had made the decision to keep the baby.

Bobbi's sister Kathy and I went through the delivery with her. She had terrible back pains during labor and spent most of it on all fours. At one point the nurse suggested taking a hot shower, so I helped Bobbi get out of her hospital gown and into the bathroom, rubbing her back all the time. She was doubled over in pain and holding on to me so hard that she pulled me—fully clothed—into the shower with her. I remember watching my new red velour sweat suit bleed all over the tile.

But I'd forgotten all about that ruined sweat suit by the time I held precious little Nicole in my arms. Her uncle—Kathy's husband, Doug—declared that she was "as sweet as a honeybee," and from that moment she became Nikki Bee.

By far the most momentous birth I ever witnessed took place a year later when my niece Amber was born. She was from my bloodline, and I knew this was the closest I would ever come to having a child of my own. I was separated from Jesse by this time, and it had been five years since my hysterectomy. I still dealt occasionally with residual anger, but I had accepted the fact that I would never have children. And I was not jealous of my friends who had babies—even those friends who had had several abortions and were still able to get pregnant. There was no way to undo what had been done; I couldn't change the past, so I moved beyond it. I rejoiced with every baby that was born, but Amber's birth was truly special.

Mark and his wife, Cathy, included me in Amber's life from the beginning. They had talked it over and knew how important this child would be to me, and they wanted me to play a significant role in her life. They were generous beyond measure in the way they tried to make me a partner in her birth and early upbringing.

We walked down the hospital corridors as a threesome while Cathy was in labor, Mark on one side of her and me on the other. At one point during the delivery I had to step in for Mark as her breathing coach; he was a nervous wreck.

Amber's birth brought so much joy to my whole family. For one thing, she was Mom and Dad's first grandchild. (That pushed Mark to the top of the List for a while, even though he hadn't managed to have a son to carry on the Graham name—something my dad pointed out to him.) For another thing, Amber's birth helped bring healing to my parents for the grandchildren they had lost because of my abortions.

Cathy and Mark always let me see Amber any time I wanted to, but my real bonding time with my little Bugaloo, my pet name for Amber, came when she was three. I injured my back in a car wreck and required physical therapy every week. I wound up being off work for ten months, so I took care of Amber all day long, Monday through Friday. It was an incredible time for me and allowed me to experience at least one aspect of what it would be like to be a mom.

Amber's brown hair had turned blonde, and Mark believed it was an answer to prayer. Since the time he was eighteen, he had known he wanted to have one child, a girl, and he wanted her to have curly blonde hair. Mark wasn't even a Christian at the time, yet he prayed for a blonde-haired daughter. When he got married, however, it was to a woman with a mixed heritage—Spanish, Puerto Rican, and Polish—who had striking black hair. I don't know what the odds are genetically, but my dark-brown-haired brother and his raven-haired wife had a daughter with curly blonde hair!

Mark still laughs about my "big hair" in those days. I wore my blonde hair long and curly and poufy, which was the style. When I'd go out with Amber, I'd curl her hair and make it big like mine. People always thought she was my daughter, and that tickled me, of course. Mark would come to pick up Amber and he'd say, "Have you big-haired blonde girls been out shopping today?"

All these memories were flooding my mind as I got ready for bed that night at the Dream Center. *Your Word says you will restore the years that the locust has eaten. You're still doing that in my life, Lord. Thank you.*

I unfastened the silver bracelet Jim had bought me and laid it carefully on the nightstand. I was as proud of that bracelet as if it had been studded with diamonds instead of rhinestone chips—it was a priceless gift to me because it represented something else the Lord was restoring in my life: the innocence and purity of first love. Through God's grace I was recapturing those emotional feelings, and I wiped away tears.

Going steady. I laughed softly as I thought of Jim happily clasping the bracelet on my arm. Now I understood why he had done it. He hadn't just wanted to buy me a present, he had wanted to put something on me to mark me as his. Like a teenage boy giving his football jacket or class ring to his girl-friend, this fifty-eight-year-old man had just claimed me with a silver bracelet.

I "belonged" to Jim now, and we both belonged to Christ. Years ago we had each made a commitment to remain celibate until such time as we remarried. There was great joy in entering into this relationship now from a position of purity. That was something I not only believed in, I preached about it; I had learned the hard way that God's way is best.

For several years I had been giving the "purity talk" to the girls at our church youth camp, and I always laid it on the line for them. It happened on Thursday morning, 9:00 A.M., every year; they called it the Lori Talk. When parents gave permission for their kids to go to camp, they knew up front that their daughters would hear a plainspoken message from someone who knew firsthand the devastating pain of promiscuity. I didn't want any of those young girls to make the same mistakes I had. I didn't just preach abstinence to them; I presented the beauty of God's plan for marriage and sexuality from Scripture. I used symbols, buy-ing every one of them a cheap silver-tone ring—fifty-cent cake decorations I bought at a craft store—that I presented to them as a reminder to stay pure until their wedding day. Years later some of those girls were still proudly wearing those cheap metal bands.

I also told the girls the story of how I literally went from Barbies to boys . . .

22

FROM BARBIES TO BOYS

I was eight years old when I discovered that my father had girl-friends. Mom was taking night classes at Arizona State University—a gutsy thing to do for a very traditional wife and mother in 1965. On the evenings when Mom went to class, Dad had to deal with the kids—something none of us looked forward to.

Dad rarely interacted with us when we were children; he simply didn't know how and was not inclined to learn. Mom says that with three kids he changed a total of three diapers—on Mother's Day following each of our births. When Dad came home from work, he expected dinner on the table and the kids to be bathed and ready for bed immediately afterward. At the table we weren't allowed to speak unless spoken to. We always walked on eggshells around my dad, and I remember dreading Tuesdays, his day off. But I loved Thursday nights, when he worked late as manager of the shoe department at J.C. Penney. On Thursdays we got to stay up late and watch *Bewitched*.

One night after Dad put us to bed, I heard him talking on the phone. I don't know why, but I got out of bed and tiptoed to the door of my room so I could eavesdrop on his conversation.

"I love you, too, doll face," Dad was saying into the telephone. "And I want to see you soon."

Who is he talking to? I wondered. *Mom's at school.* I listened as Dad continued his sweet talk, and an indefinable fear came over me. I felt something was fundamentally wrong, but I didn't know what.

After a few minutes, I got back in bed, feeling sick. "Daddy, I have a stomachache," I called out. I thought if I were sick, he would quit talking on the phone and come take care of me.

He came and stood in the doorway of my room. "You're okay, Lori. Go back to sleep," he said. Then he turned and walked away.

There was no way I could go to sleep. Not when I could still hear him talking in the next room. I could hear his voice, but I couldn't quite make out what he was saying. *Maybe he's talking to Mom,* I thought. Tiptoeing back to the door, I listened to Dad telling his unseen sweetheart how much he loved her and what he wanted to do when he saw her again.

"Daaaaaddy," I whined. "I don't feel good."

"Lori, you're just fine." He sounded angry that I had interrupted him again. "Your mother is probably on the way home from school by now, and she'll check on you when she gets here. Now, go back to bed."

It's not Mom he's talking to. It's some other woman he loves.

I didn't understand adultery at eight years old, but I knew something was very wrong at our house. Something was wrong at church too. We would ask Dad for candy or gum, and he'd always say he didn't have any. Yet we'd see him give candy to other kids at church—one particular family, anyway. I told myself it was just because she was a single mother with several young children that he paid so much attention to this family. It was much more than that, of course. The woman was one in a series of girlfriends my father had at church.

Dad was a handsome man, about six feet tall and 190 to 200 pounds then. He was very charismatic, and even when he got really heavy in later years, he was still a charmer. He was great with words and loved to talk. And because he understood that women are verbal while men are visual, he knew how to talk to women; they loved it. It wasn't as much of a sexual thing with my dad as it was the thrill of conquest. As adults, my brothers and I learned that about him; but as kids, we didn't know that husbands and fathers were calling our house and saying, "Keep Bob Graham away from my wife (or daughter), or he's dead."

My mom always tried to protect us from knowing about Dad's cheating, and she hid her emotional suffering from us, for the most part. But I have vague memories of Mom lying across the bed, crying, and people from church coming over to comfort her. I knew it had something to do with my dad.

We were in church all the time—Sunday morning, Sunday night, and Wednesday night services—and from all outward appearances, we were the perfect family. When I was born, Mom and Dad had been in charge of the youth ministry at First Nazarene Church. They gave up that activity as their family grew, but they remained active in church. Every Sunday Mom outfitted me in a frilly dress, lace anklets, patent leather shoes, and often a hat and gloves. Mark and Scott wore neatly pressed pants with jackets and bow ties. After Sunday school, our family sat all in a row on the pew, sang all the songs, listened to the sermon, and then we went to Furr's Cafeteria for Sunday dinner. Few people could have guessed what turmoil was occurring daily in our household.

Our church was very legalistic in those days. You didn't dance and you didn't go to movies. Mom let me go see *Bambi* when I was eight years old, and that was a big deal. I really wanted to be a dancer, but I never got to take ballet or tap or jazz. That was on the "can't do" list, according to my church. I always heard, "You *can't* do this, you *can't* do that. You *have* to do this; you'd *better* do that." I thought God must have been watching me from heaven with a checklist, just waiting to see if I would do something wrong. I thought God was controlling, just like my dad. And I thought God's love for me was conditional—just like my dad's. When I was a good girl, Daddy loved me; when I was bad, he didn't.

When we were really bad, we got a beating. Dad would get us in the bedroom alone—he locked Mom out—and beat us with a belt. I didn't get hit all that often; Mark bore the brunt of Dad's rage. Scott escaped, for the most part, because as he got older, Mom finally got the courage to stop Dad. While the whippings were an occasional thing, the verbal abuse was regular. Again, Mark got the biggest share of it. Dad was a man's man, and he was sorely disappointed in his firstborn son, who was shy and withdrawn. Many nights Mark cried himself to sleep as he listened to Mom and Dad arguing about him in the next bedroom.

"You're raising a wimp," Dad would yell.

Mom always came to Mark's defense. "You shouldn't hit him like that!"

"*Somebody* needs to beat some sense into that stupid boy!"

On and on it went.

We were all afraid of Dad, and as kids we rarely invited friends over when he was home.

When I was twelve, Bobbi's older sister Kathy confirmed that my dad was cheating on my mom. Kathy was sixteen and worked part-time in the shoe department with my dad. She heard him talk to his girlfriends on the phone all the time, and they even came into the J.C. Penney store where he worked. I felt nauseated when Kathy told me about it, just as I'd felt that time I was eight and overheard him on the phone.

Up until then, Bobbi and I were still playing with dolls. We weren't lucky enough to have a Barbie Dream House, but we created our own out of cardboard boxes and household items. We turned a folded washcloth into a bed, then folded another washcloth even smaller, and it became a pillow. Mom would let us keep our fully-furnished architectural wonder on the dining room table, and we peopled our pseudo-Dream House with Barbie, Ken, Midge, and Skipper in their different outfits.

When I had concrete proof of my dad's affairs, I seemed to grow up overnight. My father cheated on my mother, was angry with his kids and even abusive—yet he was a good churchgoing man who claimed to be "living for God." *If that's what church is all about,* I thought, *I don't want anything to do with it.* I still went every Sunday—never even thought about telling my parents I wouldn't—but I tuned it out. Church was no longer a positive influence in my life. Instead, I started hanging out with the bad kids at church and hooked up with the troublemakers at school. I put Barbie and Ken away and turned to boys and pot. I desperately wanted to fit in, to be accepted, to be cool. I first smoked pot in the sixth grade, and by the seventh grade, I was using speed; the pot wasn't enough to get me high anymore. I attended make-out parties at friends' homes when their parents were away, and Mark had soon given me the nickname Hot Lips.

A particular incident at home when I was around thirteen prompted me to finally confront Mom about Dad. My parents had turned our garage into a nice office with paneling and carpet.

They had a side business, similar to Amway, selling products for the home, and they used the office for meetings. While Mom was in the office during one of the meetings, Dad and another woman had come downstairs to the family room. I was in my bedroom, and when I walked into the family room, I saw the two of them holding hands. They left as I entered the room, so they didn't see me. But I watched them walk back upstairs, still holding hands, and I was shocked at his boldness. I despised him at that moment for what he was doing to my mom.

"Dad has a girlfriend," I told Mom shortly after that. She didn't say anything at first. "I *know* he does," I added.

"What makes you say that, Lori?"

"Kathy told me he has girlfriends at work. And I saw him holding hands with a lady—right here at our house!"

Mom admitted to me then that she knew about the women. I don't remember what she said about it; I just remember being upset that she knew about it and either hadn't or couldn't do anything about it.

"I hate him!" I told her. "Please make him leave—I don't want him around. He's mean and we're all scared of him."

Mom had stayed with Dad through all of his cheating, and she had endured his verbal abuse for a number of reasons. She was a very committed Christian and she did not take divorce lightly, even though she had biblical grounds for it. Dad wanted to stay in the marriage—he didn't want to stop cheating or change his behavior in any way, but he didn't want to give up his Ozzie-and-Harriet family image either. At the time, Mom thought it was better for the kids to keep the marriage together. But when she finally lost all respect for Dad, when she saw the potential for terrible violence, and when she felt a spiritual release from the marriage, then she asked him to leave.

After my angry confrontation, Mom and I didn't talk about Dad again for a while. Things rocked on as usual.

By age eleven, Mark was beginning to rebel and get in trouble at school. Dad would get angry at Scott or me or Mom, but he would find a reason to turn that anger toward Mark and take it out on him. Mostly Dad verbally abused Mark, but sometimes he would backhand Mark or throw him down the stairs. One time Mark went to school with a handprint across his face. There was no pretending he had tripped and fallen; it was obvious what had happened.

I was too scared of Dad to ever come to Mark's defense, until one day, when I was almost fourteen, I finally snapped. Dad had grabbed Mark by the shirt collar and pinned him against the wall. I knew he was about to punch Mark, and I simply exploded. Before I knew it, I was flying across the room. I hurled myself at Dad, jumping on his back and locking my arms around his neck. I was crying hysterically. "Leave him alone! Leave him alone!" I screamed over and over.

Mom tried to pull me off Dad and also tried to separate Dad and Mark. It was a nightmare come to life. I'm not sure exactly how it stopped. Perhaps it brought Dad to his senses when he realized that his little girl had actually come after him physically to stop him from beating her younger brother again.

I spent as much time as I could away from the house. I continued experimenting with drugs, trying LSD for the first time. The summer after eighth grade, I experimented with something else for the first time: sex.

Phoenix summers are hot, and you don't spend much time outdoors unless it's to swim. We didn't have a pool, but I went to a lot of swim parties at friends' houses. One weekend we had a huge party at someone's house, and we did a lot of drinking. I never did handle alcohol well, and I remember getting really drunk the night I lost my virginity. I don't remember the actual event, but I knew it had happened when I woke up crying and another guy was sitting next to me, comforting me. The recipient of my virtue was a really cute guy whose specialty was bedding every girl he could; I was simply one in a long string of conquests, and I'm sure he'd forgotten it by the next day.

My heart became even harder after that. I was smoking pot daily, doing LSD or drinking on the weekends. Mom and Dad were arguing more, and I tried to stay away from it. One argument I couldn't ignore, however. They were in the office area of the house having a huge fight. The yelling scared me, and I ran to see what was happening. When I got there, I saw that my dad was about to hit my mom. He had never struck her before, and I was both frightened and angry.

Anger beat out fear, and I stepped in between them. "If you even *think* about touching her," I said, "you'll have to hit me first." I was a little fourteen-year-old runt who wouldn't have stood a chance against my dad, but he backed down. "Get out of our lives," I screamed at him. "We hate you!"

Not long after that, he was gone. After nineteen years, Mom finally sent him packing and divorced him; he never did want to leave the marriage, but she just couldn't take it anymore.

I wanted him gone because I hated what he was doing to my mom. Yet I didn't want him to be gone because he was my dad. He would later tell me, "I always took care of you and provided for my family." But the house and the clothes and the things were not what I wanted. What I wanted was the one thing he couldn't give me: his unconditional love. I never once felt that I could crawl up on his lap uninvited. I just wanted him to love on me, just wanted him to say he was proud of me.

23

"I'll Call You Tonight"

Saturday, July 25, 1998

Jim and I spent Saturday morning in Echo Park, walking, talking, hugging, kissing—anything but saying good-bye. That afternoon I would be on a plane flying north to Danville, California, to stay with my mom. We were both subdued and sad because we would soon be apart.

"I can't stand not knowing when I'll see you again," Jim finally said.

"Me either. You have the number at my mom's house?"

"Yes. I wrote it down in big numbers and put it where I can't miss it. I'll call you tonight, as soon as I get back."

We stopped and sat on one of the park benches overlooking the lagoon and its magnificent display of lotuses. Their broad, bowl-shaped leaves turned upward, and their tall stems rose dramatically above the water to open into large, fragrant pink blossoms. The bed of lotuses—the largest stand of lotuses outside of

Asia—was an odd but beautiful contrast to the palm trees and willows that banked the lake. No one is sure of their origin, but the story is that evangelical Chinese missionaries planted the lotuses in the 1920s.

"It's already noon," Jim said as he looked at his watch. "I have to get back soon. John and Joyce Caruso are taking me to look at some property. I think you met them at my Bible study the other day."

"The name doesn't ring a bell. Describe them for me."

"John is very distinguished-looking. Gray hair, mustache, glasses. Joyce is very attractive. Frosted hair, beautiful smile. Well dressed, but not flashy—they're wealthy yet fit right in with the inner-city crowd. John and Joyce are regulars at the noon Bible study."

I shook my head. "No, I didn't meet them."

"You'll love them. I met the Carusos when I first came to the Dream Center. I preached one night on the dangers of materialism, and I said that I knew very few happy millionaires. John came up and introduced himself afterward. 'Jim, meet a happy millionaire,' he said, his face beaming."

Jim said that when John and Joyce first got married, they had learned about tithing in their Sunday school class and started putting the lesson into practice. They saved some money and started their own business, manufacturing aluminum garage doors. "Over the years, they've been faithful to the Lord," Jim said, "and he has blessed them financially. Now they have a gorgeous home in the hills, overlooking the city of Burbank. But they stay connected to God's work, and they give a lot of their time as well as their money. They're always doing something at the Dream Center."

"What kind of property are you going to see?"

"Some land up in the mountains a couple of hours from

here. John and I have been talking about starting a ranch as a place we can minister to some of the kids from the inner city. We've got to get them out of the ghetto, or they'll never make it. In discipleship programs you eventually lose 95 percent of the students—the gangs won't let go of them, and they get pulled back into the world of drugs and violence. If we had a place where we could physically remove them from the gang influence, a place where we could help them detox . . ."

Jim was animated for a few minutes as he spoke about his dream of getting kids out of the ghetto so he could make a real difference in their lives. It was a dream I shared. It had broken my heart to learn recently that Margie's son Roy—sweet little Roy, whose foot I had traced for his first pair of real shoes—had gotten in trouble and wound up in jail. I had always wished I had some way to get Margie and her family out of the projects and into a better environment.

We let the silence deepen as we sat there, not wanting to leave this quiet spot where we had shared a few romantic moments together. Jim and I knew we were headed for marriage, even though we had left those thoughts unspoken, and it hurt not knowing when we would see each other again.

When we got back to the Dream Center, the Carusos were parked in front of Casa Grande, with the car doors open, waiting for Jim. He introduced me to them, and we talked for a few minutes. I liked them immediately and thought Joyce was even more beautiful than Jim had said.

Jim hugged me good-bye and whispered in my ear, "I'll miss you, Lori Beth." Then he kissed me quickly and got in the car. "I'll call you tonight," he repeated as John started the engine.

I listened to the dull thud of the car doors shutting and waved as I watched them drive away. *He's gone!* I thought sadly.

∞

I felt forlorn as I boarded the plane for my flight to Danville. The lyrics of an old song, Peter, Paul, and Mary's "Leaving on a Jet Plane," kept running through my head. As I stared out the window at the tarmac I sang silently, "Don't know when I'll be back again—oh, babe, I hate to go."[1]

Mom was glad to see me when I arrived, and we talked a blue streak about my visit to L.A. We puttered around the kitchen preparing a meal while I told her all the details about my new relationship. I showed her my "going steady" bracelet and made her laugh about Jim dancing with a saxophone-playing Lucille Ball impersonator. Mom was so happy for me.

After dinner, I unpacked while I waited for Jim to call.

I waited. And I waited.

At eleven o'clock I started to worry. *What if they had an accident up in the mountains?* I thought as I roamed around my bedroom restlessly. Jim hadn't said what time he'd call, but surely they were back from their property inspection by now. They weren't going that far—a couple of hours away, Jim said—and not even the notorious L.A. traffic could be *that* bad.

At midnight I started to get mad, and my thoughts began to get out of hand. *This is a sign,* I told myself. *A bad sign. He said he would call and he didn't. Jim Bakker is a typical jerk—everything I thought he wasn't. I thought this was a serious relationship, but he doesn't even have the common courtesy to call me when he said he would.* Jim had not actually proposed, but we had talked about marriage, and I had opened my heart to him. Now, the longer the phone went without ringing, the more I convinced myself that Jim was an idiot.

Either that or he was dead. I went back to worrying for a while.

At 1:00 A.M. I couldn't stand it anymore. I broke down and dialed Jim's number at the Dream Center. No answer. I was furious and began to rant internally again. *The man is not even home! I leave town and he stays out all night!*

I finally turned out the light but couldn't go to sleep. I tossed and turned and punched my pillow in frustration as I tried to get comfortable. Memories of long ago traveled from my subconscious mind into my consciousness, and I began to think of all the times Jesse didn't call, all the times he stayed out all night.

I was eighteen years old, married just a little more than a year, and I knew my husband was cheating on me. He often went to bars without me because I wasn't of legal drinking age yet. In the wee hours of the morning he would come staggering home or sometimes not come home at all, and I would have a gut feeling he was with another woman. Usually I couldn't fall asleep when Jesse was out. I would stay up stewing over his neglect and infidelity. One particular night I did go to sleep, but I woke up suddenly at 3:00 A.M. I sat straight up in bed. Jesse wasn't next to me, and I knew he wouldn't be anywhere in the apartment.

For some reason, I felt I had to find him. Even though I had absolutely no idea where he could be, I threw on my clothes and got in the car. I believe what happened next was supernatural, although I'm not sure if it was from God or not. When I got behind the wheel, I somehow knew where to drive. A few miles from our apartment, I pulled up to an empty, cleared-out lot. I didn't recognize the place and didn't recall ever passing it before; I wasn't even sure what neighborhood I had reached.

In the beam of my headlights I could see a green Volkswagen parked in the middle of the field. I didn't recognize the car. I could see movement. There were people inside that car, and I immediately knew my husband was one of them. My empty stomach burned and a wave of nausea rose up in my throat, but I stifled the queasiness and got out.

I walked over to the Volkswagen, and even in the dim light there was no mistaking who was in it—my husband and some woman. They were both completely nude. It was one thing to know Jesse was cheating on me; it was another to catch him in the act, to witness the man I had completely given my heart to flagrantly betraying me in this way. For a moment I thought I would vomit.

I yanked open the car door. Jesse was so drunk, he fell out on the ground. I helped him up, saying, "If you know what's good for you, you'll get in the car." I didn't hold back. I cursed and screamed at him and then I turned on the woman.

"I didn't know he was married." She was blubbering and scrambling for her clothes. "Honest, I didn't know. He came into the club where I was dancing . . ."

I called her every vulgar name I could think of as I grabbed Jesse's clothes out of her car. I shoved his pants and shirt at him and he reeled backward, nearly falling again. "Let's go home!" I yelled at him and then half dragged, half pushed him toward my car.

He was stumbling and saying drunkenly, "I'm sorry, baby. I shouldn't have done that."

Holding the door open, I pushed Jesse into the passenger seat, then ran around to the driver's side. I couldn't get out of there fast enough. But when I got inside the car, I leaned my head on the steering wheel for a moment, overcome. *He smells like sex. My drunken sot of a husband smells like sex.* I wiped away tears with the back of my hand and then started the engine. Jesse mumbled for a minute before passing out.

I managed to get him inside the apartment and put him to bed. A few hours later he got up and went to work, apologizing as he left. "Baby, I'll never do anything like that again. I swear."

That day I moved out—took every stick of furniture, the pots, pans, everything. It wasn't a lot, but it was all we had. I moved my stuff to the apartment next door; the girl who lived there worked at the same restaurant in Sun City that I did. All I left Jesse were his clothes, piled up in a corner.

When he got home that evening, he was frantic. He called me at work and begged me to come back . . . and I did.

In the ten years we were married, Jesse and I probably lived together just a little more than seven years. We were separated a lot—a month here and a month there. One time we were separated for ten months. Jesse would go on a drug binge and leave for days, weeks, sometimes months at a time. He wouldn't come home and he wouldn't call. That was his pattern. Sometimes I would get fed up and leave Jesse, but I always came back. That was my pattern—or it was until the relationship finally unraveled and there was nothing left to patch together.

I had a hard time going to sleep that first night back at my mom's house as the anger of past hurts rose up to haunt me. Rationally, I knew Jim was not a drunk or a womanizer like my ex-husband; there was no comparison. But Jim had promised to call and he didn't keep his promise. I had lived too many years with a man who lied to me and couldn't keep his word, and I had vowed I would never live that way again. I started closing my heart.

24

"WILL YOU MARRY ME?"

Sunday, July 26, 1998

The ringing of the telephone roused me from sleep. I opened one eye enough to look at the alarm and groaned when I saw that it was almost time to get up and get ready for church. I had slept only a few hours.

Mom stuck her head in the door of my bedroom. "That was Carol Ann Murillo on the phone," she said.

"Did you tell her I'd be there this morning?" I asked. I had planned on meeting Carol Ann—the mother of Michelle Murillo, one of my girls—at church and then going out to lunch with her.

"Yes, but that wasn't why she called." Mom laughed. "Carol Ann said she had a strange phone call from Pam Miller in Tustin this morning. Pam said that Kelli had called home wanting my phone number because Jim Bakker was looking for you. And then Carol Ann wanted to know, of course, why Jim Bakker was trying to track you down."

"What did you tell her?"

"Not much, but I said it was okay to give him the phone number here."

"I can't believe it! I made sure he had the number before I left," I complained. I was aggravated and yet comforted to know Jim hadn't completely forgotten about me. "Besides, Kelli has the phone number here. Why didn't she just give it to him?"

"You know Kelli. She probably couldn't find it."

"So when Jim called her, she called her mom, who called Michelle's mom, who lives nearby . . ." *Typical Kelli,* I thought fondly. *I really am gonna kill her one of these days.* I yawned and raked my fingers through my hair. It was too early in the morning for mental gymnastics like reconstructing the circuitous route the phone message had taken.

In a few minutes the phone rang again and it was Jim. "Lori, I'm so sorry," he said. "I've been trying since last night to get hold of you, and I just now got your number. I had to jump through hoops to get it."

"What happened?" I asked. "I was worried." The apologetic tone in his voice appeased me, and he sounded suitably repentant, but I wasn't going to let him off the hook too easily.

"We didn't go back to the Dream Center last night. The property we looked at was up in the mountains near Big Bear Lake, where John and Joyce have a condo. It was getting late, so we decided to spend the night and drive back this morning. I wanted to call you, but I had left your phone number back in my room—on the nightstand, propped up against the telephone where I couldn't misplace it. I called and called, trying to find someone who knew how to get in touch with you at your mom's, but I couldn't reach Kelli and Amanda. Jamie didn't answer his phone either—I called until two this morning. I was frantic. I finally got hold of Kelli a few minutes ago."

My heart started softening as Jim explained. He really had tried desperately to call me. He wasn't a jerk after all.

We laughed about both of us wanting to kill Kelli and Jay. I had also tried calling Jim's son at one point the night before. "I called your house at 1:00 A.M.," I confessed, "and I was furious to think you were staying out all night as soon as I left town." This time I was smiling when I thought about it. He apologized all over again, and I rejoiced just to hear his voice.

"Not being able to find you proved one thing to me," he finally said. "I can't live without you, and I'm not ever leaving you again." He paused, and neither one of us said anything for a long, comfortable moment. Then he asked me a question—a short, sweet question I'd been waiting for more than a decade to hear. "Lori, will you marry me?"

I didn't hesitate. "Yes," I answered. I knew it was what I wanted, what I had prayed about for so long. Jim was God's choice for me.

"Will you marry me soon? Right away?" he asked. "I'm going overseas in September, and I'll be gone for two months. Lori, I love you too much, need you with me too much, to ever make it that long without you. If we got married, you could go with me."

"I don't want to be alone for that long either, Jim." This was right, and I knew it. I also knew we would catch a lot of criticism for getting married so soon after we met, but Jim and I weren't going to shack up like so many couples do. If he'd been the kind to want me to move in with him, I wouldn't have fallen in love with him in the first place. Jim was the marrying kind, and I was ready to trade my silver bracelet in for a wedding ring.

"You know, we've only been going steady for two days," I joked.

"When you're our age, that's long enough," Jim replied with a laugh. "Besides, I've known you for ten whole days now, Lori. Ten glorious days."

Mom and I went to church and then out to lunch with Carol Ann Murillo and another good friend, Sandy Reeza. They were buzzing about the call from Jim, and I had to tell them the whole story—in vivid detail, of course. As we talked, we realized that Carol Ann and Sandy had been sitting directly behind Mom and me the first time I'd ever seen Jim—at the Pastors' School in 1995 when Jay gave his testimony and Jim spoke briefly. In an odd coincidence, they were now the first people I told that I was going to marry Jim Bakker.

"This *is* moving fast," Carol Ann said, "but it's right for you, Lori."

"I agree. However," Sandy added, "if Jim does anything to hurt you, we'll kill him."

I passed along that message when I talked to Jim again that afternoon and evening. We spent a lot of time on the phone, making plans, discussing possible dates for the wedding, and deciding whom to tell and when. Once we had told our families, we planned to tell the people to whom we had made ourselves accountable, those who exercised a measure of spiritual oversight in our lives. Word of our engagement would be a hot topic on the Christian grapevine, and we didn't want those closest to us to hear the news from anyone else.

We started phoning on Monday morning. The number one person on my list was Lloyd Zeigler. He had been my mentor

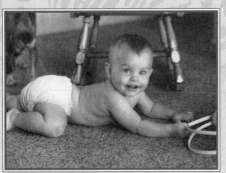

My baby picture

As a toddler, I was always
loving a baby doll.

My kindergarten picture

My senior portrait, 1975

The "picture-perfect" Graham family: my dad, Scott, my mom, me, and Mark in 1969

With my brothers, Scott and Mark,
when I was in my mid-twenties

The drug years

LaRae Silga

With my girls—front row: Jennifer Nicks Jones, Jennifer Morgan,
Michelle Murillo; back row: Nina Atuatasi Poole, Kelli Miller

Our visit with Jim's mom, Furnia (92 years old), after our engagement and just before her death in 1998

The place where Jim and I first met at the Dream Center

My "adopted" daughters: Amber, my niece, and Nicole (Nikki "Bee"), my best friend Bobbi's daughter

With pastor Tommy Barnett, members of the New Covenant staff, and others at the Dream Center—front row: Pastor Barnett, Jim, me, Irene Sanchez, Pastor Matthew Barnett; middle row: Shirley Fulbright, Armando Saavedra, Aaron Jayne, B.J. Brown (our godson), a wife of one of the pastors at LAIC; back row: Connie Elling, Harvey Martin, two other Dream Center friends, Leanne and Howard Bailey.

Reverend Lloyd Zeigler presenting the treasure chest,
which contained the black boots and glass slippers

Dr. R.T. Kendall pronouncing us man and wife

Gary Nicks

The Father/Daughter dance

Gary Nicks

Pastor Tommy Barnett with our friends Joyce and John Caruso

Gary Nicks

My matron of honor, my mom, Char Graham,
and my best friend, Bobbi Zimmerman

Gary Nicks

My prince charming on September 4, 1998

Our wedding party: Jim's two grandsons, James and Jonathan; Kelli Miller; Jay; my mom; Jennifer Nicks; and Michelle Murrillo

The first week of married life: at
Westminster Chapel, London, with
Dr. R. T. Kendall

The second week of married life:
Aussies in Australia

Our room at the Dream Center

With Margie and all the kids of my adopted family, Christmas 1998

Adopt-a-Block with
Pastor Matthew Barnett

Ministering at the Dream Center

Feeding hungry children in the inner city in Nashville, Tennessee
—in the pouring rain

With Tammy Sue's sons,
James and Jonathan Chapman

With my namesake "Little Lori"

With Mom and Tammy Sue at Jay and Amanda's wedding

With Ruth Graham and her daughter, Gigi, at Ruth's 80th birthday party

With Jane and Franklin Graham

With Larry King on *Larry King Live*

With Katie Couric on the *Today Show*

My mentors: Faithe Tines, Marge Simpson, and JoAnn Denman

Three generations—my grandma,
Lucille Thomas; my mom, Char Graham; and me

My family, Christmas 1999
My brother Scott Graham; his daughter, Katherine; his wife, Cindy; his son,
Thomas; my mom; my sister-in-law Charlene; my nieces, Mickela and Chelisa
Trinidad; and my brother Mark Graham

since I had first joined Master's Commission in 1990, and I had turned to him time after time for counsel and friendship. Lloyd had seen me through some rough times in my ministry, and I would never have made it if he hadn't stuck beside me. I've talked to many Master's Commission students over the years, and we all agree that Lloyd is more like Jesus than any other man we've ever known. We never tell him that outright because we don't want to sound fawning. But we hold that opinion of Lloyd because of his incredible compassion and courage. He's the kind of pastor who will roll up his sleeves and work alongside the flock, who will rejoice with you over every victory, weep with you over every heartbreak, and support you through every trial.

I'll never forget a particular moment one Sunday morning in 1994. I had just been through a tremendous weekend of healing, finally coming to terms with my five abortions and the loss of my children. The two friends with whom I had started Truth Ministries, Chris Harper and Jolene Dreisbach, had held a memorial service for my children, and one of the things they did for me was to print out five certificates—similar to birth certificates—with a place to write the name of each child I had aborted. That weekend I had given my children names and overtly mourned their loss. I came out of the experience a radically changed person, and it showed on my countenance. I looked so different, in fact, that the following morning in church several people asked what had happened to me. It was too personal an experience, and too fresh at the time, to share with them.

When I saw Lloyd in the hall after the service, however, I told him about it briefly. Then I pulled the certificates out of my Bible and handed them to Lloyd. He started reading the names aloud.

"'Adam' . . . the first man," he said.

"Yes, he would have been my firstborn."

He tried to blink away the tears welling up in his eyes. "'Sarah' . . . princess . . . precious Sarah," he whispered.

I watched in amazement as the children I had aborted became real to Lloyd. Looking at these simple printed sheets of paper seemed to bring them to life, to give them significance not just to me but to someone else.

"'Joseph' . . . a strong name." He was weeping openly now as he continued to read and comment on the names. "'Paul' . . . great man of God . . . and 'Hannah' . . . baby girl Hannah."

Lloyd handed the certificates back to me, too choked up to say anything for a moment. "Thank you for sharing this with me, Lori. I can't wait to meet them in heaven someday," he said.

"Don't worry," I said brightly, "I'll introduce you." I was weeping, too, yet bubbling over with joy. It meant the world to me that Lloyd not only took a few minutes to listen to me but that he cared enough to cry with me for my unborn children.

When I reached Lloyd on his cell phone that Monday morning, he and his wife, Chris, were driving to Springfield, Missouri. "Lloyd, I have something to tell you," I said, "and it's good news."

He turned to Chris and told her I was on the phone with good news. "She's getting married!" Chris guessed out loud.

"Chris is right," I said. I could hear her screaming in the background.

They passed the phone back and forth so I could talk to both of them. "I'm not coming back to Master's," I told Lloyd, "but I'll always be a part of your ministry. I'm a product of your discipleship."

"If I have to lose you," Lloyd said, "at least it's to a good man like Jim Bakker. I feel like I know his heart after reading his book.

And I have to respect a man who can put *I Was Wrong* on the cover of his autobiography. That says a lot about his character."

"We haven't set a date yet," I told him. "But it will be very soon, and we want you to be a part of the wedding."

"Of course I will." He paused for a second. "I remember something I told you years ago, when you first asked me to pray for God to send you a husband. I said it would happen very fast because you would both recognize each other immediately and you would know it was God's will. I knew even then there wouldn't be a long engagement."

"Well, Jim recognized *me* immediately—he says it was love at first sight—but it took me about twenty-four hours to realize God was up to something." I laughed and began to tell Lloyd and Chris the story of meeting Jim and falling in love.

The first person on Jim's list to call was Tommy Barnett, who was not only on the board of directors of Jim's ministry but also a close personal friend—like a father to Jim, actually, although they are close to the same age. He had taken Jim into the Dream Center, giving him a place to live and minister, when Jim feared no one in the Christian world would have anything to do with him. Tommy Barnett was also my pastor, and Jim knew he would be protective of me. Tommy's approval was so critical to Jim that he began to panic that someone else would tell Tommy before he could.

Jim called around and finally learned that Pastor Barnett was having lunch at a Mexican restaurant not far from the Dream Center. Jim knew the place so he drove there, went inside, and interrupted his good friend's meal.

"Tommy, I really need to talk to you privately," Jim said, his face somber and his soft-spoken voice urgent.

"Sure, Jim," Tommy said in his gracious way. "Let's go outside." Pastor Barnett excused himself from his guests and walked with Jim to the street corner in front of the small restaurant in the ghetto.

With the noise of blaring radios and honking cars behind him, Jim took a deep breath and said, "Tommy, I'm engaged to Lori Graham. I've asked her to marry me."

Tommy Barnett never even paused to think about it. "That's great, Jim." His face lit up and he sounded excited. "Lori's a wonderful girl, and I'm so happy for you."

"I'm so much in love—I feel eighteen again," Jim told him, and they both laughed, looking like a couple of teenage guys standing on the street corner swapping stories about their girlfriends rather than two well-known preachers. Jim related a sixty-second version of the story it had taken me over an hour to tell Carol Ann and Sandy.

"You have my blessing, friend." Tommy's voice was choked with emotion as he clasped Jim on the shoulder. "You deserve to be happy—both of you."

Jim was so relieved to have this pastoral blessing. The two of them rushed back inside the restaurant to share the good news with Matthew Barnett and the others from the Dream Center.

About the same time Jim was interrupting Tommy Barnett's lunch in L.A., I was phoning Marja Barnett in Phoenix. I thanked her for inviting me to speak at the Dream Center and told her about the unforeseen consequences my trip to L.A. had occasioned. She was very happy for me and pleased that I had called her personally with the news.

When I talked to Jim that night, he told me about his visit

with Tommy Barnett, and he also told me about an important phone call he had made to his mother.

"She's ninety-two," he told me, "and she's failing. I wasn't even sure how much she was comprehending of our conversation. It's hard to tell over the telephone sometimes. Anyway, I told her all about you, and she only had one question."

"What was that?"

"She wanted to know if you were a singer. I told her no, and she said, 'Good.'"

I wondered what she had meant by that. Perhaps it was just something an elderly person might blurt out. "Will your mom be able to come to the wedding, Jim, or is she too sick?"

"No, she can't travel," he said. "But I want to take you to meet her before the wedding. And I want you to meet Tammy Sue."

"I want to meet her as soon as possible." Jim's daughter was the one person whose reaction concerned me the most. I didn't know how she would receive the news—not just that her father was remarrying, but that he was marrying someone younger and that we were getting married so soon after we'd met—and I wanted very much to have a good relationship with her. "Have you told her, Jim?"

"Not yet. That's something I've got to do right away. Next to you, Sue is the most important woman in my life."

"How do you think she'll take it? I mean, Jay has seen us together, so it won't come as that big of a shock to him. And he's known me for several years, so we already have a basis for a relationship. But your daughter . . ."

"She'll love you, Lori. Don't worry about it."

In spite of his reassurance, I *was* worried about it—very, very much.

25

POSTENGAGEMENT STRESS SYNDROME

Jim called several times a day, and every time we talked, we would think of someone else we needed to tell. As word of our engagement spread, the telephone traffic increased. I'd end one call and the phone would immediately ring again. I went through the story again and again of meeting Jim and getting engaged.

I soon began to be overwhelmed. I had been exhausted from a grueling year before I ever went to L.A., then there had been the intense adrenaline rush of that ten-day period leading up to Jim's proposal—and now I had a wedding to plan. It was all too much; my body just wanted to shut down and sleep, but somehow I kept on going.

We set the wedding for Friday, September 4, because Jim was scheduled to leave the following Monday for England. Instead of a honeymoon, we would set out on our first ministry trip together just three days after we got married. Just thinking about it made me tired.

In discussing the plans with Jim and my mom, I said I preferred a small, private wedding with only immediate family present. But while I'd had a church wedding before, Jim hadn't, and he really wanted one. Mom wanted a church wedding too. "Think about the special people who love you," she said. "You should have a small church wedding with family and a few intimate friends."

"There's the problem," I said. "Where do I draw the line on those 'few intimate friends'?" I couldn't begin to count the number of friends and ministry associates who would want to be included. I wasn't a celebrity by any means, but I did have a wide circle of friends within my church and Master's Commission. And Jim—well, everybody in the world knew Jim Bakker. I could see the guest list easily getting out of hand and I began to have nightmares of having to hold the wedding in Dodger Stadium to accommodate the crowd.

I not only did not want the stress of planning a big wedding, I didn't want the expense. Having been in full-time ministry for nine years, I had no regular income and no savings tucked away for something like this. The reason for being in Danville with my mom for the summer was to earn enough income to see me through the next few months of ministry—and I was having a very difficult time trying to stay focused on work with all the hubbub surrounding my engagement. Whenever I thought of a church wedding, a wedding dress, a wedding cake, a reception, flowers, music . . . it was just too much.

Jim did not have the financial resources for a big wedding either. He had made it clear early on that he had almost no assets and his only source of income was from his speaking engagements. "I've got a negative net worth," he told me. "I don't even get any royalties from my books." When he was in prison, faced with huge tax bills from the demise of PTL and all the legal expenses of a trial, he had signed away his rights to any future royalties. "I didn't think I'd ever get out of prison, let alone write any books. So the IRS and the lawyers still own me," he said.

We went back and forth on the wedding plans. I naturally thought about having the wedding in Phoenix because it had always been my home. Yet I didn't want to have the wedding there because I knew it would turn into a huge wedding if I had it at Phoenix First, and I couldn't handle that—not with barely a month to pull it off. We thought about having the wedding at the Dream Center because we wanted our inner-city friends to be able to attend, but there again we were afraid it would turn into a big, unmanageable affair.

No wonder people elope, I told myself. I threw up my hands in frustration one day, completely unable to make any decisions. And then God began to work, prompting other people to get involved in what turned out to be a storybook wedding—a wedding that I watched come together from the sidelines.

First, John and Joyce Caruso said we could have the wedding at their home. "You know," Jim said, "I was at their condo in Big Bear when I proposed to you over the telephone. They were so happy for me. And when I talked to them again and told them how quickly we were trying to put together the wedding, they immediately said, 'What can we do to help?' Before I knew it, they'd offered to let us get married at their home. It will be perfect for a wedding, Lori. They have a beautiful gazebo in the backyard, with a spectacular view of the valley. It will be very romantic."

Okay, I thought. *Scratch one item off the list. We have a place to hold the wedding.*

Before I had a chance to think about it, another item was

scratched off the list: a wedding dress. That first week after Jim proposed, I was still working—or trying to work—at Mario Murillo Ministries. One day Mario's wife, Rose, showed up at the office with her wedding dress. "Lori, I want you to try this on," she said. "I think it will fit, and I'd be very happy for you to wear it for your wedding." I was thrilled that Rose had so generously offered it, and amazed that the dress fit perfectly. I could never have afforded such a beautiful wedding gown.

While I did not want the hassle of planning a big wedding, I had no hesitation about marrying Jim. My decision, while sudden, had been confirmed by virtually everyone I talked to. My mom, my dad, my brothers, my pastors, my closest friends—all of them supported me, with one exception.

Faithe Tines was one of the Phoenix First ladies who had mentored me when I first became a Christian; the Monday night ladies' Bible study she had held in her home was very influential in shaping my ministry. Faithe had remained a dear friend over the years, and I called her in Charlotte, North Carolina, where she had moved, expecting her to be excited for me. She wasn't. "Lori, you can't possibly know this man well enough to marry him. It's too soon," she told me. "I've watched the Bakkers for years. Jim's a wonderful guy, but you're rushing into this. You have no idea how intensely the media focus on this family. You need to slow down."

Her negative reaction did not sway my opinion. Instead, I asked Faithe to come out and help direct the wedding, which she did.

The only negative reaction Jim got was from his ex-wife. When he first called his daughter, Tammy Sue—who was visiting her mom in Palm Springs at the time—to tell her the news, Sue didn't quite know how to take it. She and Jim had been very close the last few years. Sue had shown loyal support to her father while he was in prison, writing him often, bringing the grandkids to visit whenever she could. Like Jay, she felt she had gotten her father back in more ways than one when he was released, and for some reason, she told me later, she had thought her father would not get remarried. Perhaps it was simply too much for her to think about. She'd been through her mother's remarriage in 1993 and all the publicity that generated. Every time one of the Bakkers did something "newsworthy," the press regurgitated the entire PTL story and the pain and upheaval of Tammy Sue's life were revisited. Her mother-in-law, with whom Sue was very close, had also recently remarried; she had known the man only a short time. Now, within a matter of days, Sue had learned from Shirley Fulbright—Jim's executive assistant for more than twenty years, who had moved to L.A. to live and work at the Dream Center and who was like a second mom to Sue—that her father was seeing someone. Jay had called and told her all about our visit to the planetarium, then Jim sent her one of my ministry brochures with my picture and bio and started telling her all about me. And then—boom—he calls and says he's getting married. It was too much for Sue to take all at once, and Jim knew she simply needed some time to adjust to the news.

So he waited a day or two and then called back a second time to talk to Tammy Sue in Palm Springs. This time he could hear Tammy Faye in the background, and he could tell that the questions Sue was asking him over the phone were being dictated by her mother, who sounded angry. Finally, Tammy Faye got on the phone with Jim.

She started right in on him. "You haven't known her long

enough," she said in a stern voice. "I'm telling you, Jim Bakker, she'd better not be some young thing under forty."

"Oh, she's definitely over forty," he replied.

"Maybe she's just after your money."

Jim laughed out loud, since he'd already told me he was not only broke but also in debt. The last person he had ever expected to lecture him about getting remarried was his ex-wife.

As tactfully as possible, he got Tammy Faye off the phone and resumed the conversation with his daughter. "I'm sorry you got caught in the middle of this," he said to Sue. "I didn't want that."

Sue agreed to bring her two boys to L.A. the next week so Jim could take them to Disneyland. While the kids enjoyed the rides, Jim and Sue would be able to visit and talk freely.

When Jim told me about the phone call later, he made me laugh about telling his ex-wife that I was definitely over forty. It wasn't a lie, but he didn't feel he had to explain to her that I was *exactly* forty. (I didn't turn forty-one until five days before our wedding.)

By the end of that first week at my mom's house, Jim and I had agreed that I should return to L.A. We couldn't stand not being together, and I wasn't able to concentrate on working anyway. Kelli and Amanda said I could stay with them as long as I wanted to, so I booked a flight.

The day before my trip to L.A., Sue brought her two sons, James and Jonathan, over from Palm Springs to see Jim, and the four of them spent the day at Disneyland. Sue agreed to stay another day so she could meet me, and I was very excited.

As I boarded my plane, however, I was unaware of the drama being played out at Casa Grande. Tammy Faye had been in town taping a television special, and she decided to show up at the Dream Center to meet me. Tammy Sue and the boys were visiting with Jim in his room when Tammy Faye arrived in Jay's room next door. (While there was a general rule against women visiting the men's rooms in Casa Grande, immediate family were allowed access.) In a few minutes, Tammy Faye came through the adjoining bathroom and breezed into Jim's room uninvited. He was so startled, he was speechless for a minute.

As if she'd known where to find it, her eyes went right to my picture on Jim's dresser. "Is this Lori?" she asked Jim as she picked up the framed photo.

"Yes . . . it is," he said. He had no idea what his ex-wife was up to and was very uncomfortable.

As Tammy Faye studied the picture and started to comment, Jim ignored her, which was difficult in the tiny, crowded room. He motioned to get Tammy Sue's attention. "Please get her out of here," he said quietly. "How would I ever explain to my fiancée that my ex-wife came to visit me in my bedroom? This isn't right." Jim was quite distraught. "Besides, I don't want you meeting Lori for the first time with your mother interjecting her opinions. It's not fair to you or Lori."

My plane from San Francisco was an hour late, which was unusual. Jim met me at the gate, carrying long-stemmed red roses and a gift bag.

"This is for you," he said after he kissed me. "I bought you something at Disneyland."

Tucked inside the folds of tissue paper was a solid white ceramic figurine of Prince Charming and Cinderella. "Did I ever tell you that Cinderella was my favorite story growing up?" I asked.

He shook his head and smiled. "No, I got lucky on that. I dragged my grandkids into every shop at Disneyland looking for a romantic gift for you, and this was the only thing I could find. Goofy and Mickey Mouse just didn't fit the bill."

"Honey, it's perfect. I love it." I kissed him on the cheek and hugged him again. "Thank you."

As we gathered my luggage and walked to the Jeep, he told me about the trip to Disneyland and how much he'd enjoyed spending the time with his grandsons and daughter.

"How is Sue?" I asked. "I'm really looking forward to meeting her."

"She's terrific. And she's really looking forward to meeting you too." He hesitated. "But we kinda have a problem."

Jim held the car door open for me and I climbed in. "What kind of a problem?" I asked. I'm not usually nervous meeting people, but the way he said it gave my stomach butterflies.

"Tammy Faye showed up," he said. "She wants to meet you." He was obviously unhappy with that development.

"That's okay. I don't have a problem with that. I'll have to meet her eventually anyway."

"Yes, but it's not fair to Sue," Jim said. "It's not right to introduce you to my daughter with her mother there. I want you and Sue to have a private time to get to know each other under the right circumstances—and this just isn't the right time."

"So what are we going to do?"

"I'm going to take you up to Kelli and Amanda's room, and you can wait there while I go back to Casa Grande and try to work things out."

"You mean I won't get to meet Sue at all?"

"Not unless I can figure a way to sneak her past her mother and bring her up to the girls' room."

But that turned out to be impossible. Because my plane was so late, Tammy Faye had tired of waiting and had already left for Palm Springs with Sue and the boys in tow. I was disappointed to have to postpone meeting Jim's daughter. She was an important part of his life, and I was eager to get to know her. I desperately wanted her approval and blessing of my marriage to her father.

During the next couple of days we scratched another big item off our wedding-planning list: an engagement ring. I knew Jim didn't have the money to buy me an expensive diamond. He would have had to charge it, and we both agreed we shouldn't start our marriage by making payments on a ring when we would need the money to live on. "Why don't we just wear plain gold bands?" I suggested to Jim when we first talked about it. He was comfortable with that.

One day around the first of August we were at the mall to pick up a few things with Armando. We hadn't planned to shop for a ring that day, but while Armando was in another store, we happened to see a display of cubic zirconia engagement rings in the jewelry department of Macy's. Set in fourteen-karat gold, they were magnificent. "You'd probably have to be a jeweler to know these weren't real diamond rings," Jim said.

"But they're so fancy," I said. "They look like they cost a fortune. I don't know if I could wear something like that."

"Sure you could." Jim grinned and motioned the salesclerk over. "Could we see some of these rings, please?" The clerk brought the tray of rings Jim had pointed to out of the case, and Jim slipped one of them on my finger. "Let's see if it fits," he said. "If not, we could always have it sized."

I stood there at the counter, trying on one ring after another, feeling like a princess. It was a moment every girl dreams about. "Look at this one," I told Jim. "I really like it." I slipped the ring on my left hand. It fit perfectly, and it was absolutely stunning. We talked it over briefly and decided it was the one we wanted. We also agreed that the fact that it wasn't a real diamond would be our little secret.

My gorgeous but inexpensive ring looked so real, however, it later became the source of much speculation. I'll share one of the ruder examples of the controversy my engagement ring has sparked. In June 2000 Jim and I were speaking at a Sunday evening church service. Jim was scheduled to speak briefly at a singles' potluck dinner afterward but, as often happens, he was waylaid by people wanting him to sign books or just wanting to say hello. He has always felt that this contact with people, many of whom have wanted to see him personally for years, is important, so it's difficult for Jim to break away from them. I could tell that the leader of the singles' group was getting antsy, so I turned to him and said, "Why don't we go ahead and start? I can speak for five or ten minutes to give Jim a chance to finish here, and then he can take over."

"I'll give you seven minutes," he said abruptly, eyeing me up and down as if he wondered if I could speak intelligently on any subject for that long.

Is this guy rude, or is it just the lateness of the hour? I wondered as we walked back to the fellowship hall, where fifty to sixty adult singles had started their meal. The leader introduced me, and I spoke for a few minutes on understanding what it was like to walk in their shoes. "I was single for thirteen years before I married Jim," I said. "People would often ask me, 'Why isn't a nice-looking, outgoing woman like you married?' They were trying to be polite about it, but you just knew that their *real* question was, 'What's wrong with you?'" Many in the audience laughed or nodded their heads; they'd heard similar questions.

"I always wanted to be married again," I continued, "but I knew it would happen according to God's timetable, so I enjoyed focusing my time and energy on ministry during those single years. It's a lot different when you're married and your time must be divided between God and your spouse. Use your single years to get to know Christ."

I wrapped up my speech in just under seven minutes and the leader, who must have been feeling somewhat more magnanimous toward me—and seeing that Jim still had not made it back to the fellowship hall—announced that we had time for a few questions from the audience. Someone asked how I met Jim, and I repeated the condensed version of our story. Someone else asked how I knew marrying Jim was God's will.

"The peace of God led me," I replied. "Over the years I had learned how to listen to God's voice in prayer and through meditating on his Word. And I just knew it was right when it happened. I had always asked God to pick a husband for me because I was a 'bad picker,' as my dad often reminded me.

"There were a lot of issues I had to work through before it was God's time for me to be married," I said. "A lot of healing needed to take place—and forgiveness too." I looked down about that time at a well-dressed man, fortyish, who was sitting right up front. He was holding a copy of R. T. Kendall's book *God Meant It for Good.* "May I?" I asked, pointing at the book. He nodded yes, and I picked it up and held it up for the audience to see.

"This incredible book, based on the life of Joseph, is available back at our book table," I told them. "If there is anyone you're struggling to forgive, you really need to read it. " I shared with them briefly how the book had ministered to Jim in prison and how he had come to know the author, then I handed the book back to its owner and handed the microphone to the singles' leader, nodding my head to indicate I was through.

"We have time for one final question," he said, "and it comes from this man in the front." The leader pointed to the man whose book I had just borrowed. "He wants to know, 'How big is that rock on your left hand, Mrs. Bakker?'" The man's voice dripped sarcasm as he asked the question and then stuck the microphone in my face.

After a second of stunned silence the man in the front row protested, "I didn't say that!"

I was too shocked at first to say anything, then I quickly realized that the question didn't deserve an answer. I simply smiled and said to the audience, "Thank you for being here. Good night." Then I walked out of the fellowship hall.

Jim was standing outside, just about to enter, when I made my exit. He took one look at my face and said, "Honey, what's wrong?"

"I was just humiliated by that singles' leader," I said, almost in tears and struggling to gain my composure. "I'll tell you about it later. Go on inside." I squeezed his hand.

"You're trembling, Lori."

"I'm okay." I took a deep breath and managed a smile. "But I'm not going back in there. I'll wait for you at the book table."

As I waited for Jim to finish speaking, I stewed over the leader's question. I knew people sometimes wondered about my ring, even though most of them were too tactful to say anything outright. But the ring raised eyebrows, and you could almost hear their minds spinning: *I heard Jim Bakker say he didn't have any money these days. So how can he afford to buy a big diamond ring for his new bride? And even if he could afford it, should a preacher be spending money on something as expensive as that?*

I even asked Jim later that night if I should stop wearing the ring or perhaps announce to the world on the upcoming Larry King show that I was wearing a fake diamond.

As a Christian and a minister, I'm sensitive to appearances and don't want anything I do or say or wear to be a stumbling block to people. But I've also learned that you can't live your life by what other people may or may not think of you. I wear my engagement ring proudly, along with a simple gold wedding band that belonged to my father's mother. My controversial cubic zirconia ring is one of the most elegant pieces of jewelry I've ever seen, and every time I look at it, I remember how delighted Jim was to find that he could afford such a beautiful "rock" to symbolize his eternal love for me.

26

JOY CAME IN THE MORNING

Early August 1998

Jamie Charles Bakker was born December 18, 1975." Jim was pretending to narrate a biography of his son.

The four of us—Jim and I, Jay and Amanda—were traveling from L.A. to Muskegon, Michigan, for the Bakker family reunion, and Jim was using the occasion to fill me in on some of the family history. Jim continued his story, but my mind stopped and focused on that date. *December 18, 1975.*

"Lori, you sure got quiet," Jay said after a few minutes. "Are you carsick? Or just mesmerized by our life stories?" The others laughed.

"No, I . . . Sorry, Jay. I just had a major reality check when I heard your date of birth." I swallowed hard. "You're the same age my firstborn son would have been." That realization had hit me like a ton of bricks. If I had carried my first pregnancy to term, the baby would have been born in late December '75 or early

January '76. I was looking at a flesh-and-blood son—soon to be *my* son, or at least my stepson—with his arm around his girl-friend, and he was the same age my firstborn would have been. "You guys could have been really good friends," I said wistfully.

The moment passed awkwardly. Jay didn't know what to say, and Jim simply looked sad. He reached over and took my hand. As much healing as I have had, the old, familiar grief can still reach out and squeeze my heart in a split second. It doesn't happen often, but when it does, it is very real. Every time I looked at Jay for the next few hours, I thought of the son I never had because of my own choices. Gradually those thoughts faded.

Such thoughts, while painful, no longer overwhelmed me because of a deep inner healing I had experienced in 1994. That event remains the single most precious moment of truth in my life.

That summer, my new friends Chris Harper and Jolene Dreisbach had been to a postabortion healing conference in Milwaukee, Wisconsin. I'd never even heard the term *post-abortion* before that time, but I knew God was dealing with me about the abortion issue, and I knew that's why he had brought Chris and Jolene into my life. I also knew it was time to leave Master's Commission but did not yet know what I would do after that. Pastor Barnett had asked me to go to L.A. and help start the LAIC, the outreach that eventually became the Dream Center. Jack Wallace, who had been teaching the singles' class the Sunday in 1989 when I made a commitment to Christ, was now pastoring a church in Detroit and wanted me on staff there. It would be a paid ministry position, and that would be a first for me.

As I prayed for direction, God started putting all the puzzle pieces together, and by August, Chris, Jolene, and I had decided to start a ministry to help bring healing to women who'd been through abortions. Before we formalized our plans to start Truth Ministries, the girls had told me they wanted to hold a memorial service for me. They'd been working on the ideas they'd learned at the Milwaukee conference, which had been not just for helping women heal emotionally after abortion but also after miscarriage and SIDS. "If we incorporated the Holy Spirit into the memorial," they told me, "incredible things could happen."

"Lori, think of it this way," Chris said. "You never had a baby shower or did any of the things that would commemorate having a child. That's what this memorial will do."

"Or think of it this way," Jolene added. "If you'd had a stillborn child or even a miscarriage, friends would have consoled you, and you would have mourned. But women who've had abortions—women like us—actually had the same kind of loss, yet we never had the experience of grieving for our children."

I thought the idea of holding a memorial service for me sounded kind of strange at first, but they persisted.

"This is a way to deal with the abortions once and for all and to bring closure on the past," Chris said.

Jolene agreed. "Please let us do this for you, Lori."

We scheduled the memorial for the last weekend in August, right before my birthday. The week prior to that, God started softening my heart. I had always been the strong one, the one people came to with their problems. That week I became mush. Pastor Barnett rarely mentioned abortion from the pulpit, but that week he mentioned it twice, Sunday morning and Wednesday night. For some reason it was on his heart; he didn't know I was that reason. He preached that abortion was wrong, but he also expressed compassion for women who had felt they had no other alternative.

On Wednesday night after church, Chris and Jolene told their families good-bye, then we drove to neighboring Scottsdale, where they had rented a one-bedroom hotel suite. We planned on staying until Friday night, so the fact that Chris and Jolene's husbands were taking care of their kids for two days so we could be free to do this was a big deal to me. I didn't think I deserved it. I was always telling people that God had great things in store for them, but I didn't believe I would ever have the great things of God because the sin *I* had committed—abortion—was so horrible. I felt I would have to live with the pain and the emptiness, the loss and the shame, no matter how great a Christian I became. As we drove to Scottsdale, I sensed God saying to me, "Let these people minister to you."

We had a beautiful suite with a separate bedroom and a kitchenette off the full-size living room. From the moment we walked in, I felt the presence of God, and I began to realize that something truly supernatural was in store for me that night. Because I knew it would be an emotional time, I went to the bathroom, took my contacts out, and washed my face. While I was putting my pajamas on, Chris and Jolene prepared the living room. They placed boxes of tissues in various spots around the room, and they decorated one of the tables with a white linen tablecloth with lace trim.

"We want to anoint you with oil and pray before we begin," one of them said. They prayed and asked God to reveal whatever memories I needed for my healing. That's an important part of post-abortion ministry, because you immediately start blocking out the memories of that event. It's a defense mechanism. You couldn't live with what you did if you had to face it, so you suppress the memories and bury the details so deep in the recesses of your mind that you're able to live in complete denial of what you've done.

After we prayed, Chris and Jolene asked me to start telling what I remembered about my abortions. "The first one was in May 1975," I said. "That's the only one I can even tell you the exact month and year." I told the story of being pregnant before I married Jesse and choosing him over the baby.

"The second abortion was in 1976," I said. "I don't remember the actual abortion; I just remember coming home to our apartment and lying on the loveseat-rocker all day. Jesse asked me, 'Are you okay?' and I remember looking up at him and thinking, *Now, you ask. I just killed my own baby—our baby— something I really wanted, and you're asking if I'm okay?* But I didn't say it.

"There were always two reasons for the abortions. One was that Jesse didn't want to have kids yet. 'Someday,' he'd always say. The other reason was drugs. I'd seen films in health class about babies who were born addicted to drugs, and it horrified me. We were so into drugs—cocaine and LSD, and even PCP, an animal tranquilizer that produced a cheap but intense high. The one time I thought I was going to die from drugs was the time I did PCP, around the time of that second abortion.

"My brother Mark and a friend brought the PCP over to our apartment; Mark had wanted to turn me and Jesse on for a change, since we were always sharing our drugs with him. Mark laced a joint with the PCP, and the four of us smoked it. The drug makes you so high, you're numb for hours; you can't feel anything. It was wintertime and raining, but I remember going outside and letting the rain pour down on me. I couldn't feel the cold or the rain. I started getting really scared. I went back inside and sat on that rocking loveseat for twelve hours without moving. I was virtually paralyzed. Jesse was sitting next to me, watching an old rerun of *The Honeymooners.* I started crying, becoming almost hysterical. 'I'm going to die,' I told him. 'I'm not making it this time.' He tried to talk me through the high, 'Don't worry. You'll be fine,' he said. But he later told me he had thought we were both going to die. At one point I cried out, 'God, if you're real, please spare me from this, and I'll never do it again.' That was one promise I made good on; I never used PCP again."

I paused to take a sip of water. Jolene and Chris encouraged me to take my time and tell it all.

"The next year, 1977, I got pregnant again. Jesse and I had moved to Farmington, New Mexico. I remember we drove there the night Elvis died, pulling a small trailer with everything we owned. Jesse was working a lot of hours as a boilermaker for a power plant there. We rented a double-wide mobile home, and it was one of the nicer places we lived. I fixed it up, and I was the typical little housewife—except that I smoked pot all the time. We weren't doing major drugs then. My grandma Graham died, and when I flew to Phoenix for the funeral, I made a doctor's appointment. I needed to have a cyst removed, and since I had just found out I was pregnant—and Jesse didn't want the baby, of course—I decided to have an abortion at the same time. That was the only abortion that was done in a hospital."

Chris and Jolene asked a question now and then to prod my memory, but mostly they just let me talk.

"Jesse and I separated for a while, and he had a girlfriend. When we got back together, we moved to Pinetop, up in the mountains; it was very beautiful there. Because of Jesse's work we moved a lot. Little towns all over Arizona and New Mexico. I once counted fifty different apartments or houses or hotels where we had lived in the ten years we were married.

"We went to Prescott for the Fourth of July. It was wild there in the '70s. The Hell's Angels would ride into town, and the police would close the streets for the holiday. Prescott is a quaint little town with antique shops, and there's a street called Whiskey Row with a bunch of saloons. Jesse and I were doing quaaludes and partying in and out of the bars. I was so spaced out, I was offering quaaludes to cops; there was no way they could control the drugs and alcohol, so they simply tried to keep the peace. We were in front of the courthouse, in the center of town, when Jesse went nuts and started hitting me, and the cops had to pull him off of me.

"Jesse screamed, 'Just get the _____ out of my life. Go find somebody else.'

"I literally took him up on it. I turned around, walked across the street, went into a bar, and met a man. Paul took me to his cabin, and I spent the night there with him. We had an off-and-on relationship for the next couple of years. Whenever Jesse beat me up, I called Paul; he came and got me and nursed me back to health. He was a very gentle guy. I don't think he ever wanted me to leave Jesse to marry him, but he was always there for me. Jesse never knew about him.

"A couple of weeks after the Fourth of July incident, I went back to Jesse, and then I found out I was pregnant. I had horrible morning sickness twenty-four hours a day. Jesse had told this guy he rode to work with that I was pregnant, even though we had already decided I was going to have an abortion. I was so upset one morning when I dropped Jesse off for his ride because this man's wife came out to congratulate me on being pregnant. She said she was happy for us. They were an older couple, and they had been trying to get pregnant for a long time.

"I knew this was not Jesse's baby, but I could never tell him; I was afraid he would kill me. I was sure the child was Paul's, so

I went to Phoenix and had another abortion, which I don't remember at all. I just know I had it. I was almost four months' pregnant, and you can tell it in pictures."

My voice was getting hoarse as I finished. "I don't remember the last abortion, either. I know we were living with Dad in the big house in Phoenix at the time, but I don't remember the details. A year later I had the infection, and that's when I had the hysterectomy."

I had gone through the entire recital of the facts about my five abortions and hysterectomy without shedding a tear. Chris and Jolene later told me they had kept praying for me to break. Although God had softened my heart in the previous week, I was still holding so much of the pain deep inside, I hadn't reached it yet.

We had talked for a couple of hours by now, so we took a break. They had brought fruit and crackers and juices with them, so we could have a light snack without leaving the hotel. As we finished our snack, I said, "I don't know how I know this, and it probably sounds weird, but I think I know the sexes of my children."

They looked at each other in surprise. "We were going to pray God would show you that."

"I already know," I said. "I think the Holy Spirit must have put that into my heart at some point. I've consciously thought about it before but never dwelled on it. Anyway, the first was a boy, the second was a girl, the third and fourth were boys, and the fifth was a girl."

"Now that you know that," Chris said, "we think it's important to name them."

"Name them? . . . But why?"

"Because they're your children, and they're in heaven now," Jolene said.

I'd already known that, but I had never considered naming my children before, and that thought began to shake me.

"We'll give you some time to think about it," they said.

I was sitting on the floor between the sofa and the coffee table. They moved behind me now, where I couldn't see them, so I had some privacy. They put some soft music on a portable cassette player. I had a note pad on the table in front of me, and I wrote the names down as I thought of them. I wanted to give them all Bible names. Eventually I came up with Adam, Sarah, Joseph, Paul, and Hannah.

I still hadn't cried at this point, but the music was beginning to melt my heart, and I started sniffling. Once I had finished naming my babies, Chris started talking about how important it was to forgive my ex-husband for wanting me to have the abortions. I also needed to forgive the doctors and nurses, she said, and the girlfriends who drove me to the abortion clinic—everyone involved.

They had cut several hearts out of construction paper, and they asked me to write on the hearts the name of every person I needed to forgive and why. "You may not feel like forgiving them," Chris said, "but you have to."

I wrote it all down, but as I was going through the people I needed to forgive, I realized that the number one person I had to forgive was *me*. I really struggled with that. I believed God had forgiven me, but I had a lot of trouble forgiving myself.

When I had finished writing on the paper hearts, Jolene said, "Now, take the hearts and put them in the basket over there." She pointed to the white-covered table I had noticed earlier. A white cross was standing on the table, and beneath it was a satin-lined basket.

"We won't look at what you've written on the hearts," she

said. "That's between you and God. But we want you to place them in the basket, symbolizing that you are leaving those people who hurt your heart at the foot of the cross."

After I had deposited my paper hearts beneath the cross, Chris said, "Now, go into the bedroom. There's a baby blanket laid out on the bed, and on it are symbols of your aborted babies." I didn't have a clue what she was talking about. "Bring the symbols back to the living room with you."

When I walked into the bedroom and saw the symbols—five handkerchief dolls made of white linen—carefully arranged on the baby blanket, I had a strong taste of the reality of what had taken place all those years ago. I was face-to-face with the fact that I had taken the lives of my children. I started breaking as I looked at the five dolls: three of them had tiny blue ribbons around the neck, and two of them had pink ribbons. They were laid out in the order I'd said my children were conceived: boy, girl, boy, boy, girl.

I folded the baby blanket around the dolls, exactly as I would tuck a blanket around a newborn baby, then I picked them up and cradled them in my arms. Jolene and Chris were struggling to maintain their composure as I walked out of the bedroom holding the symbols of the five children I had sacrificed on the altar of choice.

The girls motioned me over to the sofa, and when I sat down, I laid the symbols out on my lap, again arranging them in order. They played several songs specifically about abortion and children. I finally began the grieving process as I let the music soak into my spirit.

When the music ended, Chris said, "Now, take the symbols into the bedroom and close the door. We want you to spend two hours alone with them. Allow God to do whatever he needs to do. Express anything you've ever wanted to express to your children. It's okay to do that."

"What do you mean?" I asked.

"It would be like going to your grandfather's grave site and saying, 'Grandpa, I wish you were here to see what's going on in my life.' It's not like you're talking to the dead; you're just expressing what's in your heart, what you would say to your children if you could."

"Tell them about your niece Amber and your mom," Jolene suggested.

The two hours I spent alone in a hotel bedroom with five white handkerchiefs fashioned into dolls was by far the most supernatural experience I have ever had. When I first walked into the bedroom, I tenderly laid the symbols on the bed and then I fell to my knees, weeping. I rocked back and forth on my heels as I began to keen softly. The grief was intense. "Please forgive me," I said over and over. One by one I picked up the symbols and called them by name, asking for forgiveness. Then I picked all of them up and clutched them to my heart. "I would have made a good mommy," I sobbed. "You would have been the joy of my life . . . I would have done my best for you . . . I *wanted* you . . . Oh, God, I wanted you!" All these words came welling up from deep inside me as I began to express my sorrow. "I didn't want this to happen, but I chose your dad over you." The loss was almost more than I could take. "Oh, God, forgive me . . . please, God, forgive me."

There comes a point when you physically can't cry anymore. I reached it, and my breath came in dry, ragged sobs as I gulped for air. An incredible thing happened to me then. God started to reveal my children's personalities to me one by one. Chris and Jolene had not said anything about that happening, so I was surprised. I did not see my children's physical appearance, but I saw into their souls. God showed me what they would have been like on Earth, and what they were in heaven.

Adam, who would have been the firstborn, was very strong, and he took care of the other four. He loved God with everything inside him. It was Adam's voice I had heard twice before, and now I heard him say, "It's okay, Mommy. We forgive you . . . we love you!"

God showed me that Sarah was like me, only a million times better—me with all the flaws taken out. She was full of joy and life and passion. She loved people and children, and she was a giver.

Joseph would have been the one most like my ex-husband. He would have been a troublemaker, full of mischief, and I would have had a hard time with him. He would have kept me on my knees. At the same time, Joseph loved people, and I would have been very close to him.

Paul was very gentle and kind—a nurturer like his father, who had nursed me back to health so many times when Jesse had beaten me up.

Hannah would have been a typical baby girl, spoiled rotten and getting her way all the time. But what a delight and joy she would have been to my heart.

When I had learned all my children's personalities, I heard Adam's voice for a final time. "We're waiting here for you, Mommy, and one day you'll be here too, and we'll spend forever together."

The voice was very comforting, and I knew I wasn't crazy. The inaudible voice was really God speaking to my spirit; I heard it as a child's voice—my son's voice—because that was what I needed for my healing. God had prepared me for this moment by letting me hear that voice years earlier.

I felt I had lived a lifetime with my children in those two

hours, and I didn't want to leave the room now, but it was time to go onto the next step. I cradled the five symbols in the baby blanket and opened the bedroom door. My eyes were swollen and my nose was stuffy, but something was happening. The sadness was beginning to lift just a little.

When I sat back down on the sofa, I saw what to me was one of the most beautiful sights I'd ever seen. The linen-covered table had been transformed into a funeral bier. A tiny white casket with a padded satin lining—handmade by Chris and Jolene's husbands, I later learned—sat on top of the table. Five small, unlit candles had been placed next to the casket, together with a larger, lighted candle. The white cross was still there, but the basket had been replaced with a long-stemmed white rose. Across the front of the table were five white cards; each had either a pink or blue bow attached and a name written in calligraphy.

Without their telling me, I knew what I would have to do next: place the dolls in the casket. First they played a tape of *Tilly,* the Focus on the Family audiodrama I had heard driving to the beach with Bobbi that day. I cried quite a bit as I listened again to the story. Then they played a recording of a little girl reading the Twenty-third Psalm. It was very touching. Chris and Jolene stood behind the sofa again, where I couldn't see them. As I listened, I let everything soak in: the words, the room, the symbols, the candles, the casket.

"It's time to bring closure to this," Chris said. "Whenever you're ready, walk over to the table and lay the symbols in the casket."

It took a long time to muster the strength to say good-bye and let go of them. I felt I'd just spent a lifetime with them, and now I was going to have to give up my babies. I didn't want to, but I knew I had to. Finally, I stood up and cradled the dolls in my arms as I walked to the casket almost in a daze.

The girls had followed behind me at a respectful distance. "You can place them in the casket one by one, Lori, or all at once," Jolene said. "Whatever seems right to you."

I stood looking at the casket for a long moment, then I took the first symbol and placed it inside. "Good-bye, Adam," I whispered. Immediately I pulled the handkerchief doll out and started crying. "I can't say good-bye to you . . . I just found you." I struggled for several minutes, unable to let go of this symbol that represented the biggest loss of my life. Finally, I found the courage to place it back in the casket. I cradled the other four symbols in the crook of one elbow as I reached out with my other hand and straightened the white linen doll, carefully patting into place the creased folds of its body. Once I got Adam's symbol placed, I was able to put the others inside. It took a long time, though.

When I had placed all five dolls in the casket, I stood there staring at it. The finality of the moment penetrated my innermost being, and grief gushed out of me in a wailing sound that came from so deep within, it nearly turned me inside out. I reeled and would have collapsed, but Chris and Jolene caught me. They helped me down to the floor and rubbed my back while I continued to wail. "That's good. Just get it out, Lori. Go ahead and grieve." I've never experienced such profound mourning before or since.

As my grief began to subside, they helped me stand. "We're going to light the candles now," Chris said. "The large candle represents Jesus, the Light of the World. Take it and light the five smaller candles, signifying that you're leaving your children with the Lord."

Jolene steadied my hand, which was shaking as I bent the flame of the Jesus candle to light the candles representing my children. When I had finished, I returned to the sofa and remained seated there a long time, just looking at the beautiful, tranquil scene. No one said a word. I stared at the flickering candlelight as it danced over the casket, and in the moments just before dawn, an indescribable peace began to seep into my broken, empty soul. And on the heels of peace came a quiet joy— the kind of joy I never thought I would be allowed to have. I'd heard other Christians describe this deep inner joy, but I never thought I would experience it. I *couldn't* have experienced it until that night.

Daylight had begun filtering through the curtains, and I thought of a Scripture: "Weeping may endure for a night, / But joy comes in the morning."[1]

27

EVER AFTER? MAYBE NOT

I was surprised at how big Lake Michigan was—more like an ocean than a lake. I couldn't see all the way across it. We had arrived in Muskegon for the family reunion and were staying with Jim's brother, Norman, and his wife, June, who had rented a beachfront house.

"This is where I grew up," Jim told me. "I lived here until I moved away to attend Bible school. I've rarely come back for a visit, but this was the center of our family recreation in my youth, right here on this white sand beach. The Ovals, it was called. On this spot I had hundreds of picnics with my grandma Irwin and our extended family. They were always major feasts—food said 'love' to Grandma. But as a child I could never have imagined I would someday be staying in a place like this; renting a beachfront house was something rich people did."

Jim told me about growing up in a very tiny two-bedroom house next door to his grandma and grampa Irwin, and how his mother and father had courted, as they called it then, by Lake

Michigan. "I remember seeing old photographs from those days. The men would be in suits and ties, and the ladies in long dresses, sitting on a blanket spread on this beach."

I enjoyed hearing about Jim's early life in Michigan, and loved getting to know his family. In addition to his immediate family—his brother, Norman, and his sister, Donna—I met Jim's cousins and aunts and uncles, and all of them welcomed me warmly and accepted me as part of the family. Almost everyone I met said, "Raleigh—Jim's dad—would have loved you." I felt sad that I never got to meet his dad, who had passed away the previous year. Jim had not wanted to have a big funeral for his father at the time because he feared it would become a media circus; he wanted to be able to mourn his father in private and was almost obsessed with the family being able to control this one event in their lives. So they waited and held a memorial service at the reunion I attended. It took place outdoors, under a covered pavilion, and because it was pouring rain that day, virtually no one was in the park except the Bakker family.

At the conclusion of the short service, Jim led a procession a few hundred feet over to the channel that leads from Lake Michigan into Muskegon Lake. As a little boy, Jim had sat on the breakwater and fished with his family there. That morning Norman, Donna, and Jim had bought ninety-two roses, one for each year of their father's life. When they reached the channel, Jim distributed the roses to the entire family, and one by one they threw the roses into the channel and watched them drift toward the big lake.

Family roles took a complete reversal while we were in Michigan. Jay became very protective of his dad, and it was cute to see him hovering over Jim as a father would watch over his son. The beach house was nice but had very tiny rooms. It was like a mini-dormitory: Amanda and I shared a room with bunk beds, and Jim and Jay's room had a similar arrangement. Although the rooms were tiny, they did have a great view of the lake.

One day Jim came into my room so we could talk privately. We sat on the bunk bed and enjoyed watching the sunlight reflecting off the lake as we talked. In a minute Jay walked past the open door and stopped when he saw us. "Dad, you shouldn't be in the bedroom alone with Lori," he scolded.

We obediently moved into the living room and sat on the sofa. We continued our conversation, and before long Jim had put his arm around me and kissed me. Of course, Jay caught us. His eyebrows raised in concern. "Don't you think that's going a bit too far?" he asked.

In spite of Jay's attempts to keep us apart, Jim and I managed to talk a great deal during those few days in Michigan. We talked in-depth about every detail of our lives, about God, our families, our beliefs, our failures and defeats, our triumphs, our hopes and dreams—everything two people in love can think of to explore.

I also talked more with Amanda during that trip. She had been a sounding board and a counselor for me since the very beginning. Those first days at the Dream Center, even before Jim proposed, Amanda and Kelli and I would lie in bed and talk until two or three in the morning. Amanda had been around Jay's family for a couple of years and had spent holidays with them, so she knew them well enough to point out the pros and the cons of life with the Bakkers. But she never talked disparagingly, even when we discussed how difficult things had been for Jay and Jim, who are both sensitive by nature and sometimes a challenge to figure out. "Father and son alike have a melancholy streak," she told me, "and they tend to become negative or with-drawn. Sometimes you just have to pull them out of it."

Amanda's insight about Jim certainly proved correct during our Michigan trip. One evening the four of us went to the movies, a favorite pastime for the Fabulous Bakker Boys, as Amanda had dubbed Jim and Jay; the nickname was borrowed from the title of a movie starring real-life brothers Beau and Jeff Bridges. That night we chose the film *Ever After,* a retelling of the Cinderella story, which Jim had just learned was one of my favorites when he presented me with a Prince Charming sou-venir from Disneyland. I enjoyed the big-screen romance fea-turing Drew Barrymore, although Hollywood had turned the fairy tale heroine into a modern liberated woman disguised in lavish sixteenth-century costumes.

Jim was quiet during the movie and on the ride back to the beach house. He didn't move when Jay and Amanda got out of the car and went inside, so I stayed with him. I thought Jim seemed despondent, and it worried me.

"Honey, is something wrong?" I asked.

He looked at me briefly, his eyes full of sorrow, then looked down at his hands resting on his knees. "I've about talked myself out of it," he finally said. "I don't think it's going to work, Lori."

"What's not going to work?"

"Marrying you."

Uh-oh. He's having second thoughts. What do I do now? I won-dered. "Let's walk on the beach." I suggested. "I need some fresh air." I also needed time to consider what might have caused this sudden about-face and how I should respond.

Jim walked with his shoulders hunched, his hands in his pockets. He was a portrait of gloom.

"What makes you say it's not going to work? Please . . . talk to me." I straightened the ring on my left hand, noticing that the stone sparkled in the moonlight. "Don't you love me enough to marry me?"

"It's not that . . . not that at all." His plaintive protest rose on the wind, and I thought back to another walk on the beach, just two weeks earlier, when he'd said he was falling in love with me and practically tried to talk me out of dating him. "Maybe there are some things love just can't overcome," he said.

"Like what?"

"Like me," he said slowly. "I'm all wrong for you." He sat down on the damp sand and motioned for me to sit down beside him. "This is real life, not a movie, and I'm no Prince Charming." He paused, grappling for words or perhaps for the courage to express what was troubling him. "I'm too old for you, Lori. You deserve someone younger, someone who doesn't bring so much baggage with him, someone who doesn't have such an awful past, someone whose name isn't despised . . ." He began to talk about the past and the scandals and the scars of prison. "I feel so heavy," he said, "like I might as well be buried in this sand." His voice had dwindled to a whisper.

"You make it sound hopeless, Jim—"

"I'm just being a realist. When you've been through what I've been through, you learn to look at things objectively, and when you take a cold, hard look at *us,* Lori, you have to face up to the fact that our marriage is not going to work because there are simply too many odds against it."

"There are odds against every marriage. It's never easy to make it work."

"But we come from totally different backgrounds. And there's a seventeen-year age difference. The rock 'n' roll I grew up with in the '50s is like Sunday school music compared to today's.

Don't you see how big the gap is between us? You're forty years old, but you're part of a very youth-oriented culture. I've been in the church world for several decades now—I'm a fossil compared to you."

"Is your concern mainly the age thing? Are you worried what *other* people will think? Because I'm not. I'm only worried about what *we* think, and it doesn't bother me. Age is just a number."

"A much bigger number for some of us than others," he said.

"I think it's your mental attitude that determines how old you are. And it's not true what you said, about us not having anything in common. Yes, we grew up in different worlds, and we have different musical preferences, but every day we find something else we have in common. We have the same taste in houses and furniture and decorating. We like the same television programs and restaurants—I could name *lots* of things we have in common, but the most important is that we have the same beliefs and trust in God. It's no accident we both have the same passion for inner-city ministry and a desire to help young people.

"My point is that it's not the age difference or the taint of the past—yours *or* mine—that matters in our relationship. What really matters is whether this is God's will for us, whether we are meant to be together. If that's true, then everything else will work out. It's *never* hopeless if God is involved, and I believe he is."

As we continued to talk, Jim's despair and fear of rejection began to lessen. He had been testing me in a way by giving voice to his self-doubts, seeking reassurance that I really would stick with him if things got a little rough.

The next day it was my turn to have second thoughts when Jim got a phone call from Larry Wright, one of his closest friends from prison. Larry was a former Wesleyan pastor who had lost his church after his wife left him. Ostracized by his denomination after his marriage failed, Larry used his business and motivational gifts in the corporate world, making a lot of money. But he eventually got into some kind of business trouble and landed in prison. There he rediscovered his calling to teach and preach, leading powerful Bible studies for the inmates.

While in prison, Larry and Jim had both gone through training to become licensed counselors with the National Christian Counseling Association. They spent many long hours counseling inmates concerning their temperaments and spiritual strengths. Rather than mail my temperament-profile questionnaire to the main office, Jim had dictated my answers over the phone to Larry, who had done the analysis on his computer. Now, he was calling with the results.

Jim took the phone out to the screened-in porch to talk to Larry in privacy. I was very upset, pacing the floor inside while my fiancé and some man I didn't know discussed my personality in what I could only imagine was gruesome detail. After brooding about it while Jim continued to confer with Larry for what seemed like an hour, I finally couldn't stand the tension and went for a walk on the beach.

What on earth are they saying about me? I wondered. I began to talk to God as I walked barefoot along the dunes, sinking my toes in the clean white sand. *Now* I'm *starting to have questions about this marriage, God. The man I love is testing my temperament, and I'm scared to find out the results. I thought we worked through all of his doubts and questions last night, and now this. Maybe he was right. Maybe we* are *too different and it won't work out. Oh, God, what am I supposed to do?*

It was very late at night by this time and quiet on the beach. The solitude was soothing, and I gradually began to relax as I listened to the soft rippling of the lake and watched the stars twinkling in the sky. I thought of Psalm 19: "The heavens declare the glory of God; the skies proclaim the work of his hands."[1] *Lord, I prayed, you hung the stars in place and they've never fallen. Your word says you are faithful to all your promises and loving toward all you have made.*[2] *That includes me. I trust your faithfulness and your goodness and ask for your wisdom and direction.*

I stayed gone for a good hour before I mustered the courage to go back to the beach house and confront the situation. Jim was still sitting out on the porch when I returned, but he was no longer on the telephone.

"You were gone a long time," he said. "I didn't know whether to go find you or not."

"I went for a walk. You were on the phone a long time."

"I'm sorry it took so long."

"So what's the verdict?" I asked calmly. "What did Larry say?"

"Everything's fine." His voice was normal, but he looked spent. I couldn't assess his mood, and I was still a little edgy—and more than a little curious.

"I'd like to know what he said about my temperament profile. You obviously discussed me in great detail."

Jim stood up and moved toward me. "We'll go over it later," he said. "When Larry mails us the written report."

"I need to know, Jim. The suspense is killing me. I can't deal with a problem if I don't know what it is."

"Sweetheart, it's late and this isn't the time. And there isn't a problem." He wrapped me in his arms and held me tightly, whispering in my ear. "I love you, Lori Beth. That's all you need to know right now. The first thing I said to Larry was, 'It's too late to try to talk me out of this because I'm madly in love with this woman, and I'm going to marry her no matter what. So just tell me what I need to know to live with her and love her the way she needs to be loved.' And he did. It's going to work out."

Jim held me until all the tension and fear and worry drained out of me. Then he kissed me, and I knew in my heart that everything would be okay.

Months later, long after we were married, we went over each of our temperament profiles in great detail. Jim and I are convinced that the knowledge we gained from that analysis has saved our marriage on more than one occasion.

The first thing Larry had said to Jim on the phone that night was, "You're going to have your hands full."

"That's true," Jim told me when we finally discussed it. "You *are* a handful. In fact, as you told me yourself, you're a little pistol." I pretended to swat him and he laughed. "But I know what makes the pistol work, so my melancholy heart doesn't get wounded by your bullets anymore."

I had tried to push Jim the night Larry had called when we were in Michigan. Jim wouldn't tell me much then, and I've since learned that is one of the ways Jim works. He processes things. Timing is very important to him. At first, when Jim would have a meeting with someone or talk to someone on the phone, I would ask him about it as soon as he finished. Now I don't. I know that Jim doesn't react immediately; he needs time to process what he's heard. When he's ready to talk, he'll tell me. He's learned that I need to be filled in on all the details of an issue—not because I want to make the decision but because part of my personality is a need to be informed.

Jim and I both have a great need for love and affection, yet while I reach out to almost everyone and express affection quite easily, he does not. Knowing this has helped me understand Jim and learn how to respond when we have a disagreement or conflict. When that happens, Jim finds it extremely difficult to reach out to me because he is afraid I will reject him; he's had a lot of rejection in his life, and that is one of his deepest fears. When we have an argument, I just want to make up, to make things right—let's get it over with and go on, is my attitude. Most often I'm the one who is in the wrong, and I'm pretty quick to say so. But once in a great while he's the one who is wrong, and even though he wants to, Jim won't usually make the first move to patch things up. I know now that all I have to do is touch him—show any kind of affection toward him—and he'll melt. All he needs is a small reassurance that I won't reject him. If I hadn't learned that about his temperament, we would have been in a cold war many times.

In the two years we have been married, Jim and I have rarely been apart. About the time I started writing this book, he had to go out of town to work on a new ministry project we're starting for inner-city kids in Florida. I stayed home to work on the book. Jim was away for five days on that trip, which is the longest we had ever been separated. We were in the middle of tremendous changes in our lives and ministries, and both of us were under a lot of pressure. One day while he was gone, we got in a little tiff over the phone and rather than drag it out I said, "I'm hanging up now." Ending the conversation abruptly was progress for me. Ordinarily I would have mouthed off and kept him on the phone trying to resolve the dispute; instead I thought it was better to hang up and deal with it later. My deepest fear has been that Jim would walk out on me someday. Men have always walked out on me—my father, my husband, boyfriends. So it was risky for me to hang up on Jim, but I was finally secure enough to do it. I know he's not going to walk out on me.

Sure enough, Jim didn't call me back that day. I waited and waited. Then I thought, *Why would he call me back? He's not going to call if he thinks he'll be rejected.* So after a few hours I picked up the phone and called him.

"Weren't you going to call me back?" I asked, knowing the answer.

"Well, I didn't think you wanted me to," he said.

"Of course I do. I love you and miss you."

Instantly things were okay between us, and we were able to talk about the situation rationally.

Another thing we learned from our temperament profiles is the difference in our energy levels and the way we tackle things. I'm a night person; Jim is not. I also have a tendency to think I have to finish everything I start—right then. We'll come home from a trip and immediately I want to unpack all the bags and reorganize everything.

"Lori, it's four o'clock in the morning, and you're still lawn-mowering the place," Jim told me the night we had returned from our first extended trip. He looked around at the open suit-cases, the clothes hangers, the shoe boxes, and the laundry basket I was filling. "You're killing me with this," he said. "I can't go in the next room and get some sleep. We live in one room! I have to get some rest, and you need some too."

"But I can't function in disorganization," I told him. "This won't take much longer."

"Baby, this will all be here a few hours from now, and you'll get it done then. I'll help you."

When Jim catches me in an over-organizing binge now, he comes over to me and says he loves me, then he holds me until he can feel my body relax and let go of the tension that is driving me. He can often tell whether I've had enough rest just by looking at my face. And when we're both tired and tense, the enemy uses that if we're not careful. We used to fight for hours into the night simply because we were both exhausted; we don't do that anymore.

I've also learned that Jim is a highly creative person who begins to wear down about five in the afternoon and needs time to rebuild; he often takes an hour nap before dinner because he needs dream time in order to create. In the days of building Heritage USA, Jim used to punish himself for thinking he was lazy, pushing himself to work day and night. Years later he discovered that if he would allow adequate downtime to restore his mind, he enjoyed renewed imagination and inspiration, in addition to physical energy. Because I know that about Jim, I can protect this time for him.

And now, when melancholy strikes and Jim gets down and depressed, I pull him out of the mud. When I get hyper or in a self-destruct mode and won't stop, Jim physically holds me and gives me the security I need to let things go. We would not have known to do that for each other if we had not had the detailed information from our temperament profiles.

Jim had been right that night in Michigan when he first talked to Larry Wright. The personality issues were far too complex to deal with at that moment. The important thing was that we had faced our self-doubts and questions and reconfirmed that we loved each other deeply and knew we were supposed to be together.

28

A Teacup for Tammy Sue

Mid-August 1998

While we were in Michigan for the family reunion, Jay talked to me about his sister. "You're going to love Sue," he told me several times, "and she will take to you immediately. I'm sure about that." I appreciated his reassurance because I felt that was the big hurdle I had to jump before the wedding: establishing a relationship with Tammy Sue. I not only didn't want to do anything to weaken the close relationship Jim had developed with his children, I wanted to become close to them as well.

Just days after we returned to L.A., we were on the road again, this time heading to Charlotte, where I would finally get to meet Tammy Sue. Rick Joyner had invited Jim to speak at a Morning Star conference, and since Jim would be in town for that event, Sue had arranged for her two boys to be baptized while her father was there. Jim was thrilled that James and Jonathan, who were nine and seven, had made a profession of faith and wanted to be baptized, and especially thrilled that Sue's pastor at Indian Trail Baptist Church had given his approval for Jim to perform the baptism.

Before we left for Charlotte, I made a quick trip home to Phoenix. While there I decided on a gift for Tammy Sue. Jim had said that she loved teacups, and I happened to collect china cups and saucers and teapots. My collection is precious to me because most of the beautiful teacups were gifts and each one has a special story; I had never given one away before. But I wanted to give something special to my future stepdaughter, so I prayed about it and asked God to show me which teacup to give her. I made my selection and carefully packaged it for the trip.

It was an emotional trip for Jim for several reasons. First, of course, was the baptism of his grandsons. The oldest, James, had been only a few months old when Jim entered prison; Jonathan was born while Jim was still serving his sentence. Photos of his grandbabies had given Jim the hope to hang on to life at some of his lowest points. One time when Sue and Doug had brought baby James for a prison visit, the toddler declared, "Pawpaw Jim has a big house!" Jim laughed, knowing James was too young to understand that Pawpaw was *in* the big house.

Going back to Charlotte was also emotional because it was where it had all happened for Jim and where it had all fallen apart, the scene of his greatest success and his biggest failure. Charlotte was filled with memories, and now I would be facing them with Jim for the first time.

On the way to Michigan, I had learned Jim's family history, all about his childhood and the births of his children and grandchildren. On the way to North Carolina, Jim told me more of his ministry history and regaled me with stories of starting out as a young evangelist and later building a Christian television network from the bottom up. "I need to take you to see Heritage USA," he said. "You really can't understand my past unless you see it."

"I went there briefly a few years ago," I told him. "After Faithe Tines moved to Charlotte, I went for a visit, and her family took me to see Heritage."

"What did you think about it?"

"I felt grieved. I didn't know the history of the place, but I couldn't understand why this wonderful Christian facility wasn't operating anymore. I remember feeling sad for you and your family, even though I had never met you. I couldn't have imagined then that I would ever meet, let alone marry, the man to whom God had given the vision for such a massive undertaking."

The grief I had felt then, however, could not compare with the grief I experienced as Jim and I drove through the grounds of what had been Heritage USA, and he pointed out every feature—or what remained of them—and told me the history.

Before we even entered the park, the impact of PTL's demise could be seen. Video poker places and honky-tonks dotted the highway leading to the Heritage entrance.

Jim explained: "Some of these gambling joints were built on former Heritage property; some of our land was sold off after I left. The financial impact of our closure hit the community hard. They had to trim school budgets and restructure the tax base because the economy had become dependent on our operation. We brought in hundreds of millions of dollars in tax revenue through not just our hotels, restaurants, and food services but also by boosting local tourism in the surrounding area. We had also created thousands of jobs. All that was lost."

We turned off the highway onto a beautiful boulevard with

manicured grounds. Jim continued: "Everything you see now is what was once Heritage USA. Four square miles of development. There was such a misperception of what we did here. Most people thought I was building a resort. That's what the press told them. But that was never the goal. God had spoken to me back in the early seventies, when we first started PTL in an old furniture store, that the church would be the key to survival in the last days. I was not building a theme park but a center where the body of Christ could gather for fellowship and recreation as well as preaching and teaching—a place of physical and spiritual renewal for families."

We continued driving down the broad divided street, which had been well maintained. "At Christmastime," Jim said, "we called this Angel Boulevard. Giant angels fashioned of twinkling white lights hung over the street. During the holidays traffic coming in and out of this park would be bumper to bumper for sixteen miles. Heritage was voted one of America's top tourist destinations by the bus industry." I tried to picture the boulevard jammed with cars as people gawked at the millions of lights and listened to Christmas carols piped from loudspeakers.

Jim stopped the car at the base of a grassy hill. "This is why I went to prison," he said, pointing to a red-brick building that looked to be about twenty stories high.

"What is it?" I asked.

"It's the Heritage Grand Tower, the new addition to the hotel that the prosecutors said I never built. The judge wouldn't allow the jury to come see it. The tower was ninety days away from completion when construction was halted—we had already carpeted and wallpapered half of the five hundred rooms, and the furniture was paid for and sitting in warehouses."

"But why did you go to prison for that, Jim? I never did understand the charges against you."

"The government said I was selling securities without a license because I was offering lifetime partnerships at Heritage. But I wasn't selling anything, and the jury in the civil trial later recognized that. The people we called Lifetime Partners made a thousand-dollar donation to the ministry, and, in return, they were offered three free nights at Heritage every year. The bottom line is that I went to prison for overbooking hotel space."

"That's outrageous!"

"A lot of people thought so. Prosecutors claimed I wasn't building rooms fast enough to fulfill the Lifetime Partnership program. But we had already opened a five-hundred-room hotel, the five-hundred-room addition was ninety days away from opening, and another five hundred rooms were already on the drawing board—the land had been cleared and the blueprints were in hand. Every Lifetime Partner could be accommodated, just not at the particular time they all wanted to come. Most people wanted holidays or summer. I was building as fast as I could, but that wasn't fast enough for my enemies."

We sat in silence for a moment, staring at the huge tower that had never been occupied. *What a waste,* I thought. *Why hasn't somebody ever done something with this beautiful building?*

"It could easily have been finished," Jim finally said, as if reading my mind. "Now it will probably have to be torn down. The brick is coming loose on the side. It seems nobody cares about these buildings anymore. Even the barn auditorium, where I held my church services and camp meetings, is now leaking and in total decay. . ." His voice trailed off as he put the car in gear and drove away.

We passed the general store and the auction barn. "Every

Saturday night we had an auction," Jim said. "People donated items from toys to TV sets and toasters, and the proceeds went to one of the charities. Everybody had great fun at the auctions." We drove past the family-style bunkhouses—"something else they said I didn't build," Jim said—then continued down the road behind the auction barn and Heritage Farm.

"This must have been a beautiful home," I said as we pulled in front of a large Victorian house with a gabled roof.

"This was Kevin's House, a home for severely disabled children," Jim said. "Kevin had a very rare and fatal brittle-bone disease that caused him not to grow; he was only about two feet tall."

Huge weeds had sprouted along the wheelchair ramp leading up to the porch that ran across the entire front of the house. The blue paint and white trim were faded and peeling, yet it had obviously been an elegant home when it was new.

"Over there is Lake Carolyn, named after a wonderful little girl who had no legs—she walked on her hands. Carolyn also lived here. When the preachers who were going to 'help' me out by taking over PTL put this place into bankruptcy, they kicked the residents out. That's the behind-the-scenes pain you don't ever read about. It grieved me to think they couldn't even let Kevin die here in the dream house we had promised would be his home for the rest of his life."

"What happened to him?"

"He had to return to Michigan, where he died while I was in prison." Jim's voice choked up and he had to pause a moment. "It hit me so hard that I'd made a commitment to Kevin, and I couldn't fulfill it."

I was beginning to feel a minute portion of the heaviness that must have weighed on Jim for years. Nothing I had heard or read could have prepared me for what I was witnessing as Jim took me on a personal tour of the ruins of his ministry.

In a few minutes we parked at the entrance of the Heritage Grand Hotel and peeked in the windows of the huge lobby, now vacant. "The lobby held thousands of people," Jim said. "In fact, we did a lot of our galas right from the lobby. I remember Della Reese was here for the opening." We turned away from the windows and started walking. "The doorman always hugged the guests as they arrived," Jim continued. "It was quite a welcome."

"The hotel was still open when I was here a few years ago," I said. "And so were the shops on Main Street." I looked ahead of us, down the row of colorful three-story buildings, each with a different facade. Weeds grew through the white wrought-iron fences edging the overgrown lawn, and the pavement had cracked and buckled in places. "It looks like a ghost town now."

"These shops along Main Street were home to the most fabulous candy factory in the world . . . a big Christian bookstore . . . a beauty parlor, vitamin shop, drugstore—anything you might need for a vacation or a convention you could find right here. We had big ballrooms where we held Bible seminars as well as dinner theaters and special activities. And, of course, the water park."

Directly across from Main Street lay the remains of the water park. "It's so hot here in the summers, I wanted to bring the ocean to Charlotte. This was one of the first water parks to be built without metal towers," Jim said. "We used rock because we wanted it to look natural."

We started walking back to the car. "We had trains and trams that ran throughout Heritage, an amphitheater where we presented a nightly passion play, and even a carousel for the kids. That was one of the first things to go, the carousel." Jim paused for a moment, looking reflective. "There's some significance to what these people did. I'm talking about the preachers who took over. They sold off the fun things—the carousel and the trains—early on. I think there was a resentment that we were having so much fun. I mean, kids were telling their parents they'd rather come here than go to Disneyland. The parents loved it because of all the security; it was safe for the kids to run around and play. And everybody was ministering—seventy lifeguards a shift in the water park, and most of them were Bible school students . . ."

Jim talked about the dozens of church services, prayer meetings, and Bible studies held every week, the home for unwed mothers, the adoption agency, the rehabilitation center, the childhood home of Billy Graham, which had been moved to the grounds of Heritage USA and restored, and other ministries that operated out of PTL.

"It's no wonder you burned out," I said.

"Yes. I did so many things wrong, and I became way too obsessed with building—I got ahead of God a lot of times. Yet so much good was accomplished here. Sometimes, though, I feel it has all been in vain."

"I'm sure a lot of people still remember the good things, Jim."

"Some do, I guess. Especially those who came to know Christ here; they don't forget." He took a final look around him, obviously dismayed at what he saw. "I don't know why someone can't open this place again. It belongs to God's people—they built it. Now it seems to be rotting to the ground. I try not to get bitter over it, but every time I come and see my life's work sitting here in shambles, it's like Satan is mocking me." Jim's voice started to shake and his eyes brimmed with tears. "Corporate America can spend millions of dollars building thousands of beautiful hotels, and it never raises an eyebrow. But if anybody tries to build one nice place for God's people, it's considered exorbitant. That breaks my heart."

It hurt to see the tears spill down Jim's face. Describing the destruction of his dream—a dream of building something great for the kingdom of God—had been very painful for him. "Let's just go," I said. "This is too hard on you, and seeing it through your eyes is breaking my heart."

I was deeply affected by the time we spent at Heritage. It was a moving insight into the man I was about to marry. Now I was about to meet his daughter, and as I dressed for dinner, I couldn't help thinking of the impact all this must have had on her.

We were staying in Charlotte at the beautiful Adam's Mark Hotel, where Jim would speak at a conference the next day. Jim had a suite—courtesy of the hotel and MorningStar Ministries—on the top floor, and I had a room downstairs. I prayed a silent prayer as I took the elevator up to Jim's suite, asking the Lord to give me favor with my future stepdaughter. I was about to become a stepmom and a grandma all at once, and I was nervous because I knew how much Jim adored his daughter, and I wanted her to love and accept me.

"Is that for me?" Jim asked when I arrived, rolling his eyes at the gift bag I was carrying.

"Of course. I brought you this very feminine, frilly gift." I knew he was teasing me and trying to lighten the mood, which had been so heavy earlier that day. "No, it's for Tammy Sue." I told him about selecting one of my teacups to give her.

"She'll love it," he said. "And she'll love you."

My heart was pounding so hard I thought it would come out of my chest when I heard the knock. I was standing by the large conference table in the suite, fussing with the tissue paper spilling out of the gift bag when Jim answered the door. I pressed my palms against my skirt as I walked forward to greet the couple.

"Hi, Tammy Sue," I said. She looked exotic and lovely with her long, glossy black hair framing her fair face—a life-size china doll. "And you must be Doug." I hugged them both and we made small talk.

What Jim and Jay had predicted was true: I fell in love with Tammy Sue, and she took to me instantly. Within five minutes she had said to me, "You're so beautiful—I love you." All my fears melted away, and I knew God had answered my prayer by giving me favor with her.

From a generational standpoint, I'm closer to Tammy Sue's age than to Jim's—I'm seventeen years younger than Jim and twelve years older than Sue. And yet the age gap has never seemed to matter. Perhaps being in the middle has given me a better perspective on both father and daughter.

Sue has become a very important person in my life—and in my ministry as well. She often travels with me and sings before I speak. Her rich, honeyed voice carries the unmistakable imprint of God's anointing and, like her father, the pain of the past has given her music ministry a depth that touches people in a powerful way. On one of our recent trips, Sue told me something that remains etched in my heart. "God didn't just send you to my daddy," she said. "He sent you to me."

29

A Picture Worth
a Lot of Money

Meeting Tammy Sue was the highlight of my trip to Charlotte, yet there were other highly significant moments as well. Jim was eager for me to meet Rick Joyner, a popular author and conference speaker who served on Jim's board of directors. Rick's MorningStar conference marked the first occasion Jim and I appeared together publicly in our church circles. It was gratifying to be warmly received by both Rick and those attending the conference.

Afterward, more emotional memories surfaced as Jim took me to see the ruins of the Tega Cay house where he and Tammy Faye had raised their children. The Bakkers had moved more than twenty times during the early years of their marriage and ministry, but they had lived in this house for an entire decade while the kids were growing up. It was the one place they all thought of as home, the scene of much happier times; now it was a burned-out hull. "I learned the house was gone when I saw news coverage of the blaze from the prison television room," Jim told me.

Watching his former home go up in smoke had devastated Jim, and he couldn't help thinking that fire and destruction had become a metaphor for his life and ministry. I believe it was actually the refiner's fire—the burning away of the dross—and restoration that would become the metaphor for Jim's work for God, but in the pain of his loss, it hadn't seemed that way at the time.

At Tega Cay we crawled through the bushes that had grown over the property and climbed over charred timbers to stand on the concrete slab that had been the foundation of their lovely home. I saw the swimming pool and the playhouse that had been criticized in the press. "It's nothing like the reports made it out to be," I said. "I've seen much more elaborate ones in my friends' backyards." I felt so sad for Jim and his family.

Jim took me to see another house in Charlotte, the one where he had been living when he moved to the Dream Center. Dexter Yeager of Amway had originally built the immense "log cabin" as his home and then later used it as a corporate retreat and conference center. Sometime after that Rick Joyner leased the cabin and the surrounding acreage, which also included a large two-story brick office building, as a ministry headquarters. Bible students still lived on the top floor of the three-story log home, which was fifteen thousand-plus square feet; Jim had occupied several rooms on the bottom floor, and many of his belongings were still there.

"Living here was like coming back full circle," Jim told me as we drove up the wooded private drive that led from the highway to the cabin. We passed a small lake and the stately colonial building that now served as Rick Joyner's ministry headquarters.

"My family actually lived here for two years after I left PTL and before I went to prison," Jim said. "When I resigned, we had to move out of the Tega Cay house—it was owned by the ministry. We wound up here, thanks to Dexter Yeager."

We parked in the gravel lot in front of the L-shaped building and then walked up a few steps to the main entrance. Jim opened the beautiful double doors with leaded glass panels, and we stepped into a large, open living area. A gleaming wooden staircase led to a loft area to the right, and off to the left was a country kitchen with knotty pine walls and modern ovens set into an arched brick wall. Jim walked over to the massive stone fireplace, the focal point of the two-story great room. "Some of our last television programs were actually filmed from this room," Jim said. He looked around as if remembering where the cameras had been placed. "C'mon. I'll show you around."

Amanda had tried to prepare me for what I was about to see; she had been to this house before. "When you go to Charlotte," she had told me, "just be prepared in your heart. It will be like nothing you've ever seen before. Jim calls it his gallery."

"Gallery? . . . Like an art gallery?" I had no idea what she was talking about.

"No, a photo gallery. It's his entire life in pictures—everything . . . including Tammy Faye."

It had already been an emotional trip, seeing for the first time bits and pieces of Jim's previous life in tangible objects, the physical debris that had survived the explosion of his life. But seeing the gallery brought me face-to-face with Jim's past and how it was going to influence my future. It also brought me face-to-face with his ex-wife.

We passed through the kitchen to the central staircase that linked all three floors of the house. Reaching the basement level, we came to Jim's gallery: the walls of the long hallway were covered floor to ceiling with framed photographs. Pictures of Jim as a child and more recent pictures of him with his elderly parents. Childhood photos of Sue and Jay. Photos from every period of PTL's ministry. Jim and Tammy with Roy Rogers and Dale Evans. Jim and Tammy with Presidents Carter and Reagan. Jim and Tammy by themselves.

That took me aback. I could understand all the personal photos of the family together and all the professional photos from their ministry together. But why would he have a picture of him and his ex-wife by themselves? *Is this some kind of shrine?* I wondered. If he wasn't still carrying a torch for Tammy Faye, why did he have her pictured so prominently in his gallery?

I didn't ask him about it at that moment, but much later Jim told me the story behind the photo display. "When Tammy and I divorced," he said, "I didn't think I would ever get out of prison. I was completely hopeless. Our property settlement was simple: I told her to take whatever she wanted and to put anything she didn't want in storage for me. After I was released, I found I had several roomfuls of our old furniture, a lot of knick-knacks we had bought over the years, and an odd assortment of household items—dishes, pots, and pans. What surprised me were all the boxes of family photographs that my ex-wife apparently didn't want.

"I had lost touch with myself in prison. I almost stopped believing I was Jim Bakker—it was as if all this had happened to someone else. Going through all these photographs was my way of coming back to reality. It was like therapy. This was my history, everything I owned, and I couldn't part with any of it."

"I can understand all the pictures of you and Tammy Faye with the kids," I said. "But what I can't understand are the pictures of the two of you together. When I got divorced, I wanted to get rid of everything that reminded me of my ex-husband. So when I saw the gallery that day, it looked to me as if you were still in love with her."

"No, I'm not, and I wasn't even in love with her when I hung all those photographs. By putting up those pictures of my ex-wife, I was refusing to live in denial. She had been an important part of my life for over three decades, and she was gone. It was part of my healing process."

"Even though Amanda tried to warn me, it still shocked me."

He was apologetic. "Lori, I hadn't been back to the house in months—way before I met you—and it didn't occur to me that you would be affected that way when I took you there. I'm sorry."

In every divorce and remarriage where children are involved, the new wife has to come to terms with the existence of the former wife and her continued presence in the restructured family unit. It's seldom an easy adjustment, but our situation was complicated by the fact that Jim's ex-wife just happened to be a larger-than-life figure who, despite her remarriage, was still known worldwide as Tammy Faye Bakker.

The day after I encountered her photos in Jim's gallery, I met her in person for the first time, a memorable occasion.

For twenty-one years Jim had delegated many jobs to his assistant, Shirley Fulbright. That Sunday morning in Charlotte, he put Shirley in charge of introducing me to his ex-wife. I think Jim was even more nervous about my meeting Tammy Faye than I was.

When we arrived at the church, we went straight to the pastor's office so Jim could prepare for his grandsons' baptism. The pastor had scheduled the baptism during the early part of the service, before the sermon, because Jim and I were leaving immediately after the baptism to drive to Atlanta to see his mom. I hugged James and Jonathan and Tammy Sue, who would be staying backstage with the boys.

I dreaded venturing into the church by myself and was grateful when Shirley arrived to escort me. She greeted me graciously in her soft Southern accent. "It's so good to see a familiar face," I told her. Shirley is tall and blonde, with a high forehead and high cheekbones—very professional and poised. I had met her previously in Jim's office at the Dream Center and had learned more about her as Jim filled me in on PTL and Heritage USA. She was an important part of the Bakker family's life as well as Jim's ministry, and Sue had been very happy that Shirley could be in Charlotte for the occasion.

"We have a row of seats reserved in the balcony," Shirley said. "I'll take you up there." We walked into the sanctuary, and long before we reached the stairs to the upper level, I had spotted Tammy Faye. Even at that distance it would have been hard to miss her. She was wearing a big wide-brimmed black hat, tilted at a jaunty angle. I suddenly felt underdressed in my simple black dress with a little jacket.

I followed Shirley up the staircase, thinking what a trip it was that I was about to meet not just Jim's ex-wife but also one of the most recognizable women in America; in years past I had seen much more news coverage of Tammy Faye than I had ever seen of Jim. Shirley formally introduced me to the former Mrs. Bakker. "It's very nice to meet you," I said, and she reciprocated the greeting. Tammy Faye remained seated while she shook my hand.

"You're very blessed to have such wonderful children," I told her. "They're great kids. I've enjoyed knowing Jay for the last few years and look forward to getting to know Sue better."

"Thank you," she said. "You know, Sue and I never had a very close relationship until recently, but that's started to change."

How strange that she would immediately say that, I thought. *She must figure I know that's true, so she wants to make sure to tell me herself.*

I also met Doug's mother, stepfather, and grandmother, who had already taken their seats on one side of Tammy Faye; now Shirley sat down next to her, and I took the seat on the other side of Shirley. I was glad when Doug arrived a minute later and sat next to me; I felt a little more comfortable and not quite so alone.

Tammy Faye picked up a church bulletin and started fanning herself dramatically, batting her legendary eyelashes and sighing. "I'm having horrible hot flashes," she announced. "Just horrible."

"I can sympathize," I said. "I know how awful they can be."

"You do?" Her arched eyebrows emphasized the question, and she cut her eyes in my direction.

"Yes, I get hot flashes too. I'm on hormone replacement therapy."

"You're kidding me." She put down her bulletin for a second as she absorbed that surprising bit of information, then picked it up almost immediately and started fanning furiously again. "So am I."

"Really? I've had to take hormones for about eighteen years now."

"Just a few years for me. I take Premarin—what about you?"

"I'm on Premarin too," I said.

"Well, I'll be."

We both smiled, glad the ice had been broken. For a moment

we weren't the former and future wives of Jim Bakker but simply two women who suffered the aggravation of hormonal changes.

In a few moments the instruments began to play and the choir filed onstage. As the music minister was walking toward the pulpit to announce the opening hymn, Tammy Faye leaned across Shirley and touched my leg. "You know, honey," she said, pointing to herself and then me, "this picture would be worth a lot of money."

"Oh, yes, I'm aware of that." I grinned and silently prayed there were no camera-happy worshipers sitting nearby.

The congregation stood and Shirley reached for the hymnal. I hadn't sung out of a hymnal in years; my church sang contemporary praise music with the words projected onto a large screen. With only a few hymnals for each row, several people had to share. Our group was a trio: Shirley in the middle holding the hymnal, with Tammy Faye on one side and Lori Beth on the other. *Yes, indeed. This would make quite a picture,* I thought as we sang praises to God.

Jim did a great job baptizing James and Jonathan, who were so precious. Jim talked about the incredible experience of being a grandparent and told cute stories about the boys. I wondered what he was thinking as he looked up from the baptistry to see his ex-wife and his future wife sitting together. Tammy laughed and seemed to enjoy his comments. Then she cried as Jim immersed her grandsons in water, memorializing their commitment to Jesus Christ, and intoned the well-known words: "Upon your profession of faith, I baptize you in the name of the Father, the Son, and the Holy Spirit." We all had tears in our eyes at that moment.

After the baptism, Sue came up to the balcony to fetch Doug and me and to tell her mom and her in-laws good-bye; they would be keeping the kids while Doug and Sue drove to Atlanta with us for the afternoon.

Our four-hour drive to Atlanta was one of the most enjoyable trips I've ever made. Sue sat in the front seat with Doug, who was driving, and Jim and I relaxed in the backseat. The tension I'd felt that morning evaporated, and we laughed and told stories and sang. Sue and Doug are music people, and the three of us knew the words to every song on the radio. They also knew the older songs from the '70s that I love. I would say, "That's one of my favorite songs," and Sue would exclaim, "Mine too!" Jim opened up and even told a few jokes, which he rarely does.

Jim also talked about his mother as we rode. "My mom and dad worked with me in the ministry," he said. "They were official greeters at Heritage USA and welcomed hundreds of thousands of people. In prison I prayed every day that my parents would live to see me get out, and God granted that. When they could no longer take care of themselves in the home I'd built for them at Heritage, Norman and June moved them to Atlanta."

When we arrived, Jim was shocked to see how rapidly his mother had gone downhill in the few months since he had seen her. She was propped up in a recliner and using oxygen to help her breathe. Terribly thin and frail, she looked almost like a skeleton.

"Mother, I want you to meet someone," Jim said. "This is Lori, the girl I told you about."

I knelt down by the side of her recliner. "Hi, Furn," I said. "It's nice to meet you."

She looked confused. "Who is this?" she asked Jim.

"Lori," he said. "Lori and I are getting married."

Jim's mother looked up at him and said, "Does Tammy Faye approve?"

He looked at me and shrugged. "Well, I don't think she's very happy about it," he told her.

"Good," his mother said defiantly.

Her question and one-word answer startled me, and I wondered what the history between the two women had been.

Ironically, Tammy Faye expressed her approval of me later that day, while we were still at Norman and June's house. Sue called home to check on the kids and talked to her mom. Tammy Faye told her, "I like Lori. She's really nice, and I think we could be friends. Maybe we could even do holidays together."

Jim's mother joined us for dinner, sitting in her wheelchair. At the table she cried and asked for Raleigh, her late husband, and it upset Jim to see her like that. It was touching to see how Norman took care of his mother, who at the end of her life required the same kind of care she had given him as a baby.

It turned out to be the last time Jim ever saw his mother; she passed away not long after we were married. I was very glad I'd had the opportunity to be with her for those few hours we were in Atlanta.

We returned to Charlotte that Sunday night, and had a great time with Sue and Doug again on the drive back. The next day Jim and I left for L.A., but we did not stay there long. Soon we were on the road again, and this time Jim would be meeting my family.

30

STRAIGHT FROM THE HEART

Late August 1998

Jim, you won't believe what was waiting for me when I got home." I was pacing as I talked on the cordless phone. "I live in this huge apartment complex, but they knew where to find me. I mean, I am freaking out—"

"Lori Beth, slow down," Jim said, "and start at the beginning."

"I just got into town a few minutes ago, and someone had stuck a business card on my apartment door. There was a handwritten note that said, 'Lori Beth Graham, please call me.' Can you believe that? They knew my full name and my apartment number!"

"Who did?"

"The tabloids. The business card belongs to some reporter for the *Globe*. The note says, 'Would love to do an interview with you.'"

"Sweetheart, I tried to tell you. I knew this would happen sooner or later."

"But what do I do?"

"Nothing. Just toss the business card in the trash."

Jim had tried to tell me that life with him would include bombardment from the media at some point, but up until then, I had not come in contact with any reporters or photographers. This first experience had left me unsettled, and for the next few days I searched the shrubbery every time I left the apartment, afraid someone from the tabloids would be hiding there.

About a week after I returned to Phoenix, Jim flew in from L.A. to meet my family. But the first place I took him was the ghetto. I had been gone for most of the summer, and Margie had moved again while I was away. It had taken me a couple of days to track down where she was living, and now I was eager to see her and the kids. I also wanted Jim to meet my inner-city family, so we headed straight from the airport to the housing projects.

Although Jim had been working with inner-city people for a while, most of his contact with them had been inside the Dream Center, not in their homes. His eyes grew wide as we drove past the dingy, rundown buildings until we found the right address. The minute I stopped the car, some of Margie's kids came running; they had recognized my little tan car. "Lori! Lori!" they squealed. Maricela, Sergio, and Little Lori jumped all over me as did a couple of toddlers, who were Margie's grandchildren; her oldest girls had started having babies when they were fourteen or fifteen. The kids were dirty and sweaty, but I didn't care; I just wanted to love on them.

I introduced several of the kids to Jim. "I'm getting married next week," I told them, "and this is the man who is going to be my husband." They laughed excitedly as we walked upstairs. For eight years they had heard me talk about getting married someday.

Jim was shocked when we walked into the two-bedroom tenement where twenty people lived. Three were adults—Margie, her sister, and her cousin Joe—and all the rest were children. Jim told me later, "I couldn't believe what I saw. Why don't more people go into the inner city? Why doesn't the church know what's going on there?"

In spite of the incredible crowding, the apartment was a vast improvement over the first place I'd found Margie. Joe was mostly responsible for the changes. He had come to live with Margie a few months after I met her. Joe had once been a practicing Christian, but he had slipped back into a life of degradation. Homeless and addicted, he wound up at Margie's. I first met him when I came to pick up the kids for church one Sunday night. Joe had answered the door, and he was drunk. When he found out I was taking the kids to church, he started cussing me out. He got right in my face and let his anger erupt.

Margie had stepped between us. "Get out of my house," she yelled at him. "Nobody talks to my best friend that way! You can't live here anymore."

Later, after things had calmed down, I told her, "Margie, you can't kick Joe out. He has no place to live, and he'll wind up back on the streets."

She let him stay, and Joe ended up being wonderful to me over the years. He had become an important part of their household, taking care of the laundry and cooking, and trying to clean up their living conditions. Joe had even started saving the Christmas decorations I would bring them every year, and he kept the pictures I gave them. I was pleased now to see pictures of me on the wall, and I pointed them out to Jim.

Margie was thrilled to see me, and the feeling was mutual. "I hadn't heard from you all summer," she said, "and I didn't know what had happened to you."

"I've been away from Phoenix," I told her, "and you don't have a phone, so I couldn't call. It took me a few days to find you."

She was also overjoyed at the news of my marriage, which she had already learned. "I heard it on TV," she said. "I couldn't believe it was our Lori—and Jim Bakker!"

That week initial reports of our engagement had broken locally. Very short news blurbs announced that Jim Bakker was marrying a local Phoenix girl. Evidently the media hadn't managed to get a picture of me yet, because the television reports featured a sketch rather than a photograph. I never saw the news coverage; it wasn't extensive at that point.

Margie was also thrilled to meet Jim. In fact, she may have been more excited about that than the fact that I was getting married—and that was big news. We had often talked about my getting married, and when I was at their place the past Christmas, we joked about it while we were making videos. Margie looked right in the camera and said to my unknown future husband, "Whoever you are, you're going to have to love us, too, because we're her family!"

Now she kept saying, "I can't believe it! You're really Jim Bakker!" The older kids started running through the projects, telling their neighbors, "Jim Bakker is in our house!"

Jim had sat down in the one armchair in the living room, and the kids had flocked around him. I studied him as he sat there, looking cute in his customary ball cap, and looking compassionate and loving as a bunch of ghetto kids crawled all over him. The kids, acting like Jim was a movie star, asked him for his autograph. "I'd be glad to," he said, "but I don't have any paper."

They went and got their school notebooks, and Jim patiently

wrote a personal message to each one of Margie's eight children, filling an entire page for each child. He wanted to write something that would impact their lives in a positive way. I knew the notes wouldn't survive long unless Joe managed to save them, but I was proud of Jim's thoughtful gesture.

By this time neighbors were streaming into the already overcrowded apartment, and a couple of them started snapping pictures. When the flashes went off, Jim said, "Lori, we really need to leave. With this much attention, the news media will be here in ten or fifteen minutes."

Our visit had been short—maybe thirty or forty-five minutes—but memorable. I said my good-byes to my inner-city family, not knowing when I would see them again.

"You always promised I could be at your wedding," Margie told me as I left. "I really want to be there when you get married next week."

It grieved me deeply that I had no way to get Margie and the kids to L.A. If there had been more time, or if I hadn't been so exhausted and overwhelmed from the roller coaster of being on the road with Jim and trying to plan a wedding, perhaps I could have found someone to take up the cause and get them there. But it didn't happen, and I regretted it.

It's a great blessing when your whole family falls in love with the person you're about to marry, and that's what happened when Jim was in Phoenix. He had already met my mother, and she'd had an idea that he might be God's choice for me even before I did. Now Jim got to meet my grandmother, and they hit it off immediately.

But the biggest surprise to me—and a huge relief—was how well Jim got along with my dad. Dad could be terribly difficult, and I didn't know quite what to expect when I took Jim to meet Dad and Lita, my stepmom, at their house. My dad was an imposing figure—six feet tall and by this time four hundred pounds—so the sheer physical contrast between the two men was startling. Not only physically imposing, my dad was controlling and bombastic; I never knew what he might say, and that caused me to be nervous about their meeting. But Jim treated him with respect and seemed to know from the beginning how to handle my father, who could alternate between being very bad-tempered and supremely charming.

Lita also fell in love with Jim, and over the next few months he brought so much healing into my relationship with Lita and Dad. About two years earlier, my dad had manipulated me into doing something that put me in an untenable position with Lita, and we had been estranged ever since. When I realized what Dad had done, I immediately went to Lita and apologized, but we couldn't repair the rift, and it had deepened with time. Jim just walked into the situation and loved everybody, and it somehow broke down the barriers. Lita and I were able to renew our close relationship, and I was touched when she began referring to me as her daughter again.

The memory that stands out about Jim's first meeting with my dad was something that happened while Jim was out of the room. Dad sat me down in a chair and in his booming voice said, "Now, you listen to me, Little Girl." I knew a lecture was coming. "Jim Bakker is a good man—one of the finest men on the earth today. God has given him to you, and if you ever do anything to hurt him, you'll have your daddy to answer to." To underscore just how serious he was, he added a threat: "I will disown you."

I didn't flinch at Dad's harsh tone, as I once would have. It would have been nice if he could have simply offered me his blessing without accompanying it with a threat to disown me if I didn't treat Jim right. But he did give me his approval—in fact, marrying Jim moved me to the top of Dad's list.

He said something else that first day he met Jim, and it brought an earlier occasion to mind. "I always said Jim got a raw deal," Dad said. "Didn't I always say that?" he asked me. I remembered sitting in the same room nine years earlier, watching TV with Dad and Lita. We saw the pictures of Jim being led away in chains to serve his sentence, and Dad had announced, "They're doing that man wrong. He didn't do what they said he did." Even then, my dad had believed in Jim, and he took it very seriously that God had now brought this man into my life.

On Friday night, one week before my wedding, several friends threw a huge party for me. JoAnn Denman, one of my mentors, and her daughter Nicole Oakes hosted a wedding shower, which was held at the home of Jill and Max Arnold. Jill had been like a sister to me, and for years she had done my hair in her salon without charging me. It was her way of contributing to my ministry, and it blessed me.

I had told Jill I didn't want the typical shower with pots and pans or china and silverware. After the wedding, we would be living in Jim's one room at the Dream Center, and there would be no space to store anything. "Tell them not to bring gifts," I told Jill. "I just want to see people."

Jill argued with me about it. "But they'll want to give you something, Lori. You should allow them to do that."

I relented and we finally settled on a personal shower. I love lingerie, and that was something I knew I would appreciate and use.

That Friday night two hundred ladies, most of them members of my church, attended the event at Jill's home. The catered affair was not your typical bridal shower—it was almost a preview of the wedding. Jim and I stood at the top of the winding staircase, where everyone could see us, and I told the story of how God had brought us together. I thanked everyone for believing in me and for always telling me they knew God had someone special for me. Jim put his arm around me as he said a few words about how wonderful it was to find romance again at his age. I blushed as he told them how special I was and how much he adored me. The ladies loved it, of course.

The next day I was overwhelmed when I looked around my living room and saw the beautifully wrapped packages and elegant gift bags stacked everywhere. "Bobbi, if you hadn't come over to help me, I don't think I could have faced this," I said.

"Just think how great it will be when we've finished opening and recording all these gifts." Bobbi approached the task with gusto, and her enthusiasm began to rub off on me. Soon the floor was littered with paper and ribbons, and we giggled like teenagers as we unwrapped package after package and commented appreciatively on the contents. "Jim is gonna love this." Bobbi's eyes twinkled as she held up a beautiful red satin bra and matching panties.

"That reminds me," I said with a grin. "I'd better go check on my baby."

"He must be a really sick man if he's not in here watching you open all this lingerie."

I went back to the bedroom to check on Jim, who was sound asleep. He'd had a recurrence of an infection and his temperature had shot up. He'd been so sick, in fact, that I hadn't wanted him to stay at the hotel alone, so I insisted he take my bed and I planned on sleeping on the sofa—as soon as Bobbi and I uncovered it.

We worked on the project for several hours and still didn't finish. Bobbi agreed to come back the next day and help me. She painstakingly recorded the names in a book for me, but in transporting and cataloging all the gifts, some of the cards inevitably got mixed up, and I'm sure some friends never got a proper acknowledgment. I hope they will forgive me.

Jim's fever broke the next morning, so he went to church with me. Pastor Barnett introduced us from the pulpit and announced our upcoming wedding. Everyone applauded and wanted to congratulate us after the service.

Sunday, August 30, was my birthday, and my dad had planned a special celebration after church. Jim and I went to brunch at a nice restaurant with Dad and Lita. My mom came, and our group also included our friends Sheryl Wells, Lloyd and Chris Zeigler, and Kurt and Quanna Coahran and their son Johnny, whom we had asked to sing at our wedding.

We were enjoying our meal when the manager came over and stood directly behind Jim and me. "Excuse me," he said, "but one of the local news channels is out front, and they're wanting an interview."

Jim's face fell. "Please don't let them come inside," he said. "I'm sick and not up to an interview right now, and this is a birthday party for my fiancée. We would really appreciate some privacy."

The manager assured us he would do everything he could to keep the cameras outside.

"How on earth did they find us?" I wondered.

"Someone must have tipped them off," Jim said. "Maybe someone from church this morning."

"But the church people wouldn't have known where we were having lunch," Mom said. "Out of all the restaurants in Phoenix, how would reporters know we were here?"

Everyone at the table discussed the media intrusion, but my father remained rather quiet. That was unlike him, and it raised suspicions. I never knew for sure, but I think he may have been the one to tell the press. Later, after Jim and I had been married a while, I found out my dad had been using Jim's name to try to get good seats at the best restaurants.

The birthday brunch was my first experience of sneaking out back doors and jumping into our car to avoid the media. At that time I could not have imagined how many times Jim and I would wind up doing something similar.

That afternoon Jim went back to bed while Bobbi and I finished opening my gifts from the shower. Later, Jim helped me thin out my wardrobe.

"I'm flattered you want my opinion," he said, sounding rather surprised. He was in bed, propped up on several pillows, and still groggy from a nap.

"Well, space will be so limited in our one room that I can't take very much with me, and I want to be sure I wear clothes that are appropriate for public appearances with you. Besides, you have great taste." I held up an outfit. "What do you think of this—no, wait! I'll try it on."

I shut the door to the small walk-in closet and changed clothes. "Okay, be honest," I said when I walked back into the room.

He shook his head from side to side. "One word: teenybopper. Honey, too many of your clothes are stuff that's popular with the youth. They're not flattering to you as a great woman of God," he added in a more diplomatic tone.

"You know, you're right," I said thoughtfully. I returned to the closet. Every couple of minutes I would come back in a different outfit, and he would give me a yes or a no. If he sounded noncommittal on something, I tossed it in the give-away pile, which soon exceeded what was going back in the closet.

"That's a beautiful suit," he said on one of my modeling excursions, "but a regular suit jacket is the wrong length for you. It cuts you off. You'd look better with a short jacket that comes just to your waist, or a much longer jacket."

I was amazed at his fashion sense and so glad I had asked for his advice. He never made me feel that he was censoring my wardrobe, but simply helping me discover what looked best on me. To this day, I take Jim shopping with me, and he never steers me wrong.

After I had finished going through my closet that day in Phoenix, about three-fourths of my wardrobe was spread over the bedroom, designated for a new owner. The next day Bobbi took all the clothes, kept a few things she wanted for herself, and then gave the rest to the Bible students at Phoenix First.

In retrospect, it's funny to me that God sent me a man with a keen sense of style. I had prayed for a husband for years but hadn't thought to put that on my list of requirements for a spouse. Above all, I had simply wanted God's choice for me— and when Jim came along, I discovered God's choice was even more wonderful than I could have imagined.

Prior to Jim's arrival in Phoenix that week before we were married, I had taken time to write about him in my journal. I wish I had been more faithful in writing our story; there are only a couple of entries during our seven-week whirlwind engagement. The following is straight from those handwritten pages . . . and straight from my heart:

We have been apart for one week and I pray that is the longest we will ever be apart again! We spent hours on the phone each night. Crazy, I guess, but we are so in love and want to be together always in everything we do. I know this is possible because it has always been one of my heart's desires concerning my husband, and the Lord has blessed me with that.

Speaking of heart's desires regarding my hubby, I want to take this time to thank the Lord and to put on paper how Jim literally is all and more than I could have hoped for.

First—a humble man of God, a man after God's own heart. He is a combination of my two favorite men in the Bible: David and Joseph.

Second—a caretaker and a servant. God knows I need someone to take care of me, but I never dreamed it could be anything like this! He takes the utmost care and serves me and others with love.

The following are not necessarily in order but as I think of them I will write . . .

- He loves pouring into young people—mentoring and discipling them. That's my heart as well.
- He respects women ministers and will help develop my ministry skills.
- He provides for me.
- He protects me.
- He instructs me in the Word and so much more. He is so intelligent and knowledgeable.
- He is in God's presence but not religious. He is all about grace!
- He makes me secure, always at the right moment, when my old insecurities start rising up.

- He adores me—my heart, soul, spirit, and body.
- He loves and adores his children and grandchildren.
- He doesn't talk badly about people but gives them the benefit of the doubt.
- He is a hard worker.

I could go on and on . . .

Jim truly is the love of my life! Although the time has been very short, only a few weeks of knowing one another, it has been very in-depth. It's hard to believe I ever lived without him, and I'm sure that in the very near future I will have a hard time remembering life without him.

Those words came to pass. I do have a hard time remembering my life without Jim, and that's because we are truly one heart and one flesh and one mind. Only God could have brought us together, and only God could have put together our storybook wedding—with the help of some very special people to whom we will forever be grateful.

31

THE GIFT OF FRIENDS

September 3, 1998

It was almost 10:00 P.M. when I finally made it to John and
Joyce Caruso's home on the Thursday night before my wedding.
They had invited me to spend the night there to allow extra time
for getting dressed the next morning—the wedding was
scheduled for Friday noon.

I arrived in tears. What should have been an hour's drive from
Newport Beach—where I had been staying with my brother
Mark—had taken more than two hours because I got lost. My
cousin Mike had offered to drive me, but I had declined, thinking the Carusos' house wouldn't be that hard to find. But it was
dark, their house was up in the hills, I was exhausted, and I had
gotten completely confused by the directions. I was also upset
because Jim was still sick. When I'd talked to him on the phone
earlier that evening, he had been in bed, bundled under a pile of
blankets, sweating off a fever.

John and Joyce hugged me and fussed over me as I explained about getting lost. "We're almost ready for the big event," Joyce said. "I'm just putting some finishing touches on the flowers."

"If I know my wife," John said, "she will still be putting some 'finishing touches' on those flowers just before you walk down the aisle. The last few days our house has looked like a florist's shop—boxes of silk flowers stacked everywhere, strands of ivy carefully laid across the furniture waiting to be hung. I was afraid I'd step on something and get killed for it." He was smiling so broadly, I knew his complaint was good-natured.

"I can't believe you did all this yourself," I said. "You have such a talent for decorating, Joyce. And the expense—it looks like you spent thousands of dollars just on the flowers."

"No, most of the silk flowers were from my daughter's wedding," Joyce explained. "I bought a few extras, then added the ivy—had to get enough so it would drape just right."

"It's incredible. Unbelievably beautiful." I looked around me in awe. John and Joyce have a fabulous home to begin with, but now it looked like something out of a wedding magazine. The spacious foyer was open and almost three stories tall, and the center of attention was a magnificent curved staircase. Joyce had floral accents of mauve and burgundy silk in just the right places.

"I thought the staircase would be great for pictures," Joyce said. Speechless, I nodded in agreement.

"Come see what we've done in the backyard," John said. "That's where the ceremony will take place, of course."

"John has knocked himself out repainting the gazebo in this heat," Joyce said as we walked into the large backyard.

"The gazebo is just perfect," I said. "And the chairs—they're even white too!"

"Joyce wouldn't settle for metal folding chairs." John grinned. "Just wouldn't do. We have a friend who owns a rental company, and Joyce talked him into donating the white wooden chairs, and the kneeling bench."

"It didn't take much talking. He was glad to do it," Joyce said. "The tuxedos took a little more."

"You took care of the tuxedos too?" I asked, astonished.

"I had heard that Sears occasionally made their rental tuxedos available at no charge. I figured it wouldn't hurt to ask, so I explained the situation, and they donated the formal wear for Jim and Jay."

"I got all the easy jobs," John said with a laugh. "Like lugging the sound system out here and getting it set up. Painting, mowing, cleaning—and doing whatever Joyce told me to."

"I knew you were taking care of all the arrangements . . ." I was so overcome, my voice started to break. "But I had no idea of the scope of this wedding until now. I can't believe you've gone to all this trouble—and you barely know me!"

"We know our friend Jim is absolutely crazy about you, and that's all that matters," John said.

"We're happy to do it," Joyce added. "Although, when we first offered to let Jim have the wedding here, I hadn't quite pictured this." She pointed at the more than two hundred white chairs arranged in rows in her backyard. "He kept saying, 'It will be a small home wedding, just twenty-five guests.' I thought, *Sure, I can handle that.* And then it just kept growing. The latest estimate is around two hundred fifty."

John chuckled. "Jim just left a zero off his original estimate."

"To be honest," I said, "I don't even know who all is going to be here tomorrow. There was no time to send out formal invitations. We never even stopped long enough to make out a real guest list. Mom helped me phone invitations to a few friends and family members. And Shirley, Jim's assistant, took care of notifying his people. What a mess we've put you through . . ."

"It really wasn't that much," Joyce said as we walked back into the house. "John and I have mainly taken care of the house and decorations. A lot of other people have helped. Like Shirley and your mom. And Leanne. She was here most of the day preparing food—you should see what she's got stashed in my freezer. The buffet is going to be fabulous."

Leanne and Howard Bailey had arrived in Los Angeles four days after I met Jim. A few weeks earlier, Jim had spoken at the commencement at Christ for the Nations, a Bible school in Dallas. Howard and Leanne had been praying about what to do after graduation, and when they heard Jim speak, their hearts were stirred. They contacted Jim, who said he would love to make a place for them in his ministry, but he had no financial resources to pay them a salary. So they came as unpaid volunteers, saying, "Just put us to work."

Howard was knowledgeable in computers and began working in the office. Leanne began helping Connie prepare the meals for the noon Bible study and doing other miscellaneous jobs. When Jim found out Leanne had formerly run her own catering business, she wound up with the assignment of catering our wedding. John and Joyce had paid for the food, and Leanne planned the menu, and several volunteers from the Dream Center were helping her prepare the food for the reception.

"I'm humbled by all this," I told John and Joyce as we sat around the kitchen table having a late-night snack. "The only things Jim and I have taken care of are the wedding rings and the cake. Everything else has been donated. I just can't get over what everybody has done for us, and how quickly it's come together."

"Very fast," Joyce acknowledged. "We worked for months planning my daughter's wedding. I only had two weeks to do all the decorating and make arrangements for yours. But I think God put this wedding together. It really is a miracle."

"What will be a miracle," John said, "is if I'm still standing this time tomorrow. My feet are killing me."

"This time tomorrow," I said, "you'll have your house back—I promise—and Jim and I will be at your condo in Big Bear. That's something else you've done. Thanks for letting us spend our wedding night there." We would actually spend two nights in their condo, but it wasn't much of a honeymoon; that's all the time we had before we had to leave for London.

John looked at Joyce questioningly and she nodded. "I guess we should tell you about Big Bear," John said. "We got a call yesterday. There was a flash flood up in the mountains, and our entire complex was flooded out. Our neighbors all have water and mud damage. We couldn't take time to go check on our condo because we had so much left to do here."

"That's awful!" I said. "I'm so sorry about your condo. You should have gone up there instead of doing all this wedding stuff."

"It wouldn't have made any difference," John said. "What's done is done, and we'll go check on it Saturday. Have to get you and Jim married first. That's more important."

Joyce stood up and put her arm around me as I started to tear up at this demonstration of selfless love. "And don't worry about where to stay tomorrow night—"

"We'll get a hotel somewhere," I said.

"No, you won't. I've already taken care of it," Joyce said. "I called the nicest, most romantic bed-and-breakfast in Big Bear and made reservations for you. Our treat."

I hugged her. "Thank you both," I said. Words seemed so inadequate for all they had done.

John carried my suitcase upstairs, and Joyce showed me to one of their beautiful, spacious guest rooms. I lay in bed that night thinking that my wedding was turning out to be more than I ever could have asked for, and I thanked God for those who had put it together for me when I was too overwhelmed to plan it. I also thanked God that I was spending my last night as a single woman. I drifted off to sleep hearing a tune from a Disney movie in my mind: "Some day my prince will come . . ."[1]

32

GOD MEANT IT FOR GOOD

September 4, 1998

One of the last times my father walked without assistance was when he walked me down the aisle. He had developed diabetes because of his weight problem, and was now suffering complications from the disease. Although he was in a lot of pain, Dad was determined to give me away. "Little Girl, this is the proudest moment of my life," he told me.

The wedding party was a true family affair. My mother, who was my maid of honor, had never looked more beautiful as my brother Mark escorted her down the aisle. Jay, who was his father's best man, looked handsome in his rented-for-free tux. Jim's sister Donna played the traditional wedding march on the keyboard, and James and Jonathan, Tammy Sue's boys, carried my train as Dad escorted me to my groom.

So many people who were important in our lives played a part in the wedding. Paul Olson and Phil Shaw, two pastors who had visited Jim regularly in prison and shown him so many kindnesses, opened the ceremony with a Scripture reading and a prayer. B. J. Brown, the godson Jim and I hadn't known we had in common, read the thirteenth chapter of Corinthians—the Love Chapter—from the Bible.

Before we exchanged our vows, Lloyd Zeigler made a special presentation to me and Jim. He performed many weddings for his Master's Commission students, and what he had to say was always unique to the couple. But what Lloyd did for us that day was truly memorable.

"One of Lori's favorite stories as a child," he told the audience, "was Cinderella. That's the picture God gave me for today." I didn't remember ever having told Lloyd that was my favorite fairy tale, but it was true.

"One of the great things in ministry," he said, "is that when you work with people's lives, you get to use God's treasure chest. I never know when it will arrive in a service; an angel must bring it right on time. But there in the treasure chest is the insight God wants to give to people's hearts. It's a spiritual treasure chest, but it's very real, and today we tried to make the treasure chest visual for you."

As Lloyd talked about the treasure chest, two young men from Master's Commission walked slowly down the aisle carrying a wooden chest about three feet wide and two feet deep. They placed the chest at Lloyd's feet and then opened it.

"Two years ago," Lloyd said, "you would not have found Lori standing on a great platform, but she was doing a great ministry. She wore a certain kind of shoe for that." He stooped down and removed a pair of antique shoes from the chest. The black leather lace-up ankle boots were obviously very well-worn, even though they had been recently polished.

"These aren't the shoes Lori wore; these are from the early 1900s. They belonged to a servant girl. If you had been in the Phoenix airport two years ago, you would have found Lori shining shoes. She didn't become a shoeshine girl because she was destitute. She did it so she would have enough money to be in full-time ministry. She wore the shoes of a servant.

"When we look at someone, we notice their face or their hands or their clothes. God begins at the ground up, where no one else really looks. He looks for feet shod 'with the preparation of the gospel of peace.'"[1] Lloyd turned and spoke directly to me. "Lori, your feet were shod with the gospel of peace. That peace can be preached to one person—as you preached to Margie in the inner city, and God gave you a little goddaughter named Lori. But the gospel of peace should be preached to an entire generation—to the whole world. God has prepared you for this moment, Lori, and I believe he is trading in your shoes today."

Lloyd bent down to remove another item from the treasure chest, and I gasped in surprise as he pulled out a clear acrylic case. Inside, resting on a square of black velvet, was a pair of sparkling glass slippers. I found out later he'd had them custom-made at the Biltmore, a very upscale Phoenix mall store.

"These are the shoes of a princess," Lloyd said. "They're real shoes, by the way; you can actually wear them." I started to cry as I thought of what this pastor and friend and father figure had meant to my life and the significance of the words he was speaking to me at this moment. "You're living your dream now, Lori." Lloyd's soft voice was filled with emotion. "When you stand before an audience of women and speak to their hearts, tell them that the dream really does come true. Every part of it."

Reaching into the wooden chest yet again, this time Lloyd brought out a small hand-carved box. "Jim, you play the part of the prince in Lori's dream. You were a prince who was exiled and locked away, and you thought your life was over—you thought your ministry was over. But it wasn't." Lloyd turned the box where it faced Jim, so he could see what was carved into the top. "God once used you to operate a lighthouse," Lloyd said to Jim, "a place that saves people from shipwrecked lives by drawing them to safety, a place that shines the light of God into the darkness. Then you went through so much, it seemed all that was gone; but you still have the key to God's lighthouse."

Lloyd opened the box and removed its contents: a large antique key. "God hasn't taken it back, Jim. He isn't sorry he gave you that key, and he intends for you to use it again. Now, when you walk into the lighthouse, it won't be just a production of turning on the light. You know the fury of the storm outside. You know how real the crisis is. And you will operate God's lighthouse to rescue lives in a greater way than ever before."

Jim and I were both weeping at how in tune with our hearts Lloyd had been and how he recognized that we wanted God to use our lives together to help hurting people.

Lloyd had also said that we were a prince and princess, and he had called this "a royal wedding." At that moment I truly felt like Cinderella. Right after Lloyd spoke, Nina Atuatasi, one of my girls, sang a song she had written especially for my wedding day. One line said, "Why shouldn't this day be a fairy tale come true?" That's exactly what this day seemed to be.

Jim and I stood as Rev. R. T. Kendall, pastor of the historic Westminster Chapel in London, led us in the exchanging of our vows. Jim had trouble getting the ring on my hand, and he laughed nervously when he said, "With this ring, I thee wed." When we had finished repeating the ancient promises, Rev. Kendall pronounced us husband and wife, but he added something extra to the customary wording. He said, "Forasmuch as this man and this woman have consented together in holy wedlock . . . I pronounce that they are husband and wife together in the name of the Father, and of the Son, and of the Holy Ghost—God meant it for good!"

Few people caught the additional reference, but it was highly meaningful to us. Jim might not have made it through his prison experience without R. T. Kendall's book *God Meant It for Good*. The book's title comes from the Bible passage where Joseph tells the brothers who had sold him into slavery, "You meant evil against me; but God meant it for good."[2]

How true that was for our lives. I had lived through the devastation and degradation of sin, Jim had known the depths of humiliation and heartache, and we both had endured an aching loneliness. The enemy thought he had destroyed us, but God had turned it all to good. Our God of grace and mercy uses the broken, shattered pieces that others would throw away. That day he took all our brokenness and fashioned it into something whole, something truly beautiful.

When Jim heard the words "You may kiss your bride," he wasted no time. The audience cheered and applauded as we kissed. Afterward, I wiped a smudge of lipstick off Jim's mouth, and Pastor Tommy Barnett, who was about to officiate over Communion, spoke into the microphone. "I think there's been some practicing going on," he said, "and that violates LAIC rules. We'll take care of that after the program." That comment drew laughter from the guests familiar with the Dream Center's strict rules on dating.

After everyone present had taken Communion, Pastor Barnett officially presented us to the audience as Mr. and Mrs. Jim Bakker, and that's when the helicopter arrived overhead. As

I mentioned at the beginning, that was the first indication I had that our wedding had attracted so much media attention. I had figured a few reporters would try to get in—if our engagement had merited some brief television reports, surely the wedding would be newsworthy. But I hadn't realized what a big story it would be for the tabloids. We later heard varying reports of what the media had been willing to pay for the story. The two most reliable reports, from people who were very close to us and who were in a position to observe firsthand, were that the tabloids had offered guests ten thousand dollars for a completed roll of film, and one of the publications had offered the professional photographer two hundred thousand dollars for the official video of the wedding.

Earlier that morning, when John Caruso had discovered that the paparazzi were staking out the house, he and his son took a piece of plywood and boarded up the space between the house and the block wall a few feet away. That kept any cameras with telephoto lenses from being able to shoot into the backyard. A number of young men from the Dream Center served as an improvised security detail, wearing matching bow ties as a sort of uniform and standing out front and checking guests against a list. Armando told us later that one paparazzo had even tried to climb up the mountain behind the house into the backyard; he and Rick, another Dream Center volunteer, had bodily escorted the man off the property. Today Jim and I give interviews wherever we go; but we had wanted to keep our special day private.

After the helicopter left, Jim and I did something that was not part of our religious tradition. Jim insisted on dancing with his bride at our wedding, and he'd picked out a song for it: the old Righteous Brothers' hit "Unchained Melody." Jim held me close and looked at me with unfathomable tenderness and yearning as

Johnny Coate sang, "Oh, my love, my darling, I've hungered for your touch a long, lonely time."[3] It was so romantic. I remember thinking, *This guy is deeply in love with me, and I never knew such love existed.*

Next I danced with my dad, and Jim danced with Tammy Sue to Van Morrison's "These Are the Days," and then the reception started. The buffet tables were beautifully decorated with alternating centerpieces of vegetable and fruit trees, which Leanne had created out of Styrofoam, toothpicks, and a truckload of fresh produce. The extensive menu she had prepared was impressive, and if anyone went hungry, it was not her fault.

Halfway through the reception, Jim and I cut the wedding cake. For the cake topper, the bakery had used the glazed porcelain figurine of Prince Charming and Cinderella that Jim had given me as a souvenir from Disneyland. That simple romantic gift had turned out to be the theme for our wedding—a theme no one consciously coordinated. Jim had not bought the figurine with the idea of using it in our wedding. Nina, who wrote the song about a fairy tale coming true, and Lloyd, who had custom-ordered glass slippers as a wedding illustration, had not consulted with anyone. God was the behind-the-scenes director.

I drove everyone—including Jim, which I didn't realize until later—crazy posing for pictures at the reception. I tried to accommodate anyone with a camera who asked for a picture with Jim and me, and I coordinated many of the snapshots. The only photographers I truly wanted to avoid were the paparazzi lying in wait for us outside.

Jim and I had intended to go for a short ride in John's gorgeous 1936 Packard convertible, which was parked in the driveway with a big Just Married sign, while we were still in our formal clothes. We thought it would make a great picture for our wedding album. But by mid-afternoon it became apparent we couldn't do that because of all the media attention.

Someone finally devised a plan to lure the paparazzi away from the house so Jim and I could leave without being barraged by cameras. John moved the Packard out of the way, and Armando pulled Jim's Jeep into the garage. My friend Faithe Tines, who is taller than I am but has the same coloring, donned a white scarf; she would pretend to be me. Howard Bailey, Leanne's husband, was cast in the role of Jim. Howard threw his suit coat over their heads and he and Faithe climbed into the backseat of the Jeep. Armando and Rick jumped into the front.

John and Joyce escorted the remaining guests to the front yard, and they all waved and called good-bye as Armando backed the Jeep out of the driveway and sped off. There was a commotion, with reporters yelling, "At least give us a picture!" and a few of the paparazzi took off after the Jeep. But most of the cameras remained stationed outside, still pointed at the house.

"I wonder why they didn't fall for it?" I asked when John and Joyce came back inside.

"I hate to tell you this," Joyce said, "but I saw a couple of them pointing to the upstairs window. I think they must have seen you and Jim standing there."

"Oh, no. I can't believe we did that." I was dismayed that our curiosity had foiled their plan.

"They're used to spotting decoys, I imagine," John added. "It probably wouldn't have worked anyway. We'll just have to think of something else to get you on your way to Big Bear undetected."

Jim, who was close to collapsing by this point, said, "I think I'm just too sick to drive to the mountains."

We discussed it with John and Joyce, finally deciding that Jim and I would spend our wedding night in their house, and they would spend the night at the place they had reserved for us in Big Bear.

Around sunset the paparazzi gave up and abandoned their stakeout. Jim and I were alone at last, and the silence was glorious. We looked forward to an unforgettable wedding night, a blissful evening of romance when we would finally be able to give full expression to our love and desire for each other.

Our wedding night, however, turned out to be a little more unforgettable than we had anticipated.

33

CANDLELIGHT AND CONTENTION

Jim and I were exhausted, yet exhilarated. We decided a relaxing, intimate bubble bath would be a wonderful way to begin our first evening as husband and wife. The Carusos' spacious master bathroom had a large marble tub with whirlpool jets, and Joyce had decorated the area with a symmetrical arrangement of graduated pillars and tapers. *Candlelight—the perfect romantic touch,* I thought, feeling very glamorous in my Victoria's Secret ivory silk negligee.

I had lit the candles and started running the bathwater when a piercing siren blared throughout the house. I jumped and nearly tumbled into the tub. I had sent Jim to the garage to get something I'd left in the car; he must have forgotten and tripped the burglar alarm when he'd opened the door.

The phone in the bedroom was ringing, so I ran and picked it up. It was hard to hear over the racket, but I determined that it was the monitoring service for the security system. "Is this Mrs. Caruso?" the caller asked.

"No, she's not here. My husband and I are staying at their house," I explained, "and I think he accidentally set off the alarm—"

"What is the security code word, please."

"Code word? Just a minute." I put the phone down and ran to the staircase where we had posed for wedding pictures earlier, intending to ask Jim if he knew the code word, and then, for the second time that day I heard the roar of a helicopter. Suddenly the intense beam from the chopper's powerful searchlights hit the backyard, making it appear brighter than the sun at high noon. *Are we being raided?* I thought crazily.

From the railing I looked down and saw Jim running into the family room, clad only in his underwear, looking panic-stricken as the light poured through the French doors at the back of the house.

"I'll get you something to put on," I yelled. I dashed back to the bedroom, threw open his suitcase, and picked up a pair of Bermuda shorts lying on top. Then I ran back and tossed them over the railing to Jim. As he quickly pulled the shorts on, I heard pounding on the back door, and it dawned on me: the police are going to question Jim. *The police!* Because of some traumatic experiences with law enforcement officials during his trial and imprisonment, Jim had a childlike fear of dealing with the police. I knew he would be scared to death.

Frightened, I ran back into the bathroom to escape the incredibly bright lights and the horrible whipping of the blades. The helicopter was hovering so low over the master bedroom balcony, I thought the pilot was going to use it as a helipad; the area was probably big enough. I hunkered in the corner, covering my ears in a futile attempt to shut out the sound of the burglar alarm, which continued to shriek.

I felt as if I had landed on an episode of COPS, hiding in the bathroom while my still-sick, half-dressed husband was downstairs explaining to the police what had happened. I could picture him telling them who he was and going through the whole explanation of the wedding and the paparazzi and the flooded condo and why the Carusos were in Big Bear and we were still in their home and how he set off the burglar alarm. We found out later that John had notified the police department the day before to let them know about the wedding. In fact, a motorcycle patrol had driven by several times during the day. The police had known it would be a high-profile event, and that's why they responded to the alarm in full force.

After a few minutes—some of the longest of my life—the burglar alarm finally fell silent and the helicopter departed. The sudden quiet was almost startling. I came out of the bathroom and went downstairs. "This wasn't exactly the way I'd planned to start my wedding night," Jim said when I walked into the kitchen. "I'd counted on excitement—just not this kind," he said wryly.

I was near tears, and I didn't know which one of us was shaking the worst. "I suppose we'll laugh at this someday . . ."

"Not anytime soon."

Not knowing what to do, I busied myself straightening things on the kitchen counter; I always clean in a crisis. "Did you ever eat anything today?" I asked Jim. He shook his head no. "I didn't either," I said. "No wonder we're so shaky."

Leanne had wrapped two plates of leftovers from the reception for us, and I took them out of the refrigerator. Jim poured us each a glass of Martinelli's sparkling cider, which we had used for our wedding toast, and we shared a snack as we rehashed the alarm incident for a few minutes. Gradually, we calmed down.

"I think my heart has finally stopped pounding," I said.

"Oh, really?" Jim grinned slyly. "Maybe we should do something to get our hearts pounding again."

"You still want to soak in that bubble bath with me?" I asked with a wink.

"Don't ask dumb questions, Lori Beth."

∞

The candlelight cast a lovely glow on the walls as the warm, sudsy water swirled around us. Unfortunately, my mind was still obsessing on the events of the day, particularly about the fact that I had not been able to get all the pictures I wanted.

"I wanted to make sure everybody got their picture taken with us," I lamented. "And I couldn't do it."

"You weren't obligated to pose with every single guest, Lori."

"But a lot of people went to great trouble and expense to come to our wedding, and I didn't get the opportunity to make them feel appreciated," I said. I chattered on and on about my photographic failure.

"We took way too many pictures as it was," Jim grumbled.

"I thought you liked taking pictures."

"I hate it." He was beginning to sound testy.

"Well, you certainly have enough of them in your precious gallery," I snapped back.

"Those were pictures that *had* to be taken. They were public-ity shots with some celebrity, or layouts for a brochure, or photos for a book cover. It was part of my work. It's not like every time somebody came over to my house I thought I had to pull out the camera."

"Is that what you think I do?"

"It *is* what you do, Lori. You're Miss Picture Taker USA. You think you have to record every single moment on film."

"I'll have you know, there were some pretty special moments I wanted to record on film today, and I didn't get to. I wanted keepsake photos of you and me at our wedding with some of the most special people in my life."

"I wanted our wedding to be more than a photo op. We posed with so many people, all I can remember is cameras flashing. I can't believe you missed *anybody.*"

"I missed a *bunch* of people," I informed him. "Like Maru Oddo, who's been like a sister to me—only the *most* generous giver I've ever known. She's the one who gave you a professional pedicure and manicure the other day when she did my nails for the wedding. I didn't even get a picture of Maru!"

"Okay, if we're going to start naming all the people we neglected today, what about Jim Albert? He's the law professor who spent years researching my case and writing a book defending my innocence. He flew across the country to be at our wedding, and I never even got to say hello to him, let alone thank him for coming. Why? Because you had me posing for pictures the entire time."

If Jim had thought he could derail me with logic, he was wrong. I kept remembering people I'd missed thanking with a personal photograph.

"Look, I really don't want to fight about taking pictures," he finally said, trying to establish a cease-fire in the barrage of words.

"We're not fighting," I said impatiently.

"Great. Now we're fighting about whether or not we're fighting."

"This is not a fight," I repeated. "It's a heated discussion, maybe even a disagreement. But it is *not a fight!*"

"Then why are you yelling?"

"I'm not yelling," I said more calmly. "I just happened to raise my voice a little. That's all."

I was adamant that Jim and I were not fighting that night because I had been a battered wife for many years, and I knew what a fight was—it meant hitting and shoving and punching, not exchanging a few verbal volleys.

Jesse and I had had an explosive relationship, and we argued frequently. And occasionally, especially when he had been drinking, the arguments turned violent. Drugging usually kept him mellow, but alcohol brought out his demons.

I'd had a tiny taste of what was in store that night before I married Jesse, the first time he started pushing me around. Before long, we had established a pattern. He would get drunk and start in on me about something, and I would mouth back— I was good at that—and then he'd use his fists on me. The day after he'd made me his personal punching bag, I would be so sore all over I could barely move. I would lie on the sofa, curled up in a ball. Jesse would kneel beside me, apologize profusely, and beg me to forgive him. I didn't know what else to do, so I did. Then he would pamper me for a day or two, and things would get back to "normal."

Most of the time Jesse was laid back, and he could also be quite charismatic. But he had a deep reservoir of anger inside, and I never knew what might set it off. I lived on the emotional edge all the time.

Even though I endured a lot of battering, my injuries seldom required medical attention. Once, when we were partying in Durango, Colorado, Jesse and I were both in a drunken stupor. We got into a huge fight in the middle of the street, and he beat me to a pulp, then left me there. It was late at night and I was crying hysterically. About the time Jesse ran off, two guys came by in a truck and stopped. Fearing I was badly injured, they picked me up and took me to the hospital.

"Who did this to you?" the emergency room doctor had asked.

I lied and said I had been in a motorcycle accident.

My injuries weren't consistent with falling off a motorcycle, and he didn't believe me. "Don't you want to press charges against whoever did this?" he said.

"I told you, I was in an accident," I insisted.

I was bruised in numerous places but had no broken bones, so the ER team cleaned up my cuts, patched my busted lip, taped my twisted wrist, put an ice pack on my black eye, and let me go. The two strangers who had picked me up had stayed in the waiting room, and they offered to drive me home.

"Too far," I mumbled. "Home is Phoenix." It was difficult to talk because of the swelling.

They helped me back in the truck and drove me all the way to Phoenix. I was in too much pain to argue. Jesse had boxed my ears, so they were ringing, and I had a terrible headache in addition to the soreness all over my body. My face had stayed swollen for several days. But the bruises gradually faded, and so did the memories. Soon I was back with Jesse.

The worst beating, the one when I thought I was going to die, was shortly before I had my hysterectomy. Jesse and I were living with my dad, who had a beautiful home in Phoenix. He was divorced from his second wife and couldn't stand living without a woman in his life, so he begged me and Jesse to live with him. We didn't pay any rent, but I took care of the house for Dad. Mostly I partied with Jesse. Dad was gone a lot, running around with his women or gambling. Jesse and I had drug parties around the swimming pool in the backyard and enjoyed living the high life.

Fortunately, Dad was home the day Jesse battered me so badly. I have no recollection of what started the argument, but I clearly remember being totally nude when Jesse dragged me outside, pulling me by the hair and punching me. He beat me in the front yard, and the only thing that kept the neighbors from watching was the large hedge of oleanders surrounding the property. Jesse knocked me to the ground, then jumped on top of me and started choking me.

"Stop!" I gasped. "I can't breathe!" He wouldn't stop, and I began to black out. Everything just faded.

Dad managed to pull Jesse off of me, and he took off.

Later Bobbi came over to help take care of me. "Why do you keep putting yourself through this, Lori?" she asked me.

I didn't have an answer.

In the bathtub with Jim on our wedding night, the water grew lukewarm as I continued to enumerate the photo opportunities I'd missed. After a while I turned to naming the people who weren't at the wedding. "My baby brother didn't get to come," I whined. Scott's wife, Cindy, had just had surgery; she couldn't travel, and he had stayed home to take care of their daughter. "And Amber—my little Bugaloo—wasn't even here on the most important day of my life!"

I started crying then, and Jim reached out to comfort me. He recognized that I was arguing because I was physically exhausted and emotionally drained. And even though he was still sick, my husband's first concern was me. He held me and began to speak sweet, soothing words to me, telling me how much he loved me.

As he continued to console me, we recaptured the romantic mood with which we'd begun the evening—as if we had rewound the tape to the moment before he had triggered the burglar alarm and I had started an argument. In spite of the cops and the contention, our wedding night turned out to be just as passionate and loving as we had dreamed it would be.

Later that night I lay in bed, snuggled against Jim contentedly. *I didn't believe I could be this happy,* I thought. *This is the way it was always supposed to be.*

For a long time I lay there quietly, reliving the day in my mind. "Jim?" I said softly, thinking perhaps he had already dozed off.

"What, Lori Beth?"

"You were wrong, honey—" I yawned. "That night in Michigan."

"Hmm?"

"You *are* Prince Charming."

34

A Honeymoon?

From the moment the limo deposited us at the entrance of Claridge's and we stepped through the revolving door and onto the checkered marble floor of the grand lobby, I felt I had entered another world. The century-old five-star hotel in the heart of London was the pinnacle of refined elegance, and the restaurant where we were about to dine had served the king and queen of England and royalty from around the world.

What is a little desert girl like me doing in such a prestigious place? I wondered. It didn't seem possible.

Jim and I had married at noon on Friday and then left for England on Monday night. This ministry trip had been scheduled before I met Jim, and it was ironic that the pastor who had invited him, Rev. Dr. R.T. Kendall, had been on a speaking trip in the U.S. and had been able to fly to L.A. on short notice and perform our wedding ceremony. Jim was excited and frightened about the opportunity to travel to London and fill the pulpit at Westminster Chapel. In its almost

160-year history, the church had been pastored by some of the world's finest Bible expositors—men like G. Campbell Morgan and Martin Lloyd-Jones, a brilliant medical doctor who became one of the leading gospel preachers of his time.

We had flown all night Monday and arrived in London on Tuesday morning. A church member had picked us up at the airport in one of the vintage black English taxicabs, and even though we were suffering from jet lag, I had to take pictures of the moment of our arrival in London. Then we went straight to our hotel to rest. Westminster Chapel always arranges for its guest speakers to stay at the historic Salvation Army guest quarters across the street from the church, which is located in Buckingham Gate, adjacent to the palace. Although clean, the hotel was sparse and cramped. But our biggest complaint, as newlyweds, was that our room had twin beds, and they could not be moved together. From our bedroom window we had a less-than-panoramic view of the alley and a peek into our bathroom window. Jim had told me this trip to England would be like a honeymoon. I was beginning to have my doubts.

One evening while Jim was studying and preparing to preach, I went for a walk. As I passed a newsstand, a headline photo on one of the newspaper racks caught my eye and I stopped. It was a photo of our wedding! The front-page picture of my father walking me down the aisle was the first time I knew that the tabloids had managed to buy snapshots of our wedding. Jim had warned me this could happen, but it was still eerie finding my picture at a newsstand halfway around the world.

On Wednesday we had taken the train to Sheffield, where Jim addressed a large group of ministers and businessmen from across Europe. Rev. Kendall had arranged for Jim to speak at the meeting as a way of introducing him to the churches there. "These people only know the surface story about you," he told Jim, "and they'll want to look you over before inviting you to minister."

The large, dark auditorium was like a lecture hall, with horseshoe-shaped tiered seating around the stage area in the center. The meeting was much more formal and the people more reserved than Jim was used to. About a thousand leaders attended, and Jim sat at a table in the center and responded as the moderator read questions submitted by the audience. Jim later called it "an interrogation" and said the auditorium reminded him of the old black-and-white film footage he'd seen of the Nuremberg Trials. Nevertheless, the audience received him quite warmly.

While riding the train from London to Sheffield and back, about a two-hour trip each way, R.T. Kendall gave us the kind of counseling session he'd been unable to do before he'd married us. It was a very special time as I poured my heart out to him, and he talked to us about letting go of the past and creating a new life together. He also gave me wonderful gems of advice about how to be a minister's wife. Since then, he has spoken much wisdom into our lives, and we consider him our pastor-at-large.

Following the Sheffield meeting, we had received an invitation via Rev. Kendall to dine with a prominent figure in the business and political world, a man who advised prime ministers and presidents. He was also a parishioner at Westminster Chapel, and he had wanted to meet Jim.

As we walked into Claridge's that Friday night, Jim kidded me about cameras not being allowed inside because the royal family and other notables oftrn dined there. "Lori Beth may go through withdrawal if she can't take pictures of our dinner tonight," he warned our host and Rev. Kendall, who was joining us for the evening.

Our host was a large, imposing man who was also very charming and gracious; he treated us like royalty. I had never been in a restaurant as beautiful as Claridge's. The spacious room's tall columns with their original art deco mirrored murals and lighting gave the impression of stepping back in time, and the simplicity of decoration created an understated elegance that left me awestruck.

A small orchestra played for the diners, some of whom were dancing. After we ordered our meal, our host suggested that Jim and I dance. Uncomfortable with that prospect, Jim declined. But our host insisted, so we made our way to the dance floor.

Jim looked nervous. "It's been decades since I really danced," he said. "I don't think I remember anything but the two-step."

"We just danced at our wedding," I reminded him.

"Yes, but all I had to do was twirl you around and hold you tight, which I managed to do. Nobody was paying attention to my feet."

Fortunately, the orchestra was playing a slow number as we joined the other couples on the dance floor. "You lead," Jim whispered.

As I led my husband in the second dance of our married lives, I said, "This fairy tale is unfolding in reverse order."

"How's that?" he asked.

"A week ago I married Prince Charming; *now* I'm attending the ball."

After our sumptuous meal, we ordered dessert, and I excused myself. Inside the ladies' rest room, a uniformed attendant greeted me and opened the stall door for me. When I came out, she had filled the marble sink with warm water for me to dip my hands in. As I immersed my hands in the water, she reached for the dispenser and released some liquid soap into her palm. For a split second I wasn't sure what she was doing, then I realized she intended to soap my hands. I lifted them out of the basin, and she gently lathered my fingers in an ultimate act of personal service.

I thanked her as she handed me a towel, and since we were the only two people in the rest room, I started to talk to the woman, who appeared to be in her late sixties.

"Are you from the States?" she asked after she'd heard me speak. I said yes, and she asked what had brought me to London.

"My husband is a preacher," I said, "and he was invited to speak at Westminster Chapel."

"Oh, that's lovely, miss." Something about her soft voice and sad smile touched me, and I couldn't just walk out the door.

"We've only been married a week," I said.

She looked amazed at that. "I was married for over forty years, but my husband died recently," she said. "It's very lonely now."

We chitchatted for a few more minutes and then I asked, "Are you a Christian?" She said no, and also told me that she did not own a Bible when I inquired. That surprised me since I had thought almost everyone owned a Bible except in third-world countries where it was either illegal or the people couldn't afford one.

My heart went out to this woman as we continued to make small talk, and before I knew it, I was telling her I was married to Jim Bakker.

"You mean the preacher who was in all the newspapers and went to prison?"

"Yes," I replied, "but he is a different man than the press has reported." I began to tell her about Jim and briefly shared some of my own testimony with her. "God has done many miracles in my life," I told her. One of which, I decided later, was that no one else came into the restroom and interrupted us.

We talked for quite a while, and I eventually led her in the

Sinner's Prayer. Joy spread across her face as she asked Jesus into her heart, and I hugged her and rejoiced with her. I'd been gone a long time and knew that Jim would be wondering what had happened to me, but I hated to leave abruptly. "Why don't you come out and meet my husband?" I asked.

"Oh, no," she said, "I can't. I'd like to, but the help aren't allowed in the dining area with the guests."

I was astonished. This was the twentieth century, and we were in a free country—I couldn't comprehend that class distinctions could still be so ingrained that she could not have any association with the diners.

"Come on," I said, "let's go outside." I was determined to find some way to bridge the gap. "If you can't go in the dining room, then I'll bring Jim over to meet you."

I took her by the hand and led her out the door. We stood in the lobby, at the edge of the dining room, knowing she couldn't cross the line in her uniform. I was incensed at the injustice. This lady was now a child of the heavenly King, but apparently she was not allowed to enter the room where earthly kings dined. I didn't want to leave her to go get Jim, but he was sitting with his back to me and wouldn't be able to see me. Our host finally spotted me, and I gestured for him to get Jim's attention.

The ladies' room attendant was thrilled when I introduced Jim and he hugged her. Jim spoke to her for a minute and told her about R.T. Kendall and Westminster Chapel, encouraging her to attend church.

"Please forgive me for being gone so long," I said to our host when I returned and explained what had happened. He was very gracious about my prolonged absence at the dinner table, and being a Christian, he understood my unwillingness to pass up an opportunity to minister to someone and lead her to the Lord.

We left Claridge's, where every hotel room featured a call button to summon a valet, maid, or waiter, and returned to our twin-bed room at the Salvation Army guest house. Being at the ball had been fun, but I was ready to run back to the safe familiarity of my pumpkin.

We went from being wined and dined like royalty in London to being detained and nearly deported in Sydney.

From England we had flown home to our one room at the Dream Center. We were there a little over twenty-four hours—just long enough to unpack, do laundry, and repack—and then we were in the air crossing time zones again. We spent the seventeen-hour flight to Australia in smaller-than-normal seats by the exit door; they were the worst seats I'd ever flown in. As I had done on the flight to London—and as I did on every flight for the first few months of our travels—I hauled a huge bag full of thank-you notes and pictures, plus my address book, on board the plane. I was determined to thank everyone who had a part in our wedding and to send pictures to everyone with whom I had managed to pose.

As we neared Sydney the flight attendants passed out a customs and immigration form the passengers were required to fill out before landing. I was busy writing thank-you notes when Jim started working on our forms. He stopped suddenly. "Uh-oh," he said. "Look at this question."

He handed the form to me, and I saw what had him worried: it asked if the passenger had ever been convicted of a crime or served time in prison.

"You don't think that will be a problem, do you?" I asked.

"I don't know. It makes me uneasy having to say I'm an ex-con. But I'm not going to lie about it." He checked the YES box on the form and then turned it into the flight attendant.

"I wouldn't worry about it, honey. Our passports and visas are in order," I said, "and surely when the Women's Aglow office made the travel arrangements, they would have gotten some kind of clearance if it were necessary."

About thirty minutes later we landed. Jim and I stretched our cramped legs and gathered our carry-on bags. As we exited the Jetway and walked into the terminal, a uniformed official stopped us. "Mr. and Mrs. Bakker?"

"Yes," Jim said, a look of foreboding on his face.

"I'm sorry, sir, but you'll have to come with me."

We were in shock as he explained that we were being detained for possible deportation because of Jim's prior criminal record. We had just spent seventeen miserable hours crunched up in those awful airline seats, and we'd been exhausted before we ever started. Now it was incomprehensible to think about getting back on that plane and flying home without even a night's sleep. *This can't be happening*, I thought.

Over the next few hours I watched my husband go through an emotional gamut, knowing that he was reliving some of the feelings he'd had in prison. The holding area was a large, open room—no prison bars—and yet it felt extremely confining, knowing we couldn't leave. I had to ask for permission to go to the rest room.

The official who handled our case was very polite and kind. Because we hadn't eaten anything in hours, he brought a plate of biscuits and served us tea in china cups. He also sent someone to notify the couple who had come to pick us up at the airport; this pastor and his wife remained in the terminal, praying for us, the entire time.

Periodically we would be informed that they were making phone calls and trying to resolve the situation. I paced the floor a while, tried to write more thank-you notes, and watched Jim age visibly; the stress was almost unbearable. Finally, after four long hours, we were released. We later learned that it had taken the intervention of the highest level of government in order to get us cleared to enter the country.

The next day I was still suffering from the strain, and I was also anxious about sitting on stage behind Jim when he spoke at a national conference for Women's Aglow, an international Bible study and fellowship group of spirit-filled women. I was used to speaking to large crowds of women, but I hadn't been invited to address this one; Jim had. I would simply be on display as the new Mrs. Jim Bakker, and I knew the women would all be looking me over, and they would probably be comparing me to the former Mrs. Bakker.

By this time, I had realized that every single news story about our wedding would foster the comparison. In a newspaper or magazine article, a large photo of Jim and me would appear, accompanied by a smaller photo of Jim and Tammy Faye; the caption usually identified them as "former televangelist Jim Bakker and his ex-wife Tammy Faye Messner." That was the reality Jim had tried to prepare me for from the moment he'd said he was falling in love with me.

That morning in Sydney as I got dressed for the Women's Aglow meeting, I was fretting over my impending introduction as Jim's wife. "Five thousand women will be checking me out," I complained to Jim. "Everybody wants to see what the new Mrs. Bakker looks like."

"She looks gorgeous," he said.

"Not with this stick-straight hair, she doesn't." I fastened the adapter onto my curling iron and plugged it in, then continued putting on my makeup.

"That thing looks like a torture device," Jim said. It was the type with a large one-and-a-half-inch barrel—designed for volume without curling the hair too tightly.

"Besides," I said, "I don't want them to look on the outside; I want them to know what's in my heart. They'll just be judging my appearance, and they won't know what I've been through or what I'm like." I was getting worked up, the more I thought about it. "They don't know how I love people and how I love to minister to women . . ."

Jim listened to my litany for a while and then said, "Honey, one day everybody is going to know your heart and know the real you. Don't worry."

"Well, they won't know it today," I complained. "I won't have a chance to speak to them. This is *your* meeting." I picked up the curling iron and started working at the crown of my head. "All they'll know about me is what they see, and—"

An acrid smell suddenly penetrated the room and I heard a popping noise. I immediately lifted the curling iron and screamed when I saw that a big chunk of my hair was stuck to the sizzling metal.

"What am I going to do?" I wailed. I was so upset, I wouldn't even look in the mirror to see how bad the damage was.

Jim reassured me that everything would be okay, that nobody would be able to tell, and that I looked fine with straight hair. I got a grip on myself.

"It's okay," I said resolutely. "I have another curling iron in the suitcase."

"You do?" He sounded surprised.

I looked at him like he was crazy for asking. "Of course. I

always carry a backup when I travel." The second device had a smaller barrel, about three-quarters of an inch in diameter, so my hair would turn out slightly curlier, but that was okay. I would still look presentable.

I had finished curling one side of my hair and was starting on the other side when the exact same thing happened. Snap, crackle, pop, sizzle—and the smell of burning hair.

Now it was Jim's turn to panic. "You can't go looking like that, Lori Beth—half curly and half straight. What are you going to do?"

"Don't worry," I said. This time I was mad at the situation. I stomped over to my suitcase and started rummaging through it. "I've got another curling iron."

"You brought *three* curling irons with you?"

"Yep. And this one has fire." I dug out a butane-powered curler I used for missions trips. "No lack of electricity ever stopped me from curling my hair."

In a few minutes I was sitting on stage with Jim, still slightly frazzled from the curling-iron crisis but looking pretty good considering what I'd been through. This was the opening session for the conference, so there were a few preliminaries, and then Jim was introduced.

"How many of you ladies had a hard time getting to this conference?" he asked. Almost every woman raised her hand. "I thought so. Satan doesn't want you at these meetings because great things are going to happen here this week," he said. "My wife had a very difficult time making it to the meeting today. She was nervous getting ready. After all, she's the new Mrs. Jim Bakker—we've just been married a week and a half—and she knows you're going to be checking her out."

The audience laughed, and Jim started telling them what had just happened. He told the incident in such a funny way, I couldn't help laughing along with everyone else, and when he got to the part where I brought out the third curling iron, he made it sound like I was wielding a blowtorch and he should have been wearing safety goggles. The ladies roared at the curling-iron story; every woman has been through something similar. I was no longer nervous about their judging my appearance, and they got a glimpse of what I was really like through my husband's eyes.

Jim and I stayed in Australia for two weeks, but we were in meetings almost the entire time. One day we spent a half-hour at the beach, and that was about the only time we had for relaxation.

In the more than two years I've been married to Jim, we have traveled extensively. We've been to some wonderful places, including Hawaii, but every trip has included speaking engagements and media interviews. We still haven't had a real honeymoon, and I look forward to that day.

35

"LITTLE GIRL, DON'T EVER FORGET"

I looked at all the boxes stacked against the walls and wondered how I had ever managed to accumulate so much stuff in a one-bedroom apartment. It was the end of September, and after being on the road almost every day since we'd been married, Jim and I had returned to Phoenix to pack up my things. Mom had pitched in to help coordinate the move. She had enlisted a group of Master's Commission students because everything would have to be packed and loaded in one day. In addition to the dozen or so local recruits, Howard and Leanne had arrived from L.A.; they had offered to drive the U-Haul back for us.

With so many people working in such a small space, we kept bumping into each other—it was a scene of controlled chaos. Jim had been trying to chat with the students while they worked; they loved hearing about his ministry experiences and kept asking him questions about the Bible. I was driving everybody crazy trying to figure out what to pack and take back to our one room at the Dream Center, what to put in storage at Mom's, what to give away, and what to throw away. When Jim realized how stressed I was, he finally said, "Let's all stop for just a minute and open God's Word. If we'll get our focus back on what's really important, everything else will somehow manage to get sorted out."

We stopped working and everyone sat on the floor or leaned against the now bare walls and listened to Jim. He picked up his Bible and began to read from the apostle Paul's letter to the church at Ephesus. "For it is by grace you have been saved, through faith—and this not from yourselves, it is the gift of God."[1]

Dad arrived about the time Jim started his impromptu devotional, and as Jim began to talk about the gift of God's grace, it became a moment of divine revelation in my father's life.

Jim told the group: "Earlier, a couple of us were discussing how some people can be in church all their lives and still never comprehend the simple fact that salvation is a gift. There is no way you can ever be good enough to earn your way into heaven. It comes by grace, through faith."

Jim turned over a few pages to Colossians and read another one of his favorite Scripture passages: "Once you were alienated from God and were enemies in your minds because of your evil behavior. But now he has reconciled you by Christ's physical body through death to present you holy in his sight, without blemish and free from accusation."[2]

Calling attention to the phrase "enemies in your minds," Jim said, "There's where the problem is—it's a battle in the mind. Even Lori and I go through bouts of self-condemnation, and we're ministers of the gospel. We have to remember that it's not us—it's Christ. He has already done the work through his physical death on the cross, and all we can do is receive that through faith. It means that all of our mistakes and our failures are covered by the blood of Jesus Christ, who makes us holy and pure and blameless." Jim choked up a bit as he considered the impact of that truth, and he had to clear his throat. "Even with everything I've done in my past, with everything Lori has done in her past, we're pure before God because of what Christ has done. When you fully comprehend this, it's so awesome that all you can do is thank God for the gift of his grace."

As Jim spoke, I was watching my dad's face. I saw his countenance change, as if a light had come on in his mind. How grateful I was that my husband had made us take time out from the busyness of moving to spend a few minutes studying God's Word. I believe those few minutes had eternal consequences.

My dad became something of an evangelist after that, even preaching to his poker buddies—Dad's main source of income had been running poker games the last fifteen years of his life— and asking everyone he knew to support our ministry. He had accepted Christ as his Savior years before and had attended church off and on for decades, but I don't think Dad had fully comprehended what salvation meant until that day.

Mom had told me years earlier that Dad had been called into the ministry as a teenager. He had even preached in several churches around the Phoenix area before I was born. In October 1957, when I was two months old, my parents dedicated me to the Lord at the First Church of the Nazarene in downtown Phoenix. It's somehow appropriate to me that the old church is located in what would now be considered the inner city. That Sunday morning, Pastor Harold Daniels held me up in front of the congregation and presented me to God. "This little girl," he said, "has been born to be a bulwark against sin and the enemy." A bulwark is a fortification, something erected to defend against an invading enemy. I believe Pastor Daniels had a momentary glimpse into the future when he proclaimed the call of God on my life. I also believe that is the moment when Satan really started to work in my father's life.

My dad always had a love for the Lord, but he was never able to live for the Lord. Whenever I visited Dad after that day he responded to Jim's devotional, he would cry and tell me, "Little Girl, your daddy missed the call of God."

Jim has often said that my father would have been one of the greatest preachers of his day because of his ability to speak and to motivate. "Daddy Bob's the kind of man who could sell snowballs in Alaska," Jim said. "He can be so personable, but his temperament is so choleric that he tries to control everybody around him. His vices of women and gambling and food took over his life, sidetracking him from God's plan for his life." Eventually those vices killed him.

In November 1999 Jim and I spent a week with Dad and Lita in Phoenix. Jim had quizzed the doctor when we took my dad for an appointment that week. The doctor had said that because of the complications from diabetes, they would likely have to amputate one of Dad's legs within a year. "But he's a strong man," the doctor said, "and he could live another five years, especially if he would take care of himself."

One day that week I was driving Dad to the drugstore, and it was just the two of us in the car. Dad was a talker, so when he grew quiet I knew something was on his mind. In a minute he said, "I want to ask your forgiveness for something, Lori Beth."

I was surprised. I couldn't ever remember my father asking for forgiveness.

"Remember that Christmas you wouldn't come see me because I was so mad at you? I was wrong about that."

Several years earlier I had planned to take Amber with me to spend a few hours with Margie and the kids on Christmas Day. I wanted Amber to see what it was like in the inner city. Dad had gone nuts. "You're not dragging my granddaughter down to the ghetto and leaving me here all alone."

He had kept haranguing me about it until I had finally said, "Fine. I don't need to spend the day with you at all." I didn't go over to his house on Christmas, and Dad didn't let me live it down for several years.

Now he told me, "After I saw for myself what you did for that family, I knew you were doing the right thing. I need you to forgive me."

"Dad, it's okay," I said. "I forgave you a long time ago."

He continued apologizing to me, asking me to forgive him for everything he had done to me and for all the things he should have done for me but hadn't.

"I've forgiven you all along," I said. "All through the years. There were many times I was hurt, but I chose to forgive you."

On Saturday of the week we were there, Dad threw himself a party. It was his going-away party, although we didn't know it at the time; I think he did.

The guest list was a strange mixture of family friends, people from church, and his poker pals. Dad and Lita had started going to Phoenix First again, so many of the people at the party were old friends of mine. He put me on the spot and asked me to give my testimony and then wanted Jim to say a few words. We were uncomfortable about it, but we did it for Dad. Then he wanted everybody to sing the old hymns of the church, and he led them. He'd been singing hymns around the house all week.

On Monday afternoon Jim and I left Phoenix. We were getting in the car to drive to the airport when I turned around and went back in the house to hug Dad again. He held me to his chest and said, "Little Girl, don't ever forget. Your daddy loves you." Those were his last words to me.

The next morning Jim and Tammy Sue sat me down and broke the news that my dad had just passed away. Sue knelt down beside me and tenderly held my hand while Jim stood behind me and put his arms around me. They surrounded me with love in that difficult moment.

The first person I called was my brother Mark. I talked a bit about the week Jim and I had just spent with Dad, and I told Mark about Dad asking for my forgiveness. "He even told me he was proud of me," I said. "I'd waited all my life to hear those words."

Mark was typically quiet for a moment when I said that; he was as reflective as Dad had been talkative. I knew Mark must be thinking that he and Scott would never get to hear that from Dad. I don't know if Dad would have said it, even if they had been with him at the end. But we'd had no indication that he was about to die, so they'd had no opportunity to find out.

"Do you realize what day this is?" Mark asked finally.

"What day . . .?" I had no idea what he meant.

"It's Tuesday," he said softly. "Dad's day off."

As a child, Mark had always dreaded Tuesdays because it meant Dad would be around the house. Those old scars ran deep in my brother; he had most often taken the brunt of Dad's wrath over the years. Yet it was Mark more than anyone who had helped Scott and me understand that Dad was who he was, that he was sick, and that he couldn't change. Eventually we all came to accept that, and that's when we'd been able to forgive Dad for not being the father we had needed.

Later that day, as I was busy preparing to fly back to Phoenix for the funeral, it occurred to me that I should stop and praise

God for my father. No matter how much he had hurt me, he was my dad, and I had loved him. "I want to thank you for Dad's life, as crazy as it was," I told my heavenly Father. "Even with all the pain, there were fun times, and I'm grateful for those."

Peace filled my heart, and I felt that God was saying to me, *Your dad's here with me now, and he is happy.*

I had needed to know my dad was in heaven, and as I prayed that day, I realized that if my brothers and I could understand and love my dad, God certainly could. He knew Dad's heart. And I believe my dad had finally come to understand the gift of God's grace.

I have said more in these pages about my dad's impact on my life than I have my mom's, and that's because it was his influence that played such a key role in my bad choices early in life, many of which I've chronicled here. Mom was the ballast that kept our family ship afloat, and she remains the most significant influence in my life today, outside of my husband. My mom has never remarried; she put her needs second to ours, making a commitment to see that all three of her children succeeded in the struggle to get our lives together. We all did, thank God.

I'm grateful to my parents for taking us to church every time the doors opened and for providing Christian instruction for us when we were children. I didn't adhere to that instruction for many years, but it was there as a foundation for me when I needed it. Mom and Dad both stressed the importance of church and faith in our upbringing. The difference is that Mom was always consistent—she lived what she believed and never faltered. In preparing to write this book, my brothers helped me revisit many memories from our childhood and teenage years. Scott summed up the examples we had received from our parents in this way. "Dad preached it—" he said; then his voice broke as he continued, "—but Mom lived it."

Dad's inability to be the kind of father I needed left a gaping wound in my heart, a wound that was not completely healed until Jim came into my life. The only reason I can relive the past and talk about all these memories is that the intimate relationship I have with my husband has done so much to heal the hurts I harbored from my dad and my ex-husband. Jim does and is everything I always thought a man was supposed to do and be. He's not perfect; no one is. But Jim is the perfect man for me because he is God's man for me.

Our love is an amazing thing; it grows every day. We ask ourselves, *How can we be so much in love?* God has given us a second chance together, and it's better than the first time. Neither one of us dreamed it could be like this. It is more than we could ever ask.

36

WOMEN OF DESTINY

I put the phone down and announced to the bedroom walls, "Sheila Walsh is coming to dinner—*at my house!*"

I was so excited I could hardly contain myself. I had wanted to meet the talented singer–songwriter and Christian television personality for years because her ministry had made a tremendous impact on my life. I never thought I would have the opportunity to meet her personally, let alone welcome her as a guest in my home.

Sheila had spoken at Phoenix First, and her transparency had overwhelmed me as she related her private struggles to cope with depression while serving as cohost of *The 700 Club* with Pat Robertson. Because of her public persona, Sheila had felt there was no one she could talk to about her problems. That day, she spoke openly about lying on her bathroom floor and sobbing, overcome by a deep loneliness and physically depleted by a hectic schedule that left no time for herself. Eventually Sheila checked herself into a Christian psychiatric clinic for treatment—an incredibly courageous thing to do for a well-known woman in the fishbowl environment of the evangelical church world.

As Sheila was talking to our congregation, I sensed God speaking to my heart. *Listen closely to every word she is saying,* the message came, *because if you are not careful, this will happen to you one day.* That notion seemed impossible to me, but I accepted it because I believed it came from God.

After Sheila spoke, when Pastor Barnett gave an invitation to come forward for prayer, I was one of the first ones to move out of my seat. That wasn't unusual; almost every service I went to the altars, but I was always praying for others. This time I was the one weeping and receiving ministry, knowing that God was somehow doing a work in my heart even though I didn't understand it. Of course, at the time I couldn't have imagined that one day I *would* be living that hectic lifestyle Sheila had described, in a world where there would be very few people who could possibly know what my life was like.

Now, in late October 1999, Janet Thoma had just called to let me know that Sheila Walsh and her husband, Barry Pfaehler, would be coming for dinner the night before Sheila was scheduled to speak at a Women of Faith conference. Janet, an editorial vice president at Thomas Nelson Publishers, had just helped birth Sheila's book *Stories from the River of Mercy;* Janet also had a long association with Jim and had shepherded him through several books. I had recently told Janet that I had always wanted to meet Sheila, and Jim had said he would really like to visit with Barry, who had been a television producer at PTL. Janet had graciously offered to arrange a meeting for us, and now I had a dinner party to plan because Sheila Walsh was coming to my house.

"My" house is not quite accurate. About five months earlier, Jim and I had left our two rooms at the Dream Center (we had inherited Jay's old room, doubling our living quarters) and moved to Charlotte, North Carolina, of all places—to the very house Jim had taken me to see just before we were married. Jim and I had felt that our time at the Dream Center was over, and before we had mentioned it to anyone, Rick Joyner had confirmed it one day. "I believe God is showing me that your work in L.A. is coming to an end," Rick had told Jim. "I would love for you to be a part of our ministry and want you to know that you can have the log cabin as a place to live and work." Before moving to L.A., Jim had occupied the downstairs level of the immense "log cabin," and what few possessions he had in life were still in storage there.

Rick had also told us that his ministry would pay our rent and utilities. Our small ministry would not have been able to cover the expenses on such a facility, and we were deeply moved by Rick's generous offer. Although we would never have chosen Charlotte on our own—there were far too many ghosts from the past there—we believed it was God's provision for us personally and for our ministry, at least for a season.

In Charlotte Jim and I still had only one room to ourselves, but the two-story master bedroom suite in the log cabin was larger than our two Dream Center rooms put together, and much nicer. We were under the same roof with the New Covenant ministry offices now, and the building was also home to several people who had moved with us from L.A.—Armando Saavedra, whom we consider our foster son; Howard and Leanne Bailey, whom God had sent not just as volunteers for New Covenant but to minister to Jim and me personally; Shirley Fulbright, Jim's longtime assistant, and the wonderful man she had met at the Dream Center and married, Harvey Martin. We had held their wedding in the great room of the log cabin. My mom also made the move east with us.

By the way, Jim's large photo gallery was moved from the basement hall to the central staircase that linked all three floors of the house. The collection of framed photographs covered the stairwell's three narrow paneled walls on each level of the house; but the photos on display had been edited for my benefit and married with pictures of my family and my past.

The morning I learned that Sheila Walsh was coming for dinner, I immediately consulted with Leanne, who did all the cooking for the ministry household and constantly amazed me with the creative, delicious meals she could prepare at a moment's notice.

I also remembered that Sheila Walsh loved teacups; she had mentioned it when I heard her speak at Phoenix First. The only time I had parted with one of my precious teacups was when I had given one to Tammy Sue the first time I met her. Now I decided to relinquish a second one, and I mulled over my selection carefully, finally picking a beautiful china cup. I wrote a card for Sheila, telling her how much I appreciated her openness and honesty in sharing her story and how she had been an inspiration to me, and tucked it in a gift bag with the teacup.

Sometimes you meet a well-known person, and he or she is not at all what you had expected. But Sheila Walsh was exactly as I'd known she would be—warm, friendly, and down-to-earth. All the members of our New Covenant household joined us around the table, as well as Tammy Sue, who reminisced with Barry about double-dating back in the days when he had worked for PTL.

After dinner, everyone continued talking for a while, and then Jim took Barry and most of the others outside to see Reggie

White's tour bus, which he had left parked on our property. I had not wanted to give Sheila her present in front of the others, and we were still chatting as the group went outside, so I seized the moment.

"Sheila, I have something for you," I said.

"How sweet," she said as I handed her the gift bag. She read the card and then thanked me for the beautiful teacup when she unwrapped it. "I'll drink my first cup of tea out of this every morning and say a prayer for you, Lori."

I knew it was time for Sheila to leave; she needed to get some rest before speaking the next morning. As we made our way through the great room to the front door, Sheila put on her coat, a black hip-length leather jacket. We went out on the porch and I hugged her good-bye. As I touched her jacket, I noticed how soft and supple the leather was. "Honey," I called to Jim, who was standing by the bus with the others, "come feel Sheila's coat. This is the kind of leather I was telling you about." I had been looking for a similar jacket, waiting to find a good buy on this particular kind of leather, and I wanted Jim to know what I had in mind.

The others were trying to rush Sheila off and calling, "We've got to go." She walked down the steps into the driveway and then paused for a split second. All of a sudden Sheila whipped off her jacket, then turned around and tossed it up the steps to me.

"No!" I cried. "Sheila, I can't take this." I had been admiring the quality of her jacket, not hoping she would give it to me.

"Yes, you can. I want you to have it," she said in her lilting Scottish accent. "God said to give it to you."

Barry walked up the steps and said, "Just let me check inside." He grinned and shook his head. "Sheila's notorious for leaving things in her pockets."

Later that night I slipped the coat on and thought about how much Sheila had ministered to me with that gesture. I thanked God for giving me the opportunity to meet someone I'd admired and appreciated so much, and I asked him to help me be as honest and transparent, and as caring, as she had been. "Lord, I'll take the mantle of Sheila Walsh any day," I prayed.

Earlier that year we had braved one of the worst ice storms to hit the East coast in years to drive to Moravian Falls, North Carolina. There, at Rick Joyner's Prophetic Roundtable conference, I had met Cindy Jacobs. She and her husband, Mike, have a ministry in Colorado Springs called Generals of Intercession. Cindy and I spent quite a bit of time together that week, and I not only enjoyed her bubbly personality, but I also appreciated the special time of prayer we had together; she ministered to me in depth.

A couple of months later, I received a letter from Cindy asking me to contribute to a project she was spearheading, a new Bible designed to mentor women through the Scriptures. She asked me to write a letter commenting on Isaiah 1:18. I was flabbergasted. Me, write a teaching to be included in a Bible? I couldn't believe it.

Jim was proud that I had been asked to contribute, but I was in awe. "I'm not a woman of destiny," I told him. "I'm a nobody."

My husband set me straight. "You're a great woman of God, Lori Beth," he said firmly yet kindly. He has always built me up and encouraged me like that.

I looked at the Scripture I had been asked to write about:

> "Come now, and let us reason together,"
> Says the LORD,
> "Though your sins are like scarlet,
> They shall be as white as snow."

That verse certainly described my life.

Shortly after I submitted my mentoring letter for the Bible, Beth Clark at Thomas Nelson Publishers phoned, saying she had really liked what I had written. "Would you write another one for us?" Beth asked. The second verse she assigned me was Micah 7:8, a verse that had helped sustain Jim as he endured the isolation and humiliation of prison:

> Do not rejoice over me, my enemy;
> When I fall, I will arise;
> When I sit in darkness,
> The LORD will be a light to me.

Beth had not known how important that verse was to my husband when she asked me to write about it. Being asked to contribute those two teaching articles to the Women of Destiny Bible was a great honor—truly more than I could ever ask.

On May 29, 2000, not long after the *Women of Destiny Bible*[1] was published, Jim and I appeared on *Larry King Live*. We had been on Larry's show several times before, but this program would be an entire hour on Jim and his family, and the guests would include Tammy Faye and Roe Messner, as well as Jim and me, Jay, and Tammy Sue. It was a difficult program for me, but I did it because I thought it was important for people to see who Jim is now and what God is doing in our lives.

During the program I presented a copy of the *Women of Destiny Bible* to Larry as a gift for his wife.

The day after the *Larry King Live* show aired, we flew to Asheville, North Carolina, and there I realized another dream—meeting Ruth Bell Graham. I'd always told Jim, "I know you know a lot of famous people, and if I never got to meet any of them, that would be okay. But the two people I would most like to meet in the world are Billy and Ruth Graham."

Even when I had been estranged from God, I had loved to hear Billy Graham preach on television. Something about his fatherly demeanor and his soft Southern drawl comforted me, and his message always reached my heart. As a Christian, I had read Ruth Graham's writings, and she had touched my heart as well. I always knew she had to be somebody special, and when I met Jim and heard the story of what Ruth Graham had done for him, it only confirmed my opinion.

A few days after Jim had been released from prison, she invited him to come to Montreat Presbyterian Church with her family, and she insisted that he sit right beside her that Sunday morning. That any Christian, let alone Ruth Graham, would even be seen with him began to lift Jim out of his despair. Billy Graham had come to see Jim in prison, and their son, Franklin, had not only visited Jim regularly but also provided a place for Jim to live and a car for him to drive when Jim was released. So I knew the Grahams weren't great people simply because they were well-known Christians; they were great because they *lived* the gospel they preached. "I was a stranger and you invited me in . . . I was in prison and you came to visit me."[2]

When Jim and I had been invited to Ruth Bell Graham's eightieth birthday celebration, we rearranged our entire speaking schedule to make sure we could be there.

The Graham family is very private and rarely does large public events, so there was a great air of excitement as more than three hundred people filled the ballroom at the historic Grove Park Inn in Asheville, North Carolina, for the sit-down dinner. Built of massive granite boulders, the beautiful inn sits on top of a mountain in the Blue Ridge, overlooking the valley, and had been chosen because the restaurant there is a favorite of the Grahams. The program that evening presented Ruth Bell Graham's life through music and drama, using her own writings, and it was very moving. PBS was there filming a documentary on her life.

After dinner, Gigi Tchividjian, the Grahams' daughter, came over to our table. "Mom has asked to see you," she told us.

"Are you sure she's up to it?" I asked. "I know she hasn't been well, and we don't want to tire her out."

Gigi assured us that her mother really wanted to visit with us, so we went over to her table to greet the lovely silver-haired woman I had long wanted to know. When Jim introduced us, Ruth Graham reached up from her wheelchair and cradled my face in her hands. "You're so beautiful," she said. "God hand-picked you for Jim."

I was so touched by her words, I nearly cried. I managed to thank her for what she had done for my husband and for being such a great example of a woman of God.

As a token of appreciation for her influence on my life, I had had her name inscribed in gold on the front cover of a *Women of Destiny Bible.* I was almost embarrassed to give it to her—I mean, could Ruth Graham possibly need another Bible? I tried to sneak the gift bag in with her things, setting it down by her chair. "This is just a little something we brought you," I said.

Her eyes lit up and she reached for the gift immediately. "Oh, I hope it's what I think it is," she said. "I watched you on Larry King last night, and I want one of the Bibles like you gave his wife!"

Presenting a *Women of Destiny Bible* to Ruth Bell Graham, a true woman of destiny, was one of the greatest moments of my life.

Meeting Ruth Bell Graham and Sheila Walsh, two of my heroines of the faith, was more than I could ever ask. But I cannot pass up the opportunity to say that my number one heroine of the faith is my mother, Charlene Graham. She never gave up on me when I was a prodigal daughter. And when I came back to God and subsequently went into full-time ministry, Mom always believed in me and sacrificed to support me financially. I would never have been able to do what God had called me to do had it not been for my mom.

"Many women do noble things, but you surpass them all,"[3] Mom.

37

More Than I
Could Ever Ask

Mother's Day, 2000

I *wonder what's taking him so long,* I thought as I puttered around the hotel room while waiting for Jim to get back from Boston Market. We'd come straight to the room after Jim preached the morning service, too tired to go to a restaurant. After we'd changed clothes and rested a bit, Jim headed out to get some lunch. He'd been gone much longer than I expected.

Finally I heard the key card in the lock. "What took you so long, honey?" I asked as he entered. "I was about to get worried."

"You worry entirely too much, Lori Beth," Jim said with a grin. His arms full, he kicked the door closed behind him. "Here, hold this while I spread out the lunch." He handed me a large plastic shopping bag.

"What's that?" I peeked into the bag as he began to unpack

the containers of chicken and vegetables and laid out a mini-buffet on the coffee table.

"That's what took me so long. I had to wrap your gift."

I pulled a beautifully wrapped package out of the shopping bag.

"You didn't have to buy me a Mother's Day gift. I wasn't expecting that."

"I know. It was just something that reminded me of you, sweetheart. Wait—" he said as I started to untie the ribbon. "You have to open your cards first."

"You also don't have to get me *two* cards for every occasion, you know."

"Sure I do. I'm a romantic fool."

Jim and I are card people. We buy cards for no particular reason, just to commemorate our love and appreciation for each other. I'm often amazed at his uncanny ability to pick a card with an ideal sentiment or to write a note that expresses what I've been thinking but couldn't put into words. On special occasions Jim always gets me two cards—two mushy, sentimental cards—and I always love them.

The cards he had picked for Mother's Day were perfect, and I appreciated the gesture. It's a bittersweet day for me. Sweet, because I love honoring my mom; bitter, of course, because I lost the opportunity to have children when I had a hysterectomy at age twenty-two. People who know my past often remember me on Mother's Day. I usually get cards from my girls that say, "You're like a mother to me." Mom always gives me a card. And year after year my brother Mark has sent me a card, always with a tender note saying something like, "I know your children are proud of you."

I gave Jim a quick kiss when I read his cards, and then I opened the package, which he had meticulously wrapped himself. Inside was a darling little doll in a green travel case. The pretty blonde had on a frilly dress and tiny little socks and patent leather shoes.

"She's adorable, honey. Thank you."

"She's blonde and beautiful, just like you."

Jim served me lunch, and we chatted about our ministry schedule and upcoming events as we ate. When we finished our meal, I stood up and started to clear the coffee table.

"Leave that for a minute," he said. "I have another present for you—"

"Jim!"

"No, it's not something tangible, so don't protest." I sat back down on the small sofa beside him. "Come here, baby." He put his arm around me and pulled me close.

I studied his face for a minute. He looked very serious and yet very caring. "Tell me about this gift," I said.

"The doll reminded me of you," he began, "but it's really just a symbol of my love. It represents the one thing I'd give anything in the world to be able to give you—a baby." He paused as his eyes grew moist, and his voice was husky with emotion as he continued. "I know that the great dream of your life was to be a mother, but that's not possible anymore. So my real Mother's Day gift to you, Lori Beth, is to tell you that if you still cherish that dream of being a mother, we can adopt a baby."

I couldn't say anything at first. I simply looked into his adoring eyes, brimming with tenderness, and my eyes began to fill with tears as well. I knew in my heart this was not something Jim had said lightly or on the spur of the moment; it was something he must have thought about a great deal. God had given me a man whose unconditional love for me was almost beyond my comprehension, and his desire to make such a sacrificial gift—to become a father again at the age of sixty and to raise a child that would not even be his biologically—overwhelmed me for a few moments.

Jim kissed away my tears and embraced me tightly. I lay my head on his shoulder as he held me, and I glanced over at the doll. *A symbol of my love,* Jim had said. Looking at this symbol of my husband's love for me was a healing moment in my life, the completion of the supernatural experience that had happened six years earlier, the night I had placed five symbols in a tiny casket.

Cuddling on the sofa, we discussed this very special Mother's Day gift. "We couldn't adopt a baby right now," Jim said, "but we won't always be on the road. Things are going to settle down soon, and when they do, you could have a little buddy."

We talked about how much fun I would have dressing up a little girl and taking her places with me and doing things together. "But I no longer need a baby to fulfill me," I said. "My life has been filled with children—my nieces and nephew; my namesake, Little Lori; my "girls," who are like my grown daughters. Then there's Armando, who will always be my foster son. And especially your two children, whom I adore. I even have two grandkids now!"

"You sure are young and sexy to be a grandma," Jim kidded me.

"Oh, I'm much too young to be a grandma," I joked back. "I just inherited the grandkids when I married this wonderful man who's crazy about me."

Jim smiled broadly. "He sure *is* crazy about you, and so in love with you that he wants to give you your heart's desire, whatever that is."

Since that day we have made no plans to adopt a child. If that is in our future, God will have to orchestrate it. But my husband's willingness to give me this ultimate expression of his love was yet one more example of how God has given me back far more than I ever lost.

When I reflect on my past, I realize that the number one thing Satan tried to rob me of was family. I lost my children, but God met my need to nurture in other ways. I came from a broken home, but God put our family back together. Mark, Scott, and I all came back to our roots of faith. All of us Westerners have moved to the East Coast now. Scott lives in Maryland with his wife, Cindy, and their children, Katherine and Thomas. My niece Amber lives in the Boston area. And Mark lives in Charlotte; he is remarried to a lovely woman whose name, ironically, is Charlene Laurie.

God has also blended my family with Jim's, and I'm grateful that his children and grandchildren are not too far away. Tammy Sue and Doug and their two boys still live in Charlotte. And Jay and Amanda, who are now married, live in Atlanta.

In September 2000 Jim and I moved to Florida. Finally, for the first time since we've been married, we have a home all to ourselves, thanks to John and Joyce Caruso. A mile of lakefront property for a Christian camp has been donated to our ministry, and we are finally realizing our dream of having a place to disciple young people. We are already seeing many miracles of healing and restoration in damaged lives.

One of the dreams I always had was that my mother would someday be able to work with me in the ministry. That is another dream that has come true. Mom and Jim have had a wonderful relationship since the very beginning, and she now works with us full-time, using her business expertise to help oversee the ministry.

I continue to do postabortion work through my new organization, Mourning to Joy Ministries. By training new leaders to conduct the reconciliation memorials, we have extended our outreach to hurting women and now have chapters in several states.

All of this is far beyond anything I could ever have imagined. At times it's been a painful journey, but I found out that dreams really do come true. Mine did, and now I'm helping other people make their dreams come true . . . and that's more than I could ever ask.

Now to Him who is able to do exceedingly abundantly above all that we ask or think, according to the power that works in us, to Him be glory . . . forever and ever. Amen.

Ephesians 3:20–21

NOTES

Chapter 5: Chosen Vessels

1. John 15:16 NIV.

2. 2 Timothy 2:21.

Chapter 6: "Pay Attention!"

1. For an in-depth look at this topic, see Jim's book *Prosperity and the Coming Apocalypse* (Nashville: Thomas Nelson, 1998). This book also refutes the "prosperity gospel" that Jim once preached as a prominent television minister.

Chapter 12: Brotherly Love

1. Jim Bakker with Ken Abraham, *I Was Wrong* (Nashville: Thomas Nelson, 1996), xv.

2. Ibid., 21.

Chapter 13: Falling in Love

1. Bakker, *I Was Wrong,* photo insert.

2. Ibid., photo insert.

Chapter 16: A Little Boy's Voice

1. "Tilly" by Frank Peretti, an original radio drama for *Focus on the Family,* 1986.

2. Donald S. Smith, executive producer, *The Silent Scream* (Cleveland, OH: American Portrait Films, 1984); <http://www.silentscream.org/silent.htm> accessed 7-7-00.

3. Ibid.

4. Ibid.

Chapter 19: Empty and Angry

1. "I, even I, am He who blots out your trangressions for My own sake; / And I will not remember your sins" (Isa. 43:25). See also Isaiah 38:17; Psalm 103:12; Jeremiah 31:34; and Micah 7:19.

Chapter 21: Recovering What Was Lost

1. Joel 2:25.

Chapter 23: "I'll Call You Tonight"

1. "Leaving on a Jet Plane," written by John Denver, Cherry Lane Music Publishing Company, ASCAP, 1967.

Chapter 26: Joy Came in the Morning

1. Psalm 30:5 NKJV.

Chapter 27: Ever After? Maybe Not

1. Psalm 19:1 NIV.

2. Psalm 145:13 NIV, paraphrased.

Chapter 31: The Gift of Friends

1. "Some Day My Prince Will Come," music by Frank Churchill, lyrics by Larry Morey. From the 1937 Walt Disney animated feature film *Snow White*.

Chapter 32: God Meant It for Good

1. Ephesians 6:15.

2. Genesis 50:20.

3. "Unchained Melody," music by Alex North, lyrics by Hy Zaret. From the 1955 Warner Brothers film *Unchained*. Several hundred artists have recorded this classic love song over the years, but the Righteous Brothers' 1965 version for Phil Spector's Phillies Records remains the most popular.

Chapter 35: "Little Girl, Don't Ever Forget"

1. Ephesians 2:8 NIV.

2. Colossians 1:21–22 NIV.

Chapter 36: Women of Destiny

1. For more information about the *Women of Destiny Bible,* call 1-800-251-4000 or visit the Web site at www.nelsonbibles.com.

2. Matthew 25:35–36 NIV.

3. Proverbs 31:29 NIV.